TURN ASIDE FROM EVIL AND DO GOOD

THE LITTMAN LIBRARY OF JEWISH CIVILIZATION

Dedicated to the memory of

LOUIS THOMAS SIDNEY LITTMAN

who founded the Littman Library for the love of God
and as an act of charity in memory of his father

JOSEPH AARON LITTMAN

and to the memory of

ROBERT JOSEPH LITTMAN

who continued what his father Louis had begun

יהא זכרם ברוך

'Get wisdom, get understanding:
Forsake her not and she shall preserve thee'

PROV. 4: 5

The Littman Library of Jewish Civilization is a registered UK charity
Registered charity no. 1000784

Turn Aside from Evil and Do Good

An Introduction and a Way to the Tree of Life

ZEVI HIRSCH EICHENSTEIN

English translation by

LOUIS JACOBS

With an Introduction and Extensive Annotations

The Littman Library of Jewish Civilization
in association with Liverpool University Press

The Littman Library of Jewish Civilization
in association with Liverpool University Press
4 Cambridge Street, Liverpool L69 7ZU, UK

www.liverpooluniversitypress.co.uk/littman

Managing Editor: Connie Webber

Distributed in North America by
Oxford University Press Inc., 198 Madison Avenue,
New York, NY 10016, USA

First published in Hebrew as Sur mera va'aseh tov [1832]
First hardback edition in English 1995
First paperback edition in English 1995

Catalogue records for this book are available from the
British Library and the Library of Congress
ISBN 978-1-874774-11-2

Publishing co-ordinator: Janet Moth
Copy-editing: Connie Webber
Proof-reading: Anna Zaranko and Connie Webber
Index: Meg Davies
Design: Pete Russell, Faringdon, Oxon.
Typeset by Footnote Graphics, Warminster, Wilts.

Printed and bound by CPI Group (UK) Ltd, Croydon, CR0 4YY

IN MEMORY OF MY PARENTS AND
PARENTS-IN-LAW

Harry and Lena Jacobs
Isser and Jane Lisagorsky

Preface

THE book translated here, *Sur mera va'aseh tov*, by Zevi Hirsch Eichenstein (1763–1833), is unique in its blending of classical kabbalah with the approach of Beshtian Hasidism. The translation is fairly literal, although some concessions have been made for the modern reader. As the more technical terms defy simple translation, they are generally given in transliteration and explained in the notes.

From the second edition onwards the work has appeared with the notes and comments of R. Zevi Elimelekh of Dynow. These notes have been helpful for the elucidation of the author's meaning and are reproduced as appropriate along with my own, their source being indicated by Z.E. for Zevi Elimelekh.

Before tackling the translation itself, the reader is advised to read first the Introduction for the historical background. The section in the Introduction on kabbalah should certainly be read, since Eichenstein's text refers again and again to kabbalah and its technical terms.

Eichenstein quotes from all the traditional sources of Judaism; in the notes these are cited in the abbreviated form used in the *Encyclopedia Judaica*. Details of these works are given in the Bibliography, together with a short list of general works relevant to the book.

London L.J.
1994

Contents

Note on Transliteration

THE transliteration of Hebrew in this book reflects a consideration of the type of book it is, in terms of its content, purpose, and readership: in order to make the book as accessible as possible to the interested public, the system adopted reflects a broad approach to transcription rather than the narrower approaches found in the *Encyclopedia Judaica* or other systems developed for text-based or linguistic studies. The aim has been to reflect correct pronunciation, and to do so using conventions that are generally familiar to the average English-speaking reader of texts on Judaism rather than those that are found in very scholarly works aimed at a specialist readership.

In accordance with this approach, no attempt is made to indicate the distinctions between *alef* and *ayin*, *tet* and *taf*, *kaf* and *kof*, *sin* and *samekh*, since these are not relevant to pronunciation. The *dagesh* is not indicated except where it affects pronunciation; the often-used convention of doubling the letter in which the *dagesh* occurs would in any case not be helpful in a work in which *gematriot*—mathematical manipulations performed on the numerical value of individual letters—are so important to understanding the text. The exception has been with certain well-established transcriptions that will be familiar to the majority of readers, and which are in any case not the subject of Eichenstein's *gematriot*. Likewise, the distinction between *ḥet* and *khaf* has been retained, using *ḥ* for the former and *kh* for the latter; the associated forms are generally familiar to readers, even if the distinction is not actually borne out in pronunciation. In general, though, the use of diacritics has been avoided: the *tzadik* is rendered *tz*, and the *shin* by *sh*.

Since no distinction is made between *alef* and *ayin*, they are indicated by an apostrophe only in intervocalic positions where a failure to do so could lead an English reader to pronounce the vowel cluster as a diphthong or otherwise mispronounce the word.

The *sheva na* is indicated by an *e*, as in *devekut* and *berit*. The *yod* is represented by an *i* when it occurs as a vowel (*ein*, *peri*), and by a *y* when it occurs as a consonant (*yetzer*). The letter *e* is in fact used for the three Hebrew vowels *sheva na*, *segol*, and the diphthong *tzeré*, except at the end of words where *é* is used, in order to avoid possible mispronunciations.

Following the principle of using conventions familiar to the majority of readers, transcriptions of proper names that are well established have been retained even when they are not fully consistent with the system adopted.

All Hebrew words are italicized, except for proper nouns, which are rendered in roman characters with the initial letter capitalized. This latter convention is in fact often ignored in works on Jewish subjects, but it has been used here because it helps to clarify the nature of the reality being described. The various names of God in Hebrew are treated as other proper nouns (Elohim, Ein Sof, and so on). The same system has been followed for the names of the *sefirot* (Da'at, Binah, and so on), reflecting the fact that these represent God in His different aspects—different names of God—rather than the mere qualities ascribed to Him. The Tetragrammaton and other names of God that are acronymic in nature are rendered in small capitals.

In transliterating the titles of books, the convention followed has been to capitalize only the first word, since Hebrew in any case has no capitals. The titles of parts of works are given in roman characters; thus the *parashot* into which the Pentateuch is divided for purposes of the weekly synagogue readings (e.g. 'Mishpatim') are not italicized.

Needless to say, it is difficult to impose a transliteration system entirely rigorously and consistently, but it is hoped that the solutions that have been proposed here will indeed help readers understand the nature of the different concepts while also contributing to the typographic harmony of the printed page.

TRANSLATOR'S INTRODUCTION

ZEVI HIRSCH EICHENSTEIN was born in 1763, three years after the death of Israel Baal Shem Tov, the founder of the Hasidic movement, at a time when, under the leadership of the Maggid of Mezhirech (d. 1772), the movement had begun to win adherents in eastern Europe. Eichenstein's birthplace is given variously as Sambor or the neighbouring townlet of Safrin in eastern Galicia but he became known as R. Hirschele Zhidachover (or simply 'the Zhidachover'), after the nearby town where he functioned as a Hasidic master. He was introduced by his younger brother, Moshe, to R. Jacob Isaac of Lublin (1745–1815), the famous disciple of the Maggid known as the Seer of Lublin, and became his devoted follower while at the same time cultivating his own original approach to Hasidism.

As with many other Hasidic masters, the accounts of Eichenstein's life and career have been so mingled with pious legend that it is now extremely difficult to reconstruct his biography. Nevertheless, the salient features are known. He received the conventional Jewish education of his time, managing to become a very competent talmudist under the guidance of rabbinic scholars, as he himself relates in this work. He tells us that he also acquired a knowledge of astronomy and other natural sciences, no doubt through his reading of the few works on these subjects in Hebrew, and he was familiar with the writings of the medieval Jewish philosophers. At the age of 20 he began the study of kabbalah, a subject which came to exercise a powerful hold on his mind and heart.

Eichenstein married the daughter of a pious innkeeper in the village of Roda, within walking distance of the town of Rodzil; he was then supported by his father-in-law, after the fashion of those days, so that he could devote himself to study without having any financial worries.[1] His only son, Michel, died in his youth, but his four daughters married scholars who,

[1] Michael Braver, *Tzevi latzadik* (New York, 1976), 12–13. Eichenstein was the oldest of five brothers, all of whom became Hasidim. He was certainly well versed in Talmud and in the

together with his four learned brothers and their sons, became the representatives of the Zhidachover school in Hasidism. In fact, his foremost disciples were his nephews Yitzhak Eisik of Zhidachov (1804–72) and Yitzhak Eisik of Komarno (1806–74).[2] The latter founded a Hasidic 'dynasty' of his own (the Hasidim saw their masters as kings in a system of royal succession), but followed largely in the footsteps of his uncle and teacher; hence its name, the Zhidachov–Komarno school. It is recorded that Eichenstein had many hundreds of devoted Hasidim, to whom he refers in his writings, in humility, as his God-seeking 'companions'. Eichenstein died in a cholera epidemic in 1831, on the eleventh day of the Hebrew month of Tammuz. Until the Holocaust, Hasidim used to visit the grave on the anniversary of his death, just as the grave of R. Simeon ben Yohai, the supposed author of the Zohar, is visited at Meiron.

In Hasidic lore, Eichenstein's soul is said to have been a spark of the soul of the famous Safed kabbalist, R. Hayim Vital (1542–1620). It is certainly true that a good deal of his intellectual activity, in *Sur mera* and other works, is devoted to the elucidation of Vital's ideas.[3]

THE KABBALISTIC SCHEME

Sur mera is unintelligible without some knowledge of at least the basic vocabulary of Lurianic kabbalah. A lifetime of study is required for a full grasp of this extremely complicated system; all that is presented here are the details required to understand Eichenstein's text.[4]

Shulḥan arukh; both Braver, ibid., and Meir Wunder, in *Me'orei galitziyah* (Jerusalem, 1978), conjecture that his main teacher in these topics was R. Isaac Harif, rabbi of Sambor. It is no doubt an exaggeration, but Eichenstein's biographers state in the name of his nephew, Yitzhak Eisik of Zhidachov, that he would study seven pages of Talmud each day, such that each year he would go through the whole Talmud seven times before he advanced to kabbalistic studies. The name of his wife is given as Rachel Perl, but according to one report this was his second wife and not the daughter of the innkeeper.

[2] See H. J. Berl, *Rabbi Yitshak Eisik of Komarno* (Jerusalem, 1965). Both he and his cousin were given the name Yitzhak Eisik after their grandfather, Eichenstein's father, though he was not a follower of Hasidism.

[3] Further information on Eichenstein may be found in the following sources: Adin Steinsaltz, 'Zhidachov', in *Encyclopedia Judaica*, xvi. 1009 (but the date of E.'s birth is given incorrectly there, as 1783 instead of 1763); Y. A. Kamelhaar, *Dor de'ah: Tzadikei hador* (Bilgorey, 1933); Braver, *Tzevi latzadik*; Israel Berger, *Eser kedushot* (Jerusalem, 1973), on Eichenstein and the entire Zhidachov-Komarno dynasties; Wunder, *Me'orei galitziyah*; Aaron Walden, *Shem hagedolim heḥadash* (Warsaw, 1879), ii, *samekh*, no. 13; Mendel Bodek, *Seder hadorot* (n.p., n.d.), no. 9, pp. 76–8; Martin Buber, *Tales of the Hasidim* (New York, 1948), ii. 31–2, 216–23; and Aaron Markus, *Haḥasidut*, trans. M. Schenfeld (Tel Aviv, 1954).

[4] See Gershom Scholem, *Kabbalah* (Jerusalem, 1974), on kabbalah in general, and id., *Major Trends in Jewish Mysticism* (3rd edn., London, 1955), 244–86, for the Lurianic system. A survey of the latter in English is to be found in Louis Jacobs, 'The Uplifting of Sparks in Later Jewish

Essentially, there are two great kabbalistic systems: that of the Zohar, which first appeared at the end of the thirteenth century in Spain; and that developed by Isaac Luria of Safed (1534–72), who is known as 'the Ari' ('the Lion'). Through the writings of Luria's disciples, chief among them R. Hayim Vital, the Lurianic kabbalah came to be seen, as it is by Eichenstein, as the authentic interpretation of the Zohar; he observes that the latter is a closed book unless it is read with Lurianic eyes. That the two systems are in fact different, and even in some respects contradictory, is of no relevance for Eichenstein's thought, since as an orthodox Lurianist he believed them to be identical, the latter simply spelling out in greater detail the implications of the former. The two works by Vital considered especially in the *Sur mera* are *Etz ḥayim* ('Tree of life'), in which Vital formulates the Lurianic doctrine, and *Peri etz ḥayim* ('Fruit of the tree of life'), in which he shows how the doctrine is to be put to work in the performance of the precepts of the Torah and in divine worship generally. This involves chiefly having in mind, when engaging in prayer and worship, the special *kavanot* ('intentions'), that is, contemplations on the manner in which each detailed act has its own influence on high.

According to kabbalah, there are two aspects to the deity: (*a*) God as He is in Himself; (*b*) God in manifestation. God in His first aspect is completely inaccessible to the human mind. Of this aspect nothing whatsoever can be said, which is why it is called Nothing (in Hebrew, Ayin); that is, so far as human comprehension is concerned, It does not exist. It is also called Ein sof, The Limitless; it is the unknowable Cause of causes, not referred to directly even in the Bible but only hinted at there and in the other sacred texts of Judaism.

By a process of emanation, Ein Sof brings into being ten powers or potencies in order to create and become manifest in creation. These divine powers are known as the *sefirot* (originally meaning simply the 'numbers' one to ten, but later given the meaning of 'spheres' or 'illuminations' or other such terms). The *sefirot* are often represented anthropomorphically, one as the right arm of God, another as His left arm, and so forth. It is important to appreciate that these and similar terms are not mere metaphors. For kabbalists, God really does have, say, a 'right arm'; that is, the spiritual entity which as it becomes manifest in the material universe becomes a right arm. This is the kabbalistic understanding of 'God created man in His image'. Because of this close link with the world of the *sefirot*

Mysticism', in Arthur Green (ed.), *Jewish Spirituality* (2 vols.; New York, 1987), ii. 99–126; a full account, in Hebrew, is to be found in I. Tishby, *Torat hara vehakelipah bekabalat ha'ari* (Jerusalem, 1965).

	KETER *Crown*	
BINAH *Understanding*		ḤOKHMAH *Wisdom*
GEVURAH *Power*		ḤESED *Lovingkindness*
	TIFERET *Glory*	
HOD *Splendour*		NETZAḤ *Victory*
	YESOD *Foundation*	
	MALKHUT *Sovereignty*	

man can influence that world; in a sense, it even depends on him. When man performs wicked deeds he sends on high baneful influences that create a 'flaw' (*pegam*) in the sefirotic realm. This affects the balance of the *sefirot*, and the consequent disharmony disturbs the flow of divine grace. Conversely, every good deed causes beneficent impulses to be sent on high, promoting greater harmony among the *sefirot* and putting right the flaws: *tikun* is the term used for this rectification or 'putting right'. The divine grace can then flow freely, bringing blessing down on all creatures.

When the *sefirot* are represented anthropomorphically in the form of a human being seen from behind they are arranged as shown above. There is also what might be termed a semi-*sefirah*. This is Da'at (Knowledge), the intermediate principle between Ḥokhmah and Binah.

Keter represents the divine will to will, so to speak. It is above the other *sefirot*, hence its representation as a crown. This will to will results in a will to create, and Ḥokhmah and Binah (and Da'at) represent the processes of the divine mind in thinking out, as it were, the whole creative process. This results in the emanation of the other *sefirot* which represent the divine emotions. Thus Ḥesed is the divine love which, if it is not to engulf all in its abundance, requires to be controlled by Gevurah, thereby achieving harmony between love and power, judgement and mercy. Tiferet is the harmonizing principle. Netzaḥ and Hod are supporting principles, while it is through Yesod that all the creative power of the *sefirot* flows into Malkhut, the governing principle of the universe. In this arrangement, the *sefirot* on the right side represent mercy; those on the left, judgement; and those in the middle, harmony.

Since the seven lower *sefirot* have their origin in Ḥokhmah and Binah they are called the 'Children', Ḥokhmah being Abba ('Father'), and Binah being 'Imma' ('Mother'). The Zohar and kabbalah generally discourage too much speculation on the three higher *sefirot*; on Ein Sof only complete silence is appropriate. True to this idea, the Zohar hardly ever refers to Ein Sof except by allusion.

So much for the kabbalistic doctrine of the Zohar. The Lurianic kabbalah describes a much more elaborate process. In the Lurianic scheme, Ein Sof first withdraws 'from Himself into Himself' in order to leave room, 'the empty space', as it is called, into which the *sefirot* can emerge. This primordial act is known as *tzimtzum* ('withdrawal' or 'contraction'). But the space left after *tzimtzum* is not left entirely devoid of the light of Ein Sof. A ray of this light penetrates the empty space and this becomes Adam Kadmon ('Primordial Man'). Adam Kadmon contains in His being the ten *sefirot* but, at this stage, they are only mere 'points' with no separate identity. For the *sefirot* to acquire their separate identity they have to have vessels, *kelim*, that can absorb the divine light. The idea behind it all seems to be that the Infinite can only produce the finite, the limitless can only produce the confined, by allowing the fullness of the Infinite light to be gradually strengthened and weakened, strengthened and weakened.

Thus, in the beginning, lights—a metaphor for the incomprehensible spiritual entities—streamed forth from the nose, ear, and mouth of Adam Kadmon and then returned, leaving behind sufficient light to form 'vessels' for the *sefirot*, i.e. receptacles that could contain the light that continued to flow from the eyes of Adam Kadmon. This continuing light streaming from the eyes of Adam Kadmon now proceeded to form Keter, again comprising both essential light and the vessel to contain it, and this was then beamed back and streamed forth again to constitute Ḥokhmah, and so on to Binah. The vessels of these three *sefirot*, being closer to the powerful light of Adam Kadmon, were themselves sufficiently powerful to hold the light. But the vessels of the seven lower *sefirot*, being at a greater distance from the light of Adam Kadmon, could not contain it; this gave rise to the 'cosmic catastrophe' (in Scholem's expression) known as 'the breaking of the vessels' (*shevirat hakelim*) or the 'death of the kings' (the *sefirot* being understood as representing the divine will to reign that was frustrated at this stage). As a result, everything was in disarray; even the three higher *sefirot*, though not broken, were reduced to a lower place than they had previously occupied.

A process of reconstitution then became necessary, involving the assembling of the *sefirot* as five *partzufim* ('configurations'), each dominated by one of the *sefirot* but with all the others also present to assist in the task of sustaining the light. The five *partzufim*, in descending order, are:

1. Arikh (short for Arikh Anpin, 'Greater Countenance'), dominated by Keter
2. Abba ('Father'), dominated by Ḥokhmah
3. Imma ('Mother') dominated by Binah
4. Ze'ir (short for Ze'ir Anpin, 'Lesser Countenance') dominated by Tiferet and the *sefirot* from Ḥesed to Yesod
5. Nukba ('Female'), dominated by Malkhut

The realm of the *sefirot* is called *olam ha'atzilut*, 'World of Emanation'. Beneath this is *olam haberiyah*, 'World of Creation'. Beneath this is *olam hayetzirah*, 'World of Formation'. Beneath this is *olam ha'asiyah*, 'World of Action', the source on high of the world we inhabit and perceive. As a result of the breaking of the vessels, there was an overspill of the divine light from world to world, the overspill of each world bringing about the world beneath it. The overspill from the World of Action nourishes the demonic forces, the *kelipot* ('shells' or 'husks' surrounding the holy). There are 286 'holy sparks' imprisoned among the *kelipot*, and these can be redeemed only by human actions.

The various aspects of the *sefirot* represent all the divine names mentioned in Scripture, but the main divine creative activity is by means of the special Name, the Tetragrammaton, formed by the letters, *yod, hé, vav, hé*, YHVH. There are numerous combinations of this name formed by computations and by *gematria*, that is, by substituting one word for another with the same numerical value (each Hebrew letter has a numerical equivalent). To have in mind one or other of these combinations is to perform a *yiḥud*, 'unification' (pl. *yiḥudim*). By a kabbalistic process it is possible to spell out the Tetragrammaton in different ways so that the total numerical value of its letters is different: either 72, giving the name AV [from *ayin* (70) + *bet* (2)]; or 63, giving the name SAG [from *samekh* (60) + *gimel* (3)]; or 45, giving the name MAH [from *mem* (40) + *hé* (5)]; or 52, giving the name BEN [from *bet* (2) + *nun* (50)].[5] These four names—AV, SAG, MAH, and BEN—correspond to four of the *partzufim* (see the table below) and are also present in all the *partzufim* and in all the worlds.

The letters YHVH of the Tetragrammaton also represent the *sefirot*. Thus the letter *yod* represents Ḥokhmah. The first *hé* represents Binah. Since the numerical value of the letter *vav* is six, the *vav* represents Tiferet and the five *sefirot* that surround it. The second *hé* represents Malkhut. Keter, the link between Ein Sof and the *sefirot*, is too elevated to be represented by an actual letter but is represented by the point of the *yod*. All creative activity is by means of the *sefirot* as represented by the Tetragrammaton. For kabbalists, the letters of the Hebrew alphabet are not mere ciphers; because of their source on high, they are the divine entities that provide cosmic energy. When the kabbalist has in mind the various combinations of this and the other divine names such as Elohim, with the idea of performing a unification, as above, he assists the cosmic processes. Thus, for the kabbalist, the talmudic idea that man is a co-worker with God in creation means far more than that human beings merely co-operate with God for the fulfilment of His purposes: in the kabbalistic view, human beings who know the mysteries are, in a sense, themselves creators.

The following table shows the Lurianic scheme of correspondence. Since the *sefirot* and the *partzufim* exist in each other and in all the worlds, one can speak of, say, the Abba of Keter (meaning, the aspect of Abba in the totality of Keter) or the Imma of Asiyah, or the SAG of BEN, and so forth, leading to an infinite variety of combinations.

Letter	**Sefirah**	**Partzuf**	**World**	**Name**
'point'	keter	Arikh	Adam Kadmon	—
yod	Ḥokhmah	Abba	Atzilut	AV
hé (1)	Binah	Imma	Beriah	SAG
vav	Tiferet	Ze'ir	Yetzirah	MAH
hé (2)	Malkhut	Nukba	Asiyah	BEN

[5] The procedure by which the four names AV, SAG, MAH, and BEN are obtained is as follows. When the Tetragrammaton is infilled with *yods*, its total numerical value becomes 72: *yod* [spelled *yod* (10) + *vav* (6) + *dalet* (4) = 20], *hé* [spelled *hé* (5) + *yod* (10) = 15], *vav* [spelled *vav* (6) + *yod* (10) + *vav* (6) = 22], *hé* [spelled *hé* (5) + *yod* (10) = 15], giving a total numerical value of 20 + 15 + 22 + 15 = 72, which is equivalent, as shown above, to AV. When it is infilled with a single *alef*, the *yod* (10) in the *vav* would be replaced by an *alef* (1), reducing the total value of the infilled letters by 10 − 1 = 9 and thereby making the overall value 63, which is equivalent, as shown in the text, to SAG. When the infilling with *alef* is extended so that the *yods* in the two *hés* are also replaced with *alefs*, the overall value is reduced by a further 18 (twice 10 − 1) to 45, equivalent to MAH. When it is infilled with *hés* instead of *yods*, so that the *yods* in the two *hés* are replaced by *hés*

Sexual symbolism is used throughout, though the kabbalists never tire of warning against *hagshamah* (corporeality), that is, taking it all literally as if there are some kind of sexual relationships on high. Sexual symbolism is found in the names Abba and Imma and in the male Ze'ir and the female Nukba. The kabbalists, scandalizing their opponents, even use the term 'copulations' (*zivugim*) for these relationships, especially for the union of Tiferet and Malkhut, or of Ze'ir and Nukba. Malkhut, the female principle in the Godhead, has to succeed in awakening Tiferet's 'male waters' (*mayin dikhrin*) by means of the female waters (*mayin nukbin*). Malkhut (also known as the Shekhinah) acquires 'female waters' through the deeds of the righteous on earth and through the souls of the righteous after their death on earth.

It is hoped that this very brief survey of the kabbalistic doctrines will, together with the notes provided on the text, help the reader to understand many of Eichenstein's otherwise obscure references.

HASIDISM

Hasidism arose in Podolia, in the southeast of Poland, in the eighteenth century, an age when revivalism was in the air in Europe; there were similar manifestations in Christendom of the mysterious *Zeitgeist* whereby enthusiasm tended to overtake the more sober religious traditions, though it is unlikely that they had any direct influence on the far-flung Jewish communities of eastern Europe.[6] It seems that small Jewish groups of pneumatic God-seekers, each with it own spiritual mentor, first flourished in the Carpathian area. The name they gave themselves was the old Jewish name Hasidim, meaning 'saintly'—rather as the Mormons called themselves the Latter-Day Saints. One of these groups, led by Israel ben Eliezer, the Baal Shem Tov (also known by the acronym formed from the initial letters of his name as the Besht), eventually become dominant, the others either vanishing from the scene or becoming absorbed in the Beshtian group. This original group was not at all large, but because of the Baal Shem's teachings about God's love for the Jewish people whatever their station in

and the middle *yod* is omitted from the *vav*, the overall value is reduced by a further 5 + 10 + 5, thereby making the overall value 72 − 20 = 52, which is equivalent, as shown above, to BEN.

[6] Scholem's chapter on Hasidism in his *Major Trends*, 325–50, is still extremely valuable, but much work has been done on the movement since then; see esp. the entry on 'Hasidism' in the *Encyclopedia Judaica*, vii. 1390–435 and the bibliography cited there. To this should now be added the excellent anthology edited by Gershon David Hundert, *Essential Papers on Hasidism: Origins to Present* (New York, 1991).

life, Beshtian Hasidism attracted the Jewish masses and eventually developed from an élitist to a popular movement, offering, to use a well-worn phrase, 'mysticism for the masses'. Its adherents were known as Hasidim and their leaders as tzadikim. This was an interesting inversion of traditional Jewish terminology, in that in the Bible and the Talmud, the *ḥasid* ('saint') is spiritually and morally superior to the *tzadik*, the simple just or righteous man who follows the teachings of the Torah. But, since the members of the original group around the Baal Shem Tov and all the later followers of the movement claimed to follow the saintly way and called themselves Hasidim, the terms were reversed: the Hasid became the disciple or follower of the *tzadik* (sometimes rendered in English as Zaddik), the charismatic leader (or *rebbe*, as he was later called to distinguish him from the traditional rabbi).

The standard hagiographical work, *Shivḥei habesht* ('The praises of the Baal Shem Tov'),[7] did not appear until about fifty years after the master's death and is so full of pious legends and miracle tales that cautious scholars have been hard put to draw from it or from other early Hasidic works an accurate picture of 'the historical Baal Shem Tov' (the title of a famous essay by Gershom Scholem).[8] The preposterous notion was even entertained at one time that he never existed, the Hasidic teachings being simply fathered on him. This proposition cannot be taken seriously. Recent research by Moshe Rosman into archival material has shown not only that the Baal Shem Tov was a real person, but that he was highly respected by the Jewish community of Miedzyboz, his place of residence, which provided this 'doctor and kabbalist', as he is described, with a stipend from the communal coffers.[9] He is described as 'doctor', no doubt because he belonged at first among the *baalei shem*, 'masters of the (divine) Name', folk-healers who used the various combinations of divine names for the purpose of healing by white magic; hence, 'Baal Shem Tov', 'master of the good name'. The 'good' in the title refers to the good name of God and was never intended, as sometimes imagined, to mean that while there were 'bad' masters of the Name, the Besht was a 'good' master. In fact, the general tendency in Hasidic works is to play down the magical aspects of the hero's activity, the better to emphasize his role as spiritual guide and teacher.

[7] Published in Eng. translation as *In Praise of the Baal Shem Tov*, trans. Dan Ben-Amos and Jerome R. Mintz (Bloomington, 1970).

[8] In Heb. in *Molad*, 144–5 (1960), 1–24.

[9] Murray J. Rosman, 'Miedzyboz and Rabbi Israel Baal Shem Tov', in Hundert (ed.), *Essential Papers on Hasidism*, 209–25.

The Baal Shem Tov left nothing in writing (with the possible exception of a frequently published letter in which his ascent of soul is recorded).[10] He appears to have taught chiefly by means of Yiddish aphorisms, many of which are rehearsed by his disciple, Jacob Joseph of Polonnoye (d. *c.*1784), author of *Toledot ya'akov, yosef* ('Offspring of Jacob Joseph'), the first Hasidic work to be published (in Koretz, 1780) and by his own grandson, R. Moshe Hayim Ephraim of Sudlikov (d. 1800), in his *Degel maḥaneh efrayim* ('Banner of the Camp of Ephraim', published in Koretz in 1810). It has to be appreciated, therefore, that even these 'authentic' sayings have been transmitted to us second-hand and can by no means be said to constitute the actual words or doctrines of the Baal Shem Tov himself. This reservation has to be made with regard to all the teachings found in Hasidic works; it is difficult, to say the least, to authenticate the teachings that are attributed to the master by the Hasidic authors.

For all the importance of R. Jacob Joseph in the history of the movement, the disciple who succeeded the Besht, R. Dov Baer, the Maggid ('Preacher') of Mezhirech (d. 1772), deserves to be considered the real founder, or at the very least, the organizer, of the new movement. The Maggid gathered around him a number of learned disciples whom he encouraged to become themselves Hasidic masters, each with his own group of Hasidim, in Volhynia, Poland, Russia, and Lithuania. Under the guidance of these masters and their disciples, the movement spread rapidly; it has been estimated that by the beginning of the nineteenth century it had won over to its ranks almost half the Jewish population of eastern Europe. In the typical Hasidic fashion of interpreting the Torah so as to hint at Hasidism, the verse 'A river flowed out of Eden to water the garden; it then divided and became four branches' (Gen. 2: 10) was applied to the spread of Hasidism in Poland and Galicia. 'Eden' is the Besht; the 'river' is the Maggid of Mezhirech; the 'garden' is Elimelekh of Lyzhansk (1717–87); and the 'four branches' are Menahem Mendel of Rymanow, Israel of Kozienice, Meir of Apta (Opatow), and Jacob Isaac, the Seer of Lublin, the 'master' at whose feet Eichenstein learnt.[11] In the early days of the movement, it was generally a chosen disciple who succeeded his master through the acknowledgement of his spiritual worth by the other Hasidim of that master. But, particularly from the period of the Seer of Lublin, the idea of

[10] See Louis Jacobs, *Jewish Mystical Testimonies* (Jerusalem, 1976; London, 1977), 148–55, for a translation and notes on this letter.

[11] On the Seer of Lublin see the very comprehensive study by Rachel Elior, 'Between *Yesh* and *Ayin*: The Doctrine of the Zaddik in the Works of Jacob Isaac, the Seer of Lublin', in Ada Rapoport-Albert and Steven J. Zipperstein (eds.), *Jewish History: Essays in Honour of Chimen Abramsky* (London, 1988), 393–456.

dynastic succession took hold, in the belief that the *tzadik*'s holy thoughts when he made love to his wife could succeed in drawing down a specially elevated soul into the child conceived, who was thereby ideally suited to take his father's place when the father departed this life. This led to an enormous proliferation of *tzadikim*, each with his own 'court' and entourage, his 'crown prince' and his own special Hasidic way. It follows that it is extremely precarious to think of Hasidism in monolithic terms. There is not one official Hasidism but a great variety of Hasidisms, often in contradiction to one another.

For all that, certain ideas and practices are common to all the branches of the movement. Prominent among the institutions all Hasidim have in common is the doctrine of the *tzadik*, described by Jacob Joseph of Polonnoye as 'the channel' through which the divine grace flows to bless the created world.[12] In a different metaphor, the *tzadik* is the ladder linking earth to heaven. His function is not only to offer his Hasidim guidance in the spiritual way but to pray on their behalf that they should be blessed with children, health, and the means of earning a living. The role of the *tzadik* as spiritual guide was seen as the most important by the more intellectual members of the group, while his role of intercessor attracted the ordinary Hasidim. In any event, it was quite inconceivable for anyone to be considered a Hasid unless he was a faithful follower of a *rebbe*.

Another idea common to all the branches of the movement, one from which much else followed, was that of *devekut*, 'attachment', to God,[13] having God always in the mind. Hasidism teaches that, in language taken from the Zohar, 'there is no place empty of Him'. God's presence is all-pervasive. No single blade of grass is without an angel who strikes it and orders it to grow to its full height, and in all things there are 'holy sparks' waiting to be redeemed through man's engagement in the world in a spirit of dedication. 'Earth's crammed with heaven, and every common bush afire with God, but only he who sees, takes off his shoes.' Although ascetic practices such as fasting and self-mortification are not entirely unknown in Hasidism, the general ideal of the movement is that of 'worship through corporeality', meaning that the true Hasid must not deny himself food, drink, and other worldly pleasures but should strive to enjoy these with his mind on God, whose gifts they are, in order to rescue the holy sparks inherent in them from the demonic powers. Allied to the ideal of *devekut* is

[12] For a study of the doctrine of the *tzadik* in the writings of R. Jacob Joseph see Samuel H. Dresner's *The Zaddik* (London, 1960; paperback edn. New York, 1974).

[13] See the chapter '*Devekut*, or Communion with God', in Gershom Scholem's *The Messianic Idea in Judaism* (New York, 1971), 203–26.

the Hasidic ideal of *bitul hayesh*, 'annihilation of selfhood', in which the grasping ego is transcended and man's thought is solely on God. Humility, for the Hasid, does not mean that he thinks little of himself but that he does not think of himself at all since, in an ultimate sense, there is no independent self, an idea reminiscent of Far Eastern mystical philosophy. Even in his petitionary prayers, the Hasid does not ask that his needs be satisfied for himself but for the sake of the Shekhinah who grieves and experiences lack, as it were, when human beings suffer want. The true Hasid, who believes that God is in all things, must never be downcast but should strive to be always in a state of intense religious joy, *simḥah*, and he should pray with burning enthusiasm, *hitlahavut* (from *lahav*, 'a flame'). It was believed, however, that the higher reaches of *devekut* can only be attained by the *tzadik*, the Hasid being called upon to reach as high as he can through his attachment to the *tzadik* who, in turn, is attached to God.

The history of Hasidism is a history of struggle both from within and without the Hasidic camp. From within, because of the often intense rivalries between the various Hasidic dynasties, each claiming to be the only true representative of the Hasidic ideals. From without, because of the attack on Hasidism by the Mitnaggedim ('opponents')—the traditional rabbis and communal leaders—and by the Maskilim, the followers of the Haskalah movement who had imbibed Western culture and fought Hasidism as obscurantist and reactionary.

It says much for the success of Hasidism as a movement of rebellion against the Jewish establishment that it was not the Hasidic rebels but the establishment figures who came to be known as the Mitnaggedim—as if Roman Catholics were to be called Protestants. Many are the reasons for the Mitnaggedic opposition, apart from the obvious challenge presented to the traditional hierarchy in the Jewish community by the new type of leader, the *tzadik*, to whom the Hasidim gave far greater allegiance than to the local town rabbis. Among the theological reasons for the opposition was the suspicion that the Hasidim were crypto-Shabbeteans, secret followers of the seventeenth-century false messiah, Shabbetai Zevi. It may be the case, as Scholem and other scholars have contended,[14] that ideas stemming from the Shabbetean heresy have found their way, in disguised form, into Hasidism, but that is a far cry from the Mitnaggedic claim that the Hasidim were really Shabbeteans. Another reason was that the extreme veneration of the *tzadik* by the Hasidim was seen by the Mitnaggedim as a form of

[14] See e.g. Scholem, *Major Trends*, 327–34.

idolatry. Even though the *tzadik* is never an object of worship, the excessive role he plays in the virtual coercion of the divine will to pour out grace to the Hasidim was seen by the Mitnaggedim to be heretical in that Judaism teaches that no intermediary is required for prayers to ascend to God, still less to force God to show forth His mercies. Again, in obedience to the doctrine of *devekut*, the early Hasidim understood the old rabbinic ideal of *torah lishmah*, the study of the Torah for its own sake, to mean that God must be in the mind when studying; that study of the Torah was more of a devotional than an intellectual exercise; to which the Mitnaggedim retorted that study with God in mind rather than the actual subject studied was hardly study at all. For the Mitnaggedim, the study of the Torah for its own sake means for the sake of the Torah. It is God's will, they maintained, for Jews to study His word, but the whole of the mind is to be applied to the texts when actually studying, with God in the background only, so to speak.[15] This debate had severe repercussions. The Mitnaggedim tended to look upon the Hasidim as ignoramuses, while the Hasidim tended to see the Mitnaggedim, focused entirely on Talmud, as people totally lacking in religious devotion who studied only with the ulterior motives of acquiring the reputation of great scholars that would win them wealth and fame.

In the documents of anathema against the Hasidim produced in Vilna and Brody, the Hasidic doctrine of panentheism—that all is in God—comes under heavy attack. It is Jewish teaching, the Mitnaggedim declared, that the whole earth is full of God's glory (Isa. 6: 3), but this refers to His providence over all, not to the heretical notion that all is divine in actuality. The Mitnaggedim protested that the Hasidic idea will lead (as they put it, adapting a talmudic expression), to 'thinking on words of Torah in unclean places', meaning, to the obliteration of all distinctions between the clean and the unclean, the holy and the profane.

On a more trivial level, to the accusations of heresy were added the complaint by the Mitnaggedim that the Hasidim all too readily cultivated the notion of religious joy by means of convivial gatherings at which great quantities of alcohol were imbibed and the *rebbes* encouraged pranks of various kinds. The truth of this accusation is hard to determine, but Eichenstein takes it sufficiently seriously to warn his followers against undue hilarity and frivolity when they come together. Because the Hasidim adopted the prayer-book of Isaac Luria, in which the prayers are arranged according to the special Lurianic 'intentions', they had to establish their own prayer-houses (the Hasidic *stiebel*) so that they could follow their own

[15] See Norman Lamm, *Torah Lishmah: Torah for Torah's Sake in the Works of Rabbi Hayyim of Volozhin and His Contemporaries* (New York, 1989).

ritual, driving yet another wedge between Hasidic rebels and the *kahal*, as the official communal body.

The Maskilim attacked Hasidism on different grounds, for instance, because the movement was hostile to all secular learning. The whole Hasidic way was seen by the Maskilim as riddled with superstition. Instead of improving the lot of poor Jews by encouraging them to obtain a better general education, the *rebbes* remained content to fill the minds of the Hasidim with what the Maskilim considered hazy notions that God would help them—provided that they contributed generously to the upkeep of the *rebbe*'s court. Furthermore, the Maskilim complained, the *rebbes* tended to pay undue homage to their wealthy followers, even while Hasidism taught that all are equal in the sight of God. There is no doubt some truth in the protest of the Maskilim, but it is certainly far from being the whole truth. Some of the *rebbes* did lead lives of great opulence, residing in baronial mansions and wearing splendid robes, but others, like Jehiel Michael of Zloczow (d. 1786) and Uri of Strelisk (d. 1828), led frugal lives and gave everything they had to the poor. The rationale for the lavish style of the *rebbe*'s court was that the greater the wealth of the *rebbe*, the more successful he would be in acting as the channel to bring riches to his followers: every branch of Hasidism teaches that man is never nearer to God than when he helps the poor, 'God's near relatives'. Among the Maskilim, the most vehement opposition to Hasidism came from the ranks of the doctors—naturally so, since in their eyes, their profession was made redundant by Hasidism because the *rebbe* has the power to heal. This claim, too, may have had some truth, although generally the *rebbes* did not scorn medical methods of healing, but rather claimed that the *tzadik* has an important role to play as his prayers can be effective even when the doctors have given up. It is against this background that Eichenstein's remarks on the necessity of earning a good living and on the role of the natural healer have to be understood.[16]

The question of Hasidic attitudes to sex is complicated. We learn from the Mitnaggedic documents as well as from early Hasidic sources that it was the practice, when lustful thoughts invaded the mind of the Hasid during his prayers, not to reject these thoughts but to 'elevate' them. There are reliable reports of Hasidim thinking of pretty girls during their prayers, when their names erupted spontaneously in their minds, and then 'elevating' these thoughts by dwelling on the Source of Beauty in the higher realms. Even before the end of the eighteenth century, however, this whole

[16] On Eichenstein's positive attitude to business see Raphael Mahler, *Hasidism and the Jewish Enlightenment* (Philadelphia, 1985).

doctrine was abandoned as suitable only for the great *tzadikim*.[17] On the whole, Hasidim were chaste in thought and deed and had a rather negative attitude towards sex, which they saw as frustrating their striving for holiness—although, as Orthodox Jews, they had an obligation to marry and have children. Typical is the comment of R. Elimelekh of Lyzansk that Abraham only knew that his wife was beautiful (Gen. 12: 11) when he went down to Egypt and the lewdness that predominated there tainted his thoughts; before that time, Abraham's mind was so engrossed in heavenly matters that he had never considered whether his wife was beautiful or ugly. It was not unusual for young married Hasidim to be ashamed to come to the synagogue when their wife had given birth to a child because of the demonstration that it clearly afforded that they had engaged in marital relations. Most significant is the acceptance of Hayim Vital's demand that the mystic should have neither pleasure nor passion in the marital act but should engage in it solely as a representation on earth of the union on high of the male and female principles in the Godhead. Eichenstein's view, in contrast, reported in the name of his teacher, the Seer of Lublin, was that it is really impossible for there to be no pleasure in the act and that God should be thanked for the pleasure. This view may have been shared by other Hasidic teachers but there is no evidence of it in any of the other Hasidic writings.

ATTITUDES TO KABBALAH

Although 'kabbalah' ('tradition') means for Eichenstein and all the Hasidim the doctrines found in the Zohar and the Lurianic writings, a different form of kabbalah was taught in the thirteenth century by Abraham Abulafia.[18] Abulafia rejected the whole notion of the *sefirot*, preferring his own elaborate scheme of profound reflection on the divine names as a means to attaining the holy spirit. He considered the doctrine of the *sefirot* to be heretical, a perverse type of dualism. But Abulafia's ideas were largely ignored. The term 'kabbalah', whether in the circle of the kabbalists themselves or among authors antagonistic or indifferent to the 'hidden science', refers to the sefirotic doctrine as later elaborated by Luria. Kabbalah, in this sense, arose in Provence in the twelfth century, but obviously contains earlier Gnostic and Neo-Platonist elements. The kabbalists operated in small circles peripheral to the talmudic tradition. There was little

[17] See Louis Jacobs, *Hasidic Prayer* (New York, 1972; paperback edn. London 1993), 104–20.
[18] Moshe Idel has published a number of important studies on Abulafia; see esp. *Kabbalah: New Perspectives* (New Haven, 1988), and *The Mystical Experience in Abraham Abulafia* (Albany, 1988).

actual objection to the new ideas on the part of the talmudists. Distinguished representatives of the talmudic tradition were themselves associated with the study of kabbalah, and through their efforts the system became Jewishly respectable. Abraham Ibn David of Posquières (d. 1198) was reputed to be a kabbalist. His son, Isaac the Blind, was certainly a kabbalist. Indeed, this Isaac is known as 'the father of kabbalah'. From Provence the kabbalistic doctrines spread to Gerona in Spain, where the outstanding talmudist Nahmanides (1194–1270) was a kabbalist, referring by allusion to kabbalistic ideas in his great Commentary on the Pentateuch. Nahmanides' disciple, Solomon Ibn Adret (1235–1310) of Barcelona, known, after the initial letters of his name as Rashba (R. Shelomo ben Adret), similarly combined kabbalistic and talmudic learning in his teaching, though, like his master, he was very circumspect. The picture that emerges is one of a two-tiered system of Torah studies: (*a*) *nigleh* ('that which is revealed'); (*b*) *nistar* ('that which is hidden'). These terms are based on Deut. 29: 28: 'The secret things (*hanistarot*) belong unto the Lord our God; but the things that are revealed (*haniglot*) belong unto us and to our children for ever; that we may do all the words of this law.' Kabbalah was seen as esoteric lore suitable only for the initiates. It seems to have been acknowledged by kabbalists themselves that the system contains ideas, especially with regard to the doctrine of the *sefirot*, that could be detrimental to Jewish belief unless correctly understood, and which consequently had to be concealed from the masses. There was nothing like any determined opposition to kabbalah, but here and there voices were raised to question the claim that kabbalah was really an authentic and most valuable part of the revealed Torah.

In this connection a responsum of R. Isaac ben Sheshet Perfet (1326–1409), known as Ribash, deserves to be quoted. This renowned talmudist emigrated from Spain in 1391 to North Africa, ending his days as a foremost halakhic authority in Algiers. His teachers were Nissim of Gerona and Peretz Hakohen to whom he refers in the responsum (no. 157 in the collected responsa of Ribash) which is directed to a certain R. Amram who had asked him for an opinion on the validity of kabbalah. He replied:

> My teacher, R. Peretz Hakohen, of blessed memory, neither spoke of the *sefirot* nor had them in mind [during his prayers]. I also heard from his own mouth that R. Samson of Chinon, of blessed memory, the greatest rabbi of all his generation (I, too, knew of him, though I never met him personally) used to say: 'I pray with the intention of an infant', that is to say, he rejected the opinion of the kabbalists who have in mind one of the *sefirot* at one time and another at a different time, as the particular prayer requires it. . . . All this seems very strange to non-kabbalists

for whom it all seems a form of dualism. I once heard a man with philosophical pretensions denigrate the kabbalists, saying that the Christians believe in a Trinity while the kabbalists believe in a Decade. It once happened when I was in Saragossa that the venerable sage Don Joseph Ibn Susan came there; I had met him previously in Valencia. He was very learned in the Talmud, had an acquaintance with philosophy and was a kabbalist and he was exceedingly pious and very strict in his observance of the precepts. We became very fond of one another and I once asked him: 'How can you kabbalists have your mind on one of the *sefirot* while reciting one of the benedictions and on another of the *sefirot* while reciting a different benediction? Furthermore, are the *sefirot* divine that a man should address them in prayer?' He replied: 'Heaven forbid that prayer be directed to other than God, blessed be He, the Cause of causes. But, he said, the matter has to be understood on the analogy of a man who has a lawsuit and petitions the king that justice be done. He begs the king to order the minister of justice, rather than the minister of finance, to attend to his case, and it would be nonsensical for him to reverse the order. Similarly, if he wishes the king to give him a gift, he will not ask the king to order the minister of justice but the minister of finance to give it to him. Similarly, if he desires the king to give him wine he will ask the king to direct his request to the chief butler, and if bread to the chief baker, not the other way round. So it is in connection with our prayer. This is directed to the Cause of causes but the worshipper has the intention of drawing down the flow of divine grace to the particular *sefirah* connected to that for which he offers supplication. For instance, when he recites the benediction in which prayer is offered for the righteous he should have in mind the *sefirah* of Ḥesed, the principle of compassion; and when he recites the benediction against the *minim* ('heretics') he should have in mind the *sefirah* of Gevurah which represents judgement, and so in all such instances. This is how the aforementioned saint explained the intentions of the kabbalists and it seems to be a fine explanation. Yet, who compels us to enter into all this? Surely, it is better to pray to God, blessed be He, with unqualified intention and He knows how the request is to be granted, as Scripture says: 'Commit thy way unto the Lord; trust in Him and He will bring it to pass' [Ps. 37: 5]. As I mentioned above, this is what the great R. Samson, of blessed memory, said.'

Ribash, somewhat ambiguously, quotes his teacher, R. Nissim, saying to him in private that Nahmanides was too addicted to kabbalah; and yet he apologizes for not studying kabbalah, explaining that it was because he had not received instruction from a skilled kabbalist. As for the hints in Nahmanides' Commentary, which he admits having read, these he says are easily open to misunderstanding. This became a widely held attitude among learned non-kabbalists; they did not deny outright the truth of kabbalah but held that unless it could be taught by an expert kabbalist—of whom there were few—it was better ignored.

In his comprehensive account of kabbalah *Avodat hakodesh* ('Sacred worship'), Meir Ibn Gabbai (b. 1480) vehemently attacks Ribash. Living two hundred years after him, Ibn Gabbai is reluctant to be too critical of a scholar who had become an accepted halakhic authority, but this does not prevent him from remarking (in pt. 2, ch. 13), that Ribash should have consulted the experts in kabbalah before deciding that it is best left alone. If the claims of the kabbalists are true it is not legitimate to leave it alone; Ribash is simply begging the question. The authority of Ribash in *halakhah* is undisputed, he says, but he has no right to pass judgement on matters of which he declares himself to be ignorant and thus deter would-be kabbalists from making an effort to understand the science. The philosopher quoted by Ribash, he continues, is a fool; no less a philosopher than Maimonides admitted towards the end of his life that kabbalah is true. Ibn Gabbai refers here to the kabbalists' attempts to adopt Maimonides, the great rationalist, as their own. There can be no doubt that Maimonides would certainly have rejected kabbalah had he known of it. Shem Tov Ibn Gaon (13th–14th cent.) was the first to repeat the legend that Maimonides became convinced in his old age that kabbalah is true and that, if he were able, he would have rejected all his work not in accord with kabbalistic mysteries. Ibn Gabbai cannot accept the view that Nahmanides was 'too addicted' to kabbalah. One cannot be 'too addicted' to the truth. We know, he observes, that Nahmanides' teachers in kabbalah were Ezra and Azriel, disciples of Isaac the Blind, who received the tradition from his father, Abraham Ibn David, who in turn received it from his father, R. David. Moreover, all three—grandfather, father, and grandson—were visited by Elijah the prophet, and it was he who imparted the mysteries to them.

Ibn Gabbai's reference to both the 'tradition' and 'Elijah' is interesting. On the one hand, the very name 'kabbalah', meaning tradition, implies that it was handed down from master to disciple, a chain reaching back to Moses. But on the other hand, as even kabbalists were bound to acknowledge that some, at least, of their doctrines were new, the notion of frequent communications by Elijah had to be invoked. Elijah, who never died, is the disciple of Moses who returns to earth to communicate new mysteries to the initiates. In this way, new teachings are seen as not really new but as part of the tradition itself. The followers of Luria in the sixteenth century similarly accepted the Lurianic system as containing the true meaning of the Zoharic tradition. The Lurianic ideas are, it is true, not stated explicitly in the Zohar and were unknown until Luria discovered them there; in this sense, Luria is original. Yet, since Luria was favoured by visitations by Elijah, this amounts to a divine guarantee that the Lurianic system is the fruit of divine inspiration, the communications by Elijah being themselves an aspect of divine inspiration, a manifestation of the 'holy spirit'. Once Lurianic kabbalah spread to eastern Europe, very few voices indeed were raised to question the truth of kabbalah. Even the Mitnaggedim accepted the claims of kabbalah, taking issue only with its popularization and with specific Hasidic ideas supposedly based on kabbalah; although the arch-opponent of Hasidism, Elijah Gaon of Vilna (1720–97), is reported to have said that while the Zohar was the fruit of divine inspiration, Luria's ideas were the fruit of his own intense meditations—that is, they contain a good deal of truth, but there is no guarantee that they are all free from error.

Shabbetai Zevi's theological views were based on Lurianic kabbalah, especially on the doctrine of the holy sparks. Even after Shabbetai Zevi's conversion to Islam, some of his followers continued to believe in him, arguing that the Messiah had to descend into the realm of the *kelipot* in order to rescue the holy sparks imprisoned there.[19] This was heady stuff; but once Shabbeteanism had been exposed as a sham, the rabbis had no option but to become aware of the dangers in the study of kabbalah and take steps to ward people off. Young men were forbidden to study kabbalah, and the constant refrain of distinguished Halakhists ignorant of kabbalah became: 'We have no occupation with the mysteries', i.e. that the scholar is best advised to concentrate on talmudic studies and leave kabbalah severely alone. But none of the rabbis actually rejected kabbalah outright, and kabblistic circles such as that of Bet El in Jerusalem and that in the *klaus* in Brody continued not only to study Kabbalah but to practise the Lurianic *kavanot*.

Hasidism and Kabbalah

The Hasidim had good grounds for being circumspect in their approach to kabbalah. As we have seen, Hasidism was suspected of Shabbetean leanings. Even if this accusation was unfounded, Hasidim were especially apprehensive that any popularization of kabbalah might give credence to the suspicion, given that it was a pillar of the Shabbetean approach. In addition to the need for prudence to be exercised, the Hasidic emphasis on *devekut*, namely, on direct mystical experience, provided strong reason for restraint in the study of kabbalah. The Hasidic ideal tended to be frustrated by the practice of the Lurianic *kavanot*. It was not only, as Ribash had suggested, that 'intentions' were unnecessary, but they came to be seen in many Hasidic circles as a distraction. It was impossible for the Hasidic mystic to have his mind on God during his prayers if he was obliged to

[19] See Gershom Scholem, *Sabbatai Ṣevi: The Mystical Messiah*, 1626–1676 (London, 1973).

concentrate on the various names and combination of names. In a revealing anecdote I have heard Hasidim tell, two of Luria's disciples met on the day after the Passover *seder*. The first asked his friend what thoughts he had had in mind during the *seder*. The friend replied that at this stage he had had this *partzuf* in mind, at another a different *partzuf*, and so on. 'And what did you have in mind?' he asked in turn. 'I had my mind on God,' said the first. 'Why did I not think of that?' was the reply. The Hasidim could not deny the theurgic power of the Lurianic 'intentions'. Believing, as they did, that Luria was inspired, they were forced to acknowledge that these 'intentions' were essential for them to influence the higher worlds. Generally speaking, the Hasidic solution was to see the Lurianic 'intentions' as having their effect automatically, given that actually to have them in mind during prayer was beyond the scope of a generation of spiritual pygmies; the Hasid should offer his prayers with God alone in mind, not the *partzufim*. He should not bother himself at all with the 'intentions'. Since his devotions are sincere, God will take care of the influence of the 'intentions' on high as if prayers had been offered with these 'intentions' in mind. Some Hasidic groups went further, to argue that the whole study of kabbalah should be abandoned. The mysteries taught by the Zohar and Luria were quite beyond the scope of 'this orphaned generation'—the usual excuse among traditionalists for abandoning ideas and practices hallowed by long usage. It is true that the Hasidic works are full of kabbalistic allusions, and that they use throughout the kabbalistic vocabulary; yet all this is made to refer not so much to the sefirotic processes themselves but to the human psychological processes which mirror those on high.[20] This psychological interpretation of the Lurianic system is especially prominent in the writings of Nahman of Bratzlav (1772–1811), great-grandson of the Baal Shem Tov.[21]

The adaptation was gradual. The Maggid of Mezhirech, for instance, while using the new Hasidic ideas, still writes as a conventional kabbalist. But more and more a transformation occurred from a 'pure' kabbalah to the Hasidic interiorization of kabbalah in Hasidic vein. A statement of Menahem Mendel of Peremyshlany (b. 1728), a disciple of the Baal Shem Tov, is quoted as germane to the issue by Meshullam Phoebus of Zbarazh (d. *c.*1775) in his *Yosher divrei emet* (i. 22):

> *Nistar* refers to something it is impossible to communicate to another, the taste of food, for example, which cannot be conveyed to someone who has never tasted that

[20] See Scholem, *Major Trends*, 338–43.

[21] R. Nahman of Bratslav also told a number of fairytales into which his followers read kabbalistic ideas; see Arnold G. Band, *Nahman of Bratslav: The Tales* (New York, 1978).

particular food . . . So it is with regard to the love and fear of the Creator, blessed be He. It is impossible to convey to another how this love is in the heart. This is called *nistar*. But how can it be correct to call the kabbalistic science *nistar*? Whoever wishes to study kabbalah has the book open for him. If he cannot understand the book he is simply an ignoramus for whom the Talmud and the Tosafists would also be *nistar*. But the meaning of *nistarot* in the whole of the Zohar and the writings of the Ari, of blessed memory, is that all these are constructed on the idea of *devekut* to the Creator, for whosoever is privileged to become attached to the Chariot on High and to gaze at it, like the Ari, of blessed memory, for whom the heavenly paths were clearly illumined so that he was able to walk constantly in them guided by the eyes of the intellect . . .

What this passage seems to be saying is that the 'secrets of the Torah' are not those conveyed by the plain meaning of the kabbalistic texts but rather the personal responses of the religious mind which are 'secret' because they cannot be conveyed to another, as taste cannot be conveyed to another. The conventional distinction between the 'secret things' and the 'revealed things' is turned on its head. Where kabbalah is simply studied as a series of sacred texts, the student is simply on the 'revealed' level and there is no advantage in the study of kabbalistic texts over the study of any other sacred texts, such as the Talmud. For the Hasid whose ideal is that of personal mystical experience, the study of kabbalah is then not rejected but is relegated to a secondary status. R. Meshullam Phoebus goes on to say that the Talmud and the other 'revealed' texts can be studied in a *nistar* way, i.e. as a devotional exercise, and that, while an occasional dipping into the Lurianic texts is admirable, the Lurianic 'intentions' should not be used in prayer. In some Hasidic groups the solution adopted was that of limiting the study of kabbalah to the *rebbe* and his inner circle, who might even apply the Lurianic 'intentions' in their prayers while the main body of Hasidim were discouraged from studying kabbalah at all. The tensions were always present, and it is hard to pin down the various attitudes which prevailed in any particular Hasidic group. In any event, the general picture that emerges is of a definite neglect of kabbalistic studies in Hasidism in obedience to the ideal of *devekut*.

The Habad school in Hasidim,[22] founded by Shneur Zalman of Lyady

[22] Eichenstein refers to Habad indirectly in the text, but in his second note he attacks R. Dov Baer specifically. On Habad contemplation see Louis Jacobs (trans.), *Tract on Ecstasy*, by Dov Baer of Lubavitch (London, 1965), and Louis Jacobs, *Seeker of Unity* (London, 1966). In the appendix to the latter, pp. 159–64, there is a translation of a letter written by R. Yitzhak Isaac Epstein of Homel (1780–1857), a follower of Dov Baer, which was published in Epstein's *Ḥanah ariel* (Berditchev, 1912), 4*b*–5*a* of the final section on 'The Sabbaths and Festivals and Other Topics'. Here Epstein defends Dov Baer against the accusation that his ideas are 'philosophy' and heretical. H. I. Bunim maintained that Epstein's opponent was R. Aaron of Starosselye, Dov

(1745–1813), disciple of the Maggid of Mezhirech, and developed by his son, Dov Baer of Lubavitch (1773–1827), finds its own solution to the problem of combining the Lurianic 'intentions' with *devekut* by developing a series of contemplative exercises based on Lurianic kabbalah. In Habad, the Hasid does not simply have the Lurianic 'intentions' in mind during his prayers but reflects on the inner meaning. The 'intentions' directing the mind to this or the other *sefirah* or *partzuf* are abandoned as too mechanical. Instead, at various stages in the prayers—when the *Shema* is recited, for example—the worshipper surveys in his mind the whole Lurianic scheme, the emanations of the *sefirot* from Ein Sof, the 'breaking of the vessels', the emergence of the Four Worlds, and so forth, thus allowing his mind to wander through the whole chain of being from the highest to the lowest. Moreover, Habad interprets the details of the Lurianic scheme as metaphors; hence the accusation by Eichenstein in this book that the followers of Habad have transformed kabbalah into a system of philosophy.

Another rationalistic tendency in Hasidism is that of Simhah Bunem of Przysucha (d. 1827), furthered by his disciple Menahem Mendel of Kotzk (1787–1859) and followed by the Gerer group of Hasidim. The Przysucha school relies heavily on the writings of the Maharal, Judah Loewe of Prague (d. 1609), in whose works kabbalistic ideas are expressed in a popular, semiphilosophical manner without much use of actual kabbalistic terminology.[23]

The Specific Approach of Zevi Hirsch Eichenstein

Eichenstein's solution is peculiar to him. He believes very strongly in the Lurianic system as infallible, inspired truth and bemoans the fact that the study of kabbalistic texts has been abandoned, describing this as the work of Satan. Moreover, he understands the Lurianic texts in their plain meaning (if such texts can be said to have a plain meaning). The *partzufim* and the other features of the Lurianic system are not mere symbols or metaphors but describe processes that actually take place in the spiritual worlds on high. As he remarks in this book, the biblical statement that God is 'fire' is not a mere metaphor. God, or an aspect of deity, really *is* 'fire', in the sense of the spiritual entity that is the source on high of physical fire on earth. Although he believes that the Lurianic 'intentions' can no longer be achieved in prayer but none the less have their effects on high automatically, he insists that for this to happen the Hasid must at least be aware of how

Baer's rival in Habad; see H. L. Bunim, *Mishneh ḥabad* (Warsaw, 1936). But in the light of this note it seems almost certain that Epstein is defending Dov Baer against Eichenstein's attack.

[23] See Scholem, *Major Trends*, 339, and Berl, *Komarno*, 33.

they achieve their effects and hence is unreservedly required to be a student of kabbalah in the traditional sense. Luria, 'the angel of the Lord', as Eichenstein calls him, did not come to earth, he says, to no purpose, and to neglect the study of kabbalah is therefore a betrayal.

Eichenstein is unusual among Hasidic authors in other respects as well—in the systematic treatment of a single theme, for example. In this he resembles Shneur Zalman of Lyady in the *Tanya*. Most Hasidic texts are in the nature of discursive comments on biblical texts. These are more often than not the record, by disciples, of the *rebbe*'s teachings, which were believed to have emerged spontaneously as the spirit moved him.

Some of the other *rebbe*s were no doubt familiar to a greater or lesser degree with the works of the medieval Jewish philosophers, but in no other Hasidic texts are the views of a thinker like Bahya Ibn Pakuda quoted verbatim and keenly discussed as they are in Eichenstein's work—although, very unhistorically, Eichenstein converts Bahya himself into a kabbalist. His discussion of scientific matters is also very unusual. He evidently believes that science succeeds in accurately describing how the events in the physical world come about but that we must turn to kabbalah in order to know why they are ordered in this particular way. In this connection, Eichenstein can almost be described as a kabbalistic Maskil.

TURN ASIDE FROM EVIL: AN ANALYSIS

The essay (in the original text there are no divisions and it all reads as a single statement) is divided into three parts. The first two parts deal with the qualifications necessary for the study of kabbalah, as laid down by Vital in his introduction to the *Etz ḥayim*. In the first part, 'Turn Aside from Evil', Eichenstein tries to show how Vital's conditions can work in the circumstances in which the Jews of eastern Europe found themselves. In the second part, 'And Do Good', he describes the positive demands of kabbalistic life. The third part presents his general approach, and here he takes issue with the Maskilim of his day who reject kabbalah under the influence of Western thought. The essay opens with a fervent prayer for guidance in the true path.

The work begins by showing the importance of the study of the Zohar, the classical work of kabbalah. It is through this tremendous work that Israel will be redeemed from its long exile. But the Zohar remains a closed book without the doctrines of the Ari, who was sent from Heaven to convey its true meaning. Eichenstein is aware that many refuse to study kabbalah because they fear it will lead them astray, as it did Elisha b. Abuyah in talmudic times and Shabbetai Zevi and others in more recent times. There are great risks, he admits, but they are surely worth taking when one's spiritual life is at stake. Another reason for the reluctance to study kabbalah is because of the severe warnings R. Hayim Vital has given. Eichenstein acknowledges that it can be difficult to follow these rules, but claims that it is not impossible to do so when they are qualified somewhat so as to render them appropriate for contemporary would-be kabbalists.

The first section of the work, 'Turn Aside from Evil', expands on the ten propositions that R. Hayim Vital puts forward regarding the study of kabbalah, as follows (the numbers are Eichenstein's):

I. Kabbalistic studies should be undertaken not for one's own spiritual attainment but in order 'to remove the thorns from the vineyard' and to allow the shoots of holiness to grow to their full strength.

II. There are two types of fear; the would-be kabbalist should dwell on the fear of punishment.

III. 'Removing the thorns' can be achieved only by kabbalists.

IV. Sinfulness must be avoided, but when one does fall into sin one must not yield to despair.

V. Anger, pride, and other sins that cause friction with one's fellow men (Eichenstein terms his followers 'companions') must especially be avoided.

VI. The sex act must be performed without pleasure or passion (Eichenstein is less severe on this than Vital).

VII. Regular ritual immersion is of great significance.

VIII. Sleep and rising to perform the midnight vigil has immense religious values.

IX. Little time must be allocated to business pursuits (Eichenstein is more permissive than Vital on this).

X. Every word and deed must be aimed at the unification of God's name.

The second section, 'And Do Good', develops first the theme of the midnight vigil, a theme to which Eichenstein attaches the highest significance. He then goes on to discuss the importance of being among the first ten in the synagogue; the mystical reason why one should take upon oneself the obligation to love one's neighbour; and the question of prayer with the Lurianic *kavanot*. He expresses opposition to the latter: prayer, he says, should be in a spirit of total self-surrender. He then describes what real repentance involves.

The remainder of the part is then devoted to commenting on the passage in tractate *Shabbat* (the headings here are Eichenstein's):

And there shall be. This denotes joy in God's service. The name YHVH should be depicted in the mind. In a note, Eichenstein disapproves strongly of writing out this name.

Faith. One should not have an uncritical attitude in matters of belief but, at the same time, one must not imagine that human reasoning is in any way a substitute for faith.

Times. Everything has its appropriate time and place, and the boundaries must be preserved.

Strength. A description of spiritual and intellectual 'procreation' through discussion with suitable companions.

Salvation. A discourse on the theme of refusing to yield to despair. God helps those who have the will to survive spiritually.

Wisdom. An elaboration on the need for dialectics and of seeing problems from every angle.

and Knowledge. This involves a reluctance to rely on human reasoning to draw conclusions by analogy. Discernment is called for both with regard to the use of analogy and with attempts to become inspired by the holy spirit. The sincere kabbalist can attain to the holy spirit, but must not make this his aim.

The fear of the Lord. This is the 'treasury' (i.e. the embodiment) of all the other values.

The third part, 'Written Uprightly, Words of Truth', considers the whole question of kabbalistic studies in relation to philosophy and rationalism. The author seeks to explain how kabbalah helps in understanding the natural sciences and medicine, and he discusses the differing roles of physicians and *tzadikim* in healing. He gives a number of illustrations of how talmudic passages which on the surface seem very strange become intelligible when understood in the light of kabbalah.

The whole essay concludes with a prayer for success in the task that he has set himself.

THE HISTORY OF *SUR MERA*

The first edition of *Sur mera* was published in Lemberg in 1832, a year after Eichenstein's death, but the date was given as 1884, probably to avoid difficulties with the censor.

The publishers of the second edition (Lemberg, 1850), added notes by R. Zevi Elimelekh of Dynow (1785–1841). I have included the important ones where necessary; they are indicated by the initials Z.E. Since then, the book has gone into a number of editions, all with Z.E.'s notes. Meir Wunder refers to an edition of this and two other works by the same author in a single volume with notes published by a grandson of the author in Israel in 1969,[24] but I have not been able to obtain this edition.

The edition I have used is that of Michael David Jost (Pest, 1942). This is a second edition of the one published in Munkacs in 1901 with an approbation by a descendant of Z.E., R. Zevi Hirsch Shapira, rabbi of Munkacs (1850–1913), who states that he had delivered the first edition to the publishers together with Z.E.'s original notes. The publisher boasts that, unlike all previous editions, his is free from printing errors; a vain boast. He himself lists errata at the end of the book; and even so, many errors have been overlooked. The paper and type are very inadequate and this, as well as the frequent allusions to texts without giving the sources, has made the task of translation a difficult one. In the notes I have tried both to provide references for the sources cited and to elucidate the meaning of the more obscure passages. Nevertheless, Eichenstein's style is admirable, verging on the poetic from time to time, though he does go in for convoluted sentences and paragraphs. To help the modern reader, I have sometimes introduced additional paragraph breaks; in any case, I suspect that those in the original are not Eichenstein's but the publisher's. The note attacking the view of R. Dov Baer of Lubavitch (p. 116) would seem to be misplaced; I think it should come rather later than it does. The author does not give the source of the many scriptural verses quoted, evidently relying on the reader to be familiar with them. From the occasional incorrect quotation it looks as if he was quoting from memory. I have supplied the missing sources in square brackets in the body of the text but it is only right to emphasize to the reader that the author does not supply them himself.

[24] Wunder, *Me'orei galitziyah*.

TURN ASIDE FROM EVIL AND DO GOOD

An Introduction and a Way to the Tree of Life

With the help of the Lord, Blessed be He

THE BOOK

Introduction to the Tree of Life

known as

TURN ASIDE FROM EVIL AND DO GOOD

By his holiness, the holy and renowned GAON,
man of God, light and teacher of Israel etc., to him silence is praise,
his name itself is a greater title even than that of Rabban, our teacher
RABBI ZEVI HIRSCH OF ZHIDACHOV
his memory is for a blessing for the life of the World to Come,
may his merits shield us and all Israel.

Together with the

SUPPLEMENTS OF MAHARTZA
(*Complete*)

By his holiness, the holy and renowned GAON,
man of God, light and teacher of Israel etc., to him silence is praise,
his name itself is a greater title even than that of Rabban, our teacher,
RABBI ZEVI ELIMELEKH SHAPIRA
his memory is for a blessing for the life of the World to Come,
may his merits shield us and all Israel, Head of the Court of the Community of Dynow

I now bring the work to light from the holy autograph copy of the author of Supplements of Mahartza, of blessed memory, together with many additions and restoration of those matters missing from earlier editions, as explained in the Approbation.

The humble publisher, Zevi Aryeh Hammermann of Munkacs

And now the afore-mentioned edition has gone entirely out of print and is no longer to be purchased on the market. Consequently, I bestirred myself, with the help of God, Blessed be His name, to republish the work with all its additions, in the most splendid and beautiful form, as it was previously.

The Humble Michael Dov Jost, here in Pest, may the Rock protect and save it, in the year 702 according to the smaller reckoning.

Printed in the city of Pest by the printer Shalom Friedmann, may his light shine, in the printing house mentioned below

Bard Jakab konyvaondaja Bpest, Miksa-u 17, 1942
Felelos kiado: Jaszi Miksa

TURN ASIDE FROM EVIL

For the sake of the unification of the Holy One, blessed be He, with his Shekhinah

O LORD, Thou art my God, I will extol Thee, I will praise Thy name, for Thou hast done wonderful things, even counsels of old in faithfulness and truth.* I will give thanks unto Thee, for I am fearfully and wonderfully made. Wonderful are Thy works; and my soul knoweth right well* my low spirit and lack of discernment. Who am I, what is my house, that Thou hast brought me thus far*; that Thou hast placed my portion among loving companions hearkening to the voice of the living God in the paths of wondrous wisdom to walk in the garden, giving me to taste the fruit of the plants of the Tree of Life* for the sake of the Torah and testimony and the reasons for the command of the King for His worship; and that Thou hast trained me in the ways of unification of the glorious and tremendous Name, to prepare the throne of David* and to establish it! O Lord our God, Thou hast not forsaken us in our poverty and Exile, and Thou hast sent us the salve and the balm to give us the strength to endure the yoke of Exile; to select and to sift the roots of our souls in order to elevate all good things* to become attached to the root and source of life. In Thy light do we see light to understand and be wise in the light of the King of Life's countenance. The intelligent shall shine as the brightness* casting

Note: Eichenstein is referred to throughout as 'E.', Zevi Elimelekh as 'Z.E.'

O Lord, Thou art my God ... in faithfulness and truth Isa. 25: 1.

I will give thanks ... my soul knoweth right well Ps. 139: 14.

Who am I ... that Thou has brought me thus far 2 Sam. 7: 18. The reference is to the saying (*Zevaḥim* 102*a*) 'thus far' means kingship. E. hints at the fact that he has become a Hasidic master, a 'king' or 'ruler'.

Tree of Life Heb. *Etz ḥayim*; a reference to R. Hayim Vital's book of the same name.

throne of David the Shekhinah. (Note of Z.E.)

elevate all good things elevate the 'holy sparks' fallen among the *kelipot*. (Note of Z.E.)

the brightness Heb. *zohar*; see Zohar i. 15*a*, where the verse 'And the intelligent shall shine as the brightness of the firmament, and they that turn many to righteousness like the stars for ever and ever' (Dan. 12: 3) is applied

sparks on all sides, as the Zohar, our fortress in our Exile and our soul's redemption. Let our King come,* he is triumphant and victorious.

And what shall we say unto Thee, O Lord our God, in this last generation,* in which for long seasons Israel has been without the true God, and without a teaching priest and without Torah,* every man doing that which is right in his own eyes,* and the power of heresy prevails. We have been left orphaned without a father. But Thou, O Lord our God, because of the love Thou hast borne for our ancestors, Thou hast fulfilled for us the verse: 'It shall not be forgotten out of the mouths of their seed' [Deut. 31: 21]. Thou hast revealed Thyself in the splendour of Thy glorious majesty to reveal for us, in our days, the secret reasons for Thy Torah, the hidden things* that belong to the Lord our God. Thou hast sent us the teacher of righteousness, the angel who descended in heavenly clouds, the celestial holy one from the high heavens, our holy teacher, the Ari, of blessed memory, and his holy disciples, chief of whom was our master, R. Hayim Vital, of blessed memory. They have illumined the eyes of those who dwell in darkness and have opened the eyes of the blind to take delight in the light of wisdom, Torah, and divine worship; to understand words of discernment; to become wise in the things hidden in the Zohar—[all] in order to return to Thee, O Lord our God, with all our heart and with all our soul, and to Thy delightful Torah. And we give thanks unto Thee, O Lord our God, for all the goodness Thou hath wrought for us in giving us to taste of the fruit of the Tree of Life* that we may serve Thee and fear Thee. May the Lord our God be with us. May he give us length of days and years of goodness, and may He reverse the captivity of Zion and Jerusalem.* May we go from strength to strength to walk before the Lord in the lands of life, and may the gates of light be opened for us that we may be illumined in the light of life together with the souls of the righteous, the living souls, Amen.

to the mystical adepts. It has been conjectured (though E. would not have had this in mind) that this passage was originally the beginning of the Zohar, and that the name Zohar was given to the work as a whole on the basis of this opening; see Eliakim Milsehagi, *Sefer raviah*, ch. 19, pp. 19*c*–20*a*.

let our King come Zech. 9: 9; i.e. the study of the Zohar prepares the way for the advent of the Messiah.

in this last generation E. thought that the time of the Messiah was at hand.

for long seasons . . . Israel has been without Torah 2 Chron. 15: 3.

every man doing that which is right in his own eyes Judg. 17: 6.

the hidden things Deut. 29: 8.

the fruit of the Tree of Life meaning, R. Hayim Vital's work *Peri etz ḥayim*. (The phrase is a literal translation of the Hebrew title.)

and may He reverse the captivity of Zion and Jerusalem based on Ps. 127: 1.

Hear me, my brethren and companions, who long for the real truth regarding worship in the heart, who seek to behold the graciousness of the Lord and to visit forthwith in His temple.* Let his soul long for and become attached to the Zohar. For the mystical power* of the Zohar is well known from the teachings of our early sages. See the ruling of the *gaon* R. Isaac de Lattes* (he was a famous *gaon*, quoted many times in the responsa of Ran),* and especially in *Or ne'erav** and in the *Shelah** and in the Introduction of R. Hayim Vital,* of blessed memory. In particular many works quote passages from the Zohar which imply that the final generation will be sustained by this work, and in the *Raya mehemna** 'Naso', p. 124*b*, the passage beginning 'If any man's wife go aside', states: ' "And they that are wise shall shine as the brightness of the firmament", by means of this book of yours, the Zohar, from the brightness of the Supernal Mother,* Repentance. For these no test is required.* And because Israel is destined to taste of the Tree of Life, that is, the Zohar, they will be delivered from Exile with compassion, in fulfilment of the verse: "The Lord alone did lead him, and there was no strange god with Him" [Deut. 32: 12].' Consult there the whole passage. Consequently, I beseech my colleagues, men like myself, to tremble at the word of the Lord, to set aside time to study the Zohar so as to know the source of the light that is so sweet to the eyes, and not to be content with merely mouthing the words* [of the Zohar] as if one were reciting some hymn. Rather it is necessary to study the work and to seek its basic ideas, which deal with the clarity of the illuminations and the

to behold the graciousness of the Lord and to visit forthwith in his temple Ps. 27: 4.

the mystical power Heb. *segulah*, 'special property', used in medieval Hebrew for supernatural as opposed to natural efficacy.

Isaac de Lattes Italian sage (d. *c.*1570), printer of the Mantua edition of the Zohar. His ruling (*pesak*) that it is permitted to print the Zohar despite rabbinic opposition to revealing the mysteries is printed at the beginning of many editions of the Zohar.

in the responsa of Ran Ran is the acronym by which R. Nissim of Gerona (*c.*1310–*c.*1375) is commonly known. E. has confused this sage with the Italian scholar with the same name. (Note of Z.E.)

Or ne'erav by R. Moses Cordovero (1522–70).

Shelah abbreviation of *Shenei luḥot haberit*, by Isaiah Horowitz (d. 1610).

Introduction of R. Hayim Vital to the *Etz ḥayim*.

Raya mehemna 'Faithful Shepherd', a section of the Zohar dealing with the mystical significance of the precepts. The reference here is to Zohar iii. 124*b*.

Supernal Mother The *sefirah* Binah, the 'Mother' of the seven lower *sefirot*, also called Teshuvah, 'Repentance' or 'Return', because the lower *sefirot* return to Her, and hence representing on earth the return of the sinner to God.

no test is required i.e. those who study the Zohar are not brought into temptation in order to demonstrate their faithfulness.

merely mouthing the words there was a widespread belief that reciting the Zohar, even without any understanding, is beneficial to the soul. (Note of Z.E.)

dimensions of the Creator,* concerning which a man is asked in the future life: 'My son, did you gaze at the Chariot? What is the distance from the top of His head to His forehead?', as it is stated at length in the *Midrash shoḥer tov** on Proverbs, as quoted in all the books of the God-fearing; and the whole of the Zohar is based actually on this. And great virtues are implied in this, especially to become a vehicle* for the unification of the Holy One, blessed be He, and His Shekhinah. It awakens the eyes of the upright from their slumbers and it removes the heart of stone (if it is stone it will dissolve),* and it also has the special property of warding off the waters of presumption, the bitter and cursed waters of external sciences.* Whoever tastes of it will see for himself that no science in the world can compare with the science of the deep mysteries of the reasons for the Torah, and that all other sciences are regarded as nothingness and void, as I shall explain later. He will taste what David referred to when he said: 'More to be desired are they than gold ... Sweeter also than honey and the honeycomb' [Ps. 19: 11]; consult the Talmud on this verse.* Whoever desires truly to taste will agree with these remarks of mine. This brief note will suffice if the dear and faithful reader is not to be bored.

However, the Zohar is an opaque and sealed book, concealed from the eye of every living creature. It is true that the earlier sages such as the holy Recanati* and his colleagues, R. Meir Ibn Gabbai* and R. Judah Hayat,* did explain many of the Zoharic passages, and, especially, the holy

dimensions of the Creator *shiur komah*, the mystical dimensions of the Deity; described in Midrash *Shiur komah*.

Midrash shoḥer tov The Midrash on Psalms, a name deriving from the opening words, which are a quotation from Prov. 11: 29: 'He that diligently seeketh good' (*shoḥer tov*). But there is an obvious error here. R. Hayim Vital, *Etz ḥayim*, Introd. 3*b*, quotes it as the Midrash on Proverbs and says nothing about Midrash *Shoḥer tov*. The passage is in Prov. 10: 3. See *EJ* xi. 1517. Referring to the Midrash on Proverbs as Midrash *Shoḥer tov* was not an unusual mistake.

to become a vehicle lit. to become a chariot, resembling the *merkavah*, the Chariot on high (Ezek. 1).

if it is stone it will dissolve based on Kid. 30*b*: 'If this repulsive creature [the evil inclination] attacks you, draw it into the house of study; if it is of stone, it will dissolve, if it is of iron, it will be shattered.' E. applies this to the study of the Zohar.

the bitter and cursed waters of external sciences meaning, extraneous to Judaism; the Hasidic masters saw the study of secular subjects as bound to lead to heresy.

the Talmud on this verse Sot. 48*b*, where a number of explanations are given to *nofet tzufim*, translated as 'the honeycomb'. One of these, to which E. probably refers, is that the bees spring forth and fly in the heights of the world to collect honey from the herbiage on the mountains. E. evidently understands this in a mystical sense as referring to the high places of the *sefirot*.

Recanati The Italian kabbalist Menahem Recanati (13th–14th cent.), author of *Perushal hatorah*.

Meir Ibn Gabbai Turkish kabbalist (d. 1480), author of *Avodat hakodesh*.

Judah Hayat Spanish kabbalist (d. *c*.1510), author of a work known as *Sefer haḥayat* but correctly entitled *Minḥat yehudah* (a commentary on *Ma'arekhet ha'elohut*).

R. Moses Cordovero,* who laboured in the study of the Zohar to explain completely and adequately all its hints, as if it were actually the Torah. For all that, my brethren, whoever has not tasted the Tree of Life and the wisdom of the Ari, of blessed memory, the profundities of the lily of the valley,* all of it delightful, pleasant to the taste, has never really tasted the Zohar. For our master, the Ari, of blessed memory, was great in counsel and he increased wisdom, and it is he who illumined the paths of Heaven as if they were the streets of Nehardea,* the wondrous divine wisdom in the light of the reasons for the Torah and divine worship upon which the doors of the Zohar hinge. Whoever studies his works will see with his own eyes and understand in his heart that the human mind has no capacity, that there is no ability anywhere in the world, to grasp the subtle paths, except for he whom the Lord has sent for our illumination, to open the eyes of the blind to understand the Zohar. Therein he will perceive the profundities of our holy Torah, whether it be of Scripture, the Talmud, Sifra and Sifrei, Tosefta and Baraita, and the strange sayings in the Midrashim and the words of our holy teachers, all of whose words are based on the secrets of the Torah, as it is stated in the *Raya mehemna*,* 'Pineḥas', p. 244*b*. And how he will rejoice and delight in the sayings of our teachers, in their wondrous riddles, which remained sealed and closed until now. May the Lord illumine for us the waves of darkness and remove blindness from our eyes. Happy are we that we have had this merit in this final generation.*

Therefore, O men of heart, men of my ilk, my companions, since the Lord has made it known to us and has revealed it to us through His angel, the Ari, of blessed memory, and has shown us the entrance to the gate which opens the doors of wisdom—gird yourselves, be strong, and see to it that you engage in the study of the Ari's doctrine; for whoever has not seen the light of his doctrine has never seen light in all his days. And if not now, when? As R. Simeon said to the companions at the beginning of the *Idra rabba*:* ' "For how long will we sit supported by a single pillar?" (See ch. 3

Moses Cordovero Moses Cordovero (1522–70), the foremost Safed kabbalist and author of *Pardes rimonim*, who instructed Luria in kabbalah (though Luria went on to develop a different kabbalistic system).

the profundities of the lily of the valley in the older kabbalistic doctrine, the lily of the valley (S of S 2: 1) represents the Shekhinah.

illumined the paths of Heaven as if they were the streets of Nehardea based on Ber. 58*b*: 'Samuel said: I am as familiar with the paths of heaven [the courses of the stars and planets] as with the streets of Nehardea [a town in Babylon].' E. applies this to the paths and channels of the *sefirot*.

Raya mehemna Zohar iii. 244*b*, which says that the talmudic passages also contain mystical meanings.

this final generation E. believed that the advent of the Messiah was very close.

Idra rabba The 'Great Idra'—the section in the Zohar where R. Simeon ben Yohai re-of the gate 'The Breaking of the Vessels').* It is written: "It is time to work for the Lord, they have made void Thy Law" [Ps. 119: 126]. The days are short and the creditors are pressing ...'*

Now many companions are afraid for their souls, if they study the *Tree of Life*, to walk in the Orchard in the Garden,* lest it happen to them what happened to Aher,* Heaven forfend, especially when they observe that which R. Hayim Vital, of blessed memory, himself warns in his introduction to the *Tree of Life*. This in brief is what he says. A person's main aim in knowing this science should be in order to remove the thorns from the vineyard; hence those who engage in this study are called 'the pruners of the field'.* It is obvious that the Outside Ones* will rouse themselves against such a person, Heaven forfend, in order to seduce him and cause him to sin. Consequently, he must take care never to sin, not even unwittingly, so that they can have nothing to do with him. Consequently, he must abstain from eating meat and drinking wine during weekdays and he must take care to turn from evil and do good. See there for the numerous conditions and stipulations, to be explained later with God's help; not everyone is able to achieve them, especially in this generation, which is weakened by the severities of the Exile. So who dares to draw near to enter the holy place?

You must know, my brother, my dear reader and beloved friend, it is true that the Outside Ones do attack anyone who engages in the study of this science and they seek to cause him to sin since his whole aim is to prune them from the vineyard.* The Ari, of blessed memory, writes in the *Sha'ar hayiḥudim** that this is the reason why, of those who entered the Orchard, only R. Akiba* emerged safely, for the others were attacked by

veals the deepest mysteries to his companions (Zohar iii. 127*b*–145*a*).

'The Breaking of the Vessels' 'Sha'ar shevirat hakelim' in the *Etz ḥayim*, ch. 3, p. 42, where the 'single pillar' is said to refer to the 'World of the Points', i.e. to the stage in the process of the divine unfolding at which the *sefirot* have not as yet been differentiated but are as 'points' in a single entity.

The days are short and the creditors are pressing based on Avot 2: 20.

to walk in the Orchard in the Garden the Orchard (Heb. *pardes*) is Paradise, the Garden is the Garden of Eden.

Aher 'The Other One', Elisha ben Abuyah, one of the four who entered Paradise but became an apostate as a result of what he saw there (Ḥag. 14*b*–15*a*).

pruners of the field or 'cutters of the field', *meḥatzdei ḥakla*, an expression used at the beginning of the *Idra rabba* (Zohar iii. 127*b*) to mean the mystical adepts.

Outside Ones the demonic powers who are 'outside' the realm of the sacred.

to prune them from the vineyard i.e. removing the unholy forces from the domain of the sacred, cutting away the 'weeds' to enable the 'shoots' in the divine vineyard to grow to their full strength.

Sha'ar hayiḥudim from the school of R. Hayim Vital.

only R. Akiba of the four who entered Paradise (Ḥag. 14*b*), only R. Akiba emerged without mishap.

the denizens of the deep.* Thus far his words. Yet hearken to my voice and I shall give you counsel, and the Lord will be with you. Do not keep yourself fearfully away from proceeding with this study, for what is your aim in life? Surely without wisdom and knowledge, Heaven forfend, your life is no life at all. As Scripture states: 'See, I have put before thee this day life ... therefore choose life' [Deut. 30: 15, 19]. Supposing a man would seek to take away your life from you, would you not engage in battle with him whether the outcome will be—* Heaven forfend, or life? Whether you will be the victor or, Heaven forfend, the opposite? A man will give everything he possesses in order to save his life; it is a small thing in his eyes to use every means and every stratagem, even to the extent of crossing the sea* or ascending to heaven (thus writes Ramban,* in his commentary on the Torah, on the verse: 'And now, Israel, what doth the Lord require of thee' [Deut. 10: 12] resolving the difficulty raised in the Talmud:* 'Is fear a small matter?' For the text continues [v. 13]: 'for thy good'; consult it there), until he humbles his attacker who wishes to deprive him of his life. How much more than this must we say with regard to eternal life—real, not illusory: each person is obliged to fight in defence of the very soul of his life and to sacrifice himself in order to engage in this study, in order to prune the vineyard and to cut down the thorns. If he wins out, so much the better. But if, Heaven forfend, he loses the war—well, that is why it is called a war, as the saintly author of *Ḥovot halevavot** states in connection with the war against the evil inclination: 'Observe how in warfare, where the danger is great, yet the soldier risks his life though he is not sure that he will win, because he knows that if he wins he will gain much spoil. How much more so with regard to the great war against the evil inclination. How can you refuse to take the risk? How great will be your joy and gladness, how much glory and satisfaction will be yours if you win the victory.' And see the ruling of R. Isaac de Lattes and the Introduction of

the denizens of the deep the demonic forces lurking in the depths of the 'deep sea', the realm of the unholy.

will be— death, which E. does not want to mention explicitly.

extent of crossing the sea see Eruv. 55*a* on Deut. 30: 12–13: 'if it were in Heaven you should have to go up there and if it were beyond the sea you should have to go over the sea to get it'.

Ramban Nahmanides (1194–1270). Spanish kabbalist, talmudist, and author of a commentary on the Pentateuch. The passage quoted is on p. 390 of the Chavel edn.

the difficulty raised in the Talmud Ber. 33*b*. 'Moses said: "what doth the Lord require of thee but to fear". Is fear such a small thing?' Ramban's solution is that since it is for a man's own good it is indeed easy and only a 'small thing'. The suggestion that this solves the question in the Talmud is not Ramban's but E.'s.

Ḥovot halevavot 'Duties of the Heart', by Bahya Ibn Pakuda (11th cent.). The reference here is to gate 5, ch. 5.

R. Hayim Vital in the name of the Ari, of blessed memory, in his own handwriting. Therefore, my brethren, be not afraid and be not in dread, for the Lord will be your protection and He will guard your feet from stumbling.

To be sure, my brethren, every intelligent and spiritually minded person is obliged generally to follow the rules stated at the beginning of the *Tree of Life*, quite apart from the question of studying this science. But hear, O my friends: with regard to these matters it is said that it all depends on the intention of the heart. The basic principle is that a man should engage in this study with the pure motivation, as R. Hayim Vital says, of pruning the thorns from the vineyard. Later on, God willing, it will be explained what is meant by removing the thorns, and how this is achieved by those who engage in this study, called the 'pruners of the field'. First, however, I must explain the simple rules that those who engage in this study are required to observe. These are stated in the Introduction to the *Etz ḥayim*, and with God's help we shall speak of them.

I

R. Hayim Vital writes as follows: 'He whose soul has the desire to enter the halls of this science must resolve to keep faithfully everything of which I shall write, and then the Creator will guarantee that he will suffer injury neither to his wealth nor to his life because of his pursuit of the good.'

Now it is good advice that a man should not engage himself in this study for the purpose of attaining some mystical state* or the holy spirit or a prophetic vision. Rather, there should be a firm resolve to keep all that is stated in the book. If you see that it deals with the supernal illuminations in Heaven you must know that the main purpose is practical, namely, to draw conclusions for divine worship, as I shall explain later. Then, the Creator will guarantee that you will suffer no harm and no evil mishap, but will enter in safety and emerge in safety.

II

From the remarks of R. Hayim Vital: 'To purify oneself in order to attain to the fear of the Lord, the first step is to experience fear of divine punishment. For it is only possible to experience inner fear after one has acquired great wisdom. And the main purpose should be ...' as stated above.

mystical state Heb. ***hasagah***, lit. 'awareness', 'comprehension', 'gnosis', but used by E. and many others in the sense of an advanced mystical state.

It is necessary to understand what is meant by to experience fear* of divine punishment. My friend, you should know that all fear which comes clothed in the garments of the Torah, with its punishments, its warnings and its detailed rules, is called 'the fear of divine punishment'; as it is stated in the Introduction to the Zohar,* there is fear and fear;* consult it there. Every kind of fear clothed in the garments of this world is the fear of divine punishment. It is to this that the Mishnah refers* when it states: 'Where there is no fear there is no wisdom.' For, at first, it is necessary to acquire fear of divine punishment, namely, fear that stems from the plain meaning of the Torah, the numerical value of *yirat*.* And 'Where there is no wisdom there is no fear', namely, inner fear, stemming from the great and elevated knowledge of His name, blessed be He, because He is great and He rules, the main principle and the root of all worlds, and all worlds are as naught before Him, as stated in the above-mentioned passage in the Zohar. Here five praises are mentioned: 'great and He rules' are represented by *vav* and *hé*;* 'the main principle and the root' are represented by *yod* and *hé*. For the letter *vav* represents 'great', according to the mystery* of the elongated, tapering letter, as it is stated in the *Raya mehemna*, 'Pineḥas',* p. 232*a*, and according to the mystery of the One who is Great is Small.* The letter *hé* represents Malkhut,* ruler of those above and those beneath. And 'the main principle' is represented by the mystery of *yod*, the mystery

what is meant by to experience fear i.e. the term *hasagah* refers not only to the emotion of fear but to a real intellectual perception.

Introduction to the Zohar Zohar i. 11*b*.

fear and fear i.e. the fear of punishment and the higher fear that is dread in the experience of the holy; what Rudolf Otto in *The Idea of the Holy*, trans. J. W. Harvey (Oxford, 1957) calls the 'numinous'.

the Mishnah refers Av. 3: 17, 'Where there is no wisdom there is no fear. And where there is no fear there is no wisdom.' E. understands 'fear' here as meaning fear of punishment, and 'wisdom' as referring to the mystic lore, the kabbalistic doctrines.

numerical value of *yirat* *yirat* is the construct form of *yirah*, 'fear'. The numerical value of the word is equivalent to that of *torah*, as follows: *yirat* = *yod* (10) + *resh* (200) + *alef* (1) + *tav* (400) = 611. *Torah* = *tav* (400) + *vav* (6) + *resh* (200) + *hé* (5) = 611.

vav* and *hé the letters of the Tetragrammaton, *YHVH*, represent the ten *sefirot*. Thus, Y (*yod*) is Ḥokhmah; the first H (*hé*) is Binah; V (*vav*) is Tiferet (together with the five lower *sefirot*, since *vav* is six); and the second H (*hé*) is Malkhut. Keter is represented by the point of the *yod*, it being too elevated to be represented by an actual letter.

***Raya mehemna*, 'Pineḥas'** Zohar iii. 232*a*.

according to the mystery the term 'mystery' (Heb. *sod*) is used frequently to denote the secret lore of kabbalah.

the mystery of the elongated tapering letter . . . and the One who is Great is Small the letter *vav* extends downwards, corresponding to the six lower *sefirot* descending from Binah in a straight line. In the Lurianic kabbalah, the *vav* corresponds to Ze'ir Anpin, 'The Lesser Countenance', the male principle. Hence the 'one who is great', the largest of the letters when it is extended or elongated, is 'small', that is, the *Lesser* Countenance. The expression 'The one who is great is small and the one who is small is great' occurs in Zohar i. 122*b*.

Malkhut 'Sovereignty'.

of Wisdom: 'In wisdom thou hast made them all' [Ps. 104: 24]. 'The root' is the first *hé*, the mystery of Binah, the root of *vav* and *hé*,* as is well known to those who know the mystery of the writing of the divine name. 'All worlds are as naught before Him' is the mystery of the upper point* of the *yod*, the One who is Small is Great.* This is how I have explained in my notes on the Zohar. See the Zohar, 'Vayakhel', p. 216*a*: 'It is written, "thou shalt fear the Lord thy God" [Deut. 10: 20]; and it is also written, "and thou shalt fear *of* thy God"* [Lev. 19: 14], implying from some part. What is meant by "fear of thy God"? The meaning is of that place which surrounds the brain from above,* and it is to this that "of thy God" refers. For in that place judgement resides, the judgement which is drawn down from the Judgement on high.* In that place there is fire and another fire. Therefore one must be in fear of that fire in which fear resides, and from there fire spreads outside* to another type of fear, of which it is written, "ye shall not fear the gods of the peoples" [Judg. 6: 10], namely, it is forbidden to fear them.' Consult the passage and the commentary *Zohar harakia** and you will discover many pleasant things. This is what R. Hayim Vital means when he says that one should not have an external fear, namely, the holy external fear that appertains to the *kelipot*.* It is forbidden to entertain such fear.* The fear one should have is the fear of divine punishment, the fear of

the root of *vav* and *hé* the seven lower *sefirot* stem from Binah.

upper point the upper point in the sefirotic system is Keter. All worlds are as naught in relation to Keter, which is also called Nothing because 'nothing' can be said of this stage: it is beyond all comprehension.

the One who is Small is Great Keter, the 'great', the Greater Countenance, is represented by the 'small' point of the *yod*.

***of* thy God** the letter *mem* can mean 'from', i.e. fear of that which is *from* God, implying only a part and not the whole, that which is taken from.

surrounds the brain from above i.e. surrounding Malkhut—the Shekhinah—called 'thy God', there is the fire of judgement, and of this one should be afraid; hence 'from thy God', from that which surrounds the Shekhinah.

drawn down from the Judgement on high from Gevurah, the source of judgement.

spreads outside the fear of God extends to the fear the idolators have of their gods.

Zohar harakia a series of commentaries on the Zohar by R. Hayim Vital and others. Z.E.'s note gives the gist of this comment as follows. When Malkhut extends to the World of Action it is among the *kelipot* (see next note) which it nourishes. Fear must be only of Malkhut above the World of Action, otherwise the fear is tainted by the *kelipot*. The love of God, on the other hand, stems from Ze'ir Anpin, which comprises the *sefirah* of Ḥesed, 'love', whereas Malkhut is judgement and represents the fear of God.

to the *kelipot* the *kelipot* are the 'shells' or 'husks', the demonic forces which feed on the sacred. Hence 'the holy external fear' i.e. it is sacred because it stems from Malkhut, but has extended to the Outside Ones.

It is forbidden to entertain such fear E. seems to mean that the 'numinous' fear the pagans have of their gods is unholy, unlike the fear of divine punishment for sin. Z.E.'s note adds: 'There are inner meanings to this subject but I am afraid to rely on my own opinion and may God, blessed be He, who

the Lord. Take note of this and study and become wise to understand this essay of mine. I shall not expound at greater length in order not to digress from my purpose.

III

'A person's main aim in this study should be for the purpose of pruning the vineyard from the thorns', etc. You should know, my brother and friend, that the ultimate purpose of divine worship by means of the Torah is to select the good and throw away the bad, that which stems from the dross of the seven kings.* Now without knowledge of this science a man is like a beast; the Zohar calls such persons 'those whose hearts are stopped up and whose eyes are blind'. Concerning these David said: 'They have a mouth ... They have eyes' [Ps. 115: 5], as R. Hayim Vital remarks in his Introduction, quoting from the *Tikunim*,* *Tikun* 30: ' "All flesh is grass" [Isa. 40: 6]. They are like beasts who eat grass. "And all the goodliness thereof is as the flower of the field" [Isa. 40: 6]. All the good they do is for themselves.'* Consult the passage.

Thus you can see, my brethren, that whoever performs a *mitzvah* [religious precept] without understanding the reason for it but only by rote is like a beast that eats grass, that which human beings find tasteless. Now even of fear Scripture says: 'And their fear of Me is a commandment of men learned by rote' [Isa. 29: 13], stressing 'their fear'.* One who fears God and worships Him must direct his deeds toward Heaven, as the rabbis say:* 'Let all thy deeds be for the sake of Heaven.' This is clearly stated in all works of religion.

Now, whoever has not studied the ways of the Ari, of blessed memory, may still, in a general way, direct his deeds towards Heaven. For example, he can eat in order to have strength to worship the Creator, or sleep in order for his mind to be clear, and so forth, with physical acts all for the sake of Heaven. For all that, happy is he who knows the details regarding

knows the things hidden in the heart, lead us in the paths of righteousness.'

the dross of the seven kings the cosmic catastrophe of the 'breaking of the vessels' is described as the 'death of the seven kings', i.e. of the seven lower *sefirot*, which shattered under the impact of the divine light they were unable to contain. After they had been reconstituted, the 'holy sparks' became embedded in the *kelipot*, the 'dross' that remained. The task of divine worship is to elevate the holy from the dross.

the *Tikunim* lit., 'Rectifications'; a section of the Zoharic corpus.

is for themselves i.e. even the good they do is tainted by self-interest.

stressing 'their fear' i.e. they fear only for themselves.

as the rabbis say Av. 2: 12.

everything in the world according to the ways of the Ari, of blessed memory, the root of everything done on earth from beginning to end; for instance, why God so made man that he has to eat when he could have made him able to live without having to eat and such-like severe and extremely difficult questions (and consult part II of R. Hayim Vital's *Sha'arei kedushah*)* regarding the tremendous acts of the Lord. But according to the way of this science derived from the Ari, of blessed memory, it is all based on the pillar of wisdom, each movement and each limb of the body and all that is in existence exists to point to the divine wisdom and to teach the people of the Lord the way in which they should walk in order to select and refine the residue of the seven primordial kings who died so that reward and punishment should come into being.* In reality it is that upon which is centred the whole mystery contained in the *Idrot** and the *Sifra detzeniuta.** (And all the mysteries of the Torah, as stated in *Likutei torah*,* 'Pineḥas', with regard to the laws of inheritance, consult the passage.)

Go forth and study the *Tree of Life*, eat of its fruit and you will eat and be satisfied and bless. You will find sweet reasons in every movement, even in the way in which the limbs are designed, the hair, the forehead, the ears, the eyes, the hands, the feet—all are designed as subtle channels for the worship of our Creator, blessed be He and blessed be His name. Then in every act and every deed you will discover desirable things, how to throw away the bad and elevate the good. This is in general; consult *Likutei torah*, 'Behar', and the 'Gate of Prayer' and 'The Intention of *Ahavah rabah*'.*

IV

'Depart from evil and do good' [Ps. 34: 15]. Consult the Introduction by R. Hayim Vital, and particularly his *Sha'arei kedushah*, at length: 'To keep all the prescriptions of the rabbis,* to put right everything that is crooked,

Sha'arei kedushah R. Hayim Vital's guide to holy living.

so that reward and punishment should come into being the 'kings' had to 'die' in order for the divine light to be sufficiently weakened so that it could produce a world in which there is evil as well as good, and hence reward for the righteous who choose good and punishment for the wicked who choose evil.

Idrot the *Idra rabba* ('Greater Gathering') and the *Idra zuta* ('Lesser Gathering'), the first in Zohar iii. 127*b*–145*a*, the second in Zohar iii. 284*b*–296*b*.

Sifra detzeniuta 'Book of Concealment', a section of the *Idra rabba* describing the mystical measurements of the deity (the *shiur komah*) as if there is a representation on high of the human form with bodily limbs.

Likutei torah from the school of the Ari.

'Gate of Prayer' and 'The Intention of *Ahavah rabah*' in *Peri etz ḥayim*, 4*a* f.

all the prescriptions of the rabbis rabbinic law in addition to biblical law.

not to come to sin even unwittingly.' Consult the passage. You should know, my brother, the main principle is that it is the heart that the All Merciful requires. The root principle behind it all is that a person's thought and heart should be naturally disposed (see R. Hayim Vital's *Sha'arei kedushah*, part 1, gate 3) to take upon himself to practise and to keep [the commandments] and to unify the Holy One, blessed be He, and His Shekhinah, with every limb of his body and with every act, in order to give satisfaction to his Creator, who has formed him and made him with heart, *nefesh*, *ruaḥ*, *neshamah*, *ḥayah*, and *yeḥidah*,* and to comprehend all that it is in his power to achieve. But if, Heaven forfend, on occasion he stumbles and does that which should not be done, let him not retreat from his sacred path and consequently give up his studies, his way and his path. Concerning this it is said: 'Look not behind thee' [Gen. 19: 17]. I have heard my master* give this turn to the verse 'turn not aside after your heart' [Num. 15: 39]. It means: You must not let go because of your heart, namely, do not loosen your bond to the Creator if your heart happens to turn backwards. If your heart has not been fully in your control, do not as a result relinquish your efforts in worship. Rather, you must repent and offer supplication to the Merciful; He will forgive you, for He is great in goodness and He pardons. And he said further that even a person who has sinned by a flaw in the covenant* and repented, confessed his sin, experienced remorse with all the strength of his heart, his heart broken, knocking at the doors of mercy—he is called one who keeps the covenant. He will not be lost* in relation to a more righteous person since he has done all that is in his power to do. Thus his words. And many proofs can be adduced for this idea; see the Zohar, 'Lekh',* pp. 93*a*–*b*. Note it well; there is no cause to go into the matter at length.

The general principle is: 'Happy is the man who does not forget Thee.'* The man who remembers his Creator all the time, who scrutinizes his deeds as far as his strength and reason reaches to search in the recesses of

nefesh, ruaḥ ... yeḥidah according to kabbalah there are five degrees of the soul, different levels of psychic life; given here in ascending order.

my master Jacob Isaac, the Seer of Lublin (1745–1815).

flaw in the covenant the 'covenant' in the flesh, i.e. circumcision; the reference is to a sexual offence such as masturbation, but the term is often applied even to an involuntary emission of semen.

He will not be lost his value will not be lost, he will not be considered inferior.

Zohar, 'Lekh' Zohar i. 93*a*–*b*, in praise of circumcision. Z.E. remarks that he cannot see how the Zoharic passage is relevant to E.'s contention here.

'Happy is the man who does not forget Thee' quote from the Rosh Hashanah *musaf* prayer.

his being, as is stated in the Zohar, 'Balak',* p. 195*b*—at all times he should allow his heart, his brain, and his reason to elevate his body and his deeds to unify them all.

And if, on occasion, his inclination gets the better of him and seizes hold of him in some matter, he should at once experience remorse and be ashamed and he will then be pardoned immediately. As the sages say:* 'Whoever sins and is ashamed of it is immediately pardoned.' And they said further:* 'Better is one admonition in the heart than a hundred lashes.' For this is the final end of repentance and remorse until the soul has been chastened to the uttermost degree. See the *Raya mehemna*, 'Naso',* p. 122: 'This precept is of repentance. This is a divine command. And from the time of the destruction of the Temple, for our sins, the only thing left to us is verbal confession, this is Malkhut. The letter *hé* is undoubtedly verbal confession,* the mystery of the word: 'Take with you words and return unto the Lord'* [Hos. 14: 3]. And see the passage on p. 123. 'There are many types of repentance by means of which people become wholly good. There is a man who was completely wicked all his life, transgressing many negative precepts, but then he experiences remorse and confesses that he has transgressed, yet afterwards he does neither good nor evil. To be sure the Holy One, blessed be He, pardons such a person, but he cannot attain the stage of supernal repentance.* But another person, after he has repented of his sins and has been pardoned, walks in the way of the *mitzvot* and engages himself with all his might in the fear and love of the Holy One, blessed be He. Such a person reaches the stage of the lower repentance* ... And there is still another who, after he has repented of his sins, engages in the practice of the Torah without thought of reward for it. Such a person attains to the letter *vav**—that is, the son of *yod* and *hé*, called Binah*—because of this, with the result that *vav* returns to *hé*.'* Consult the passage.

Zohar, 'Balak' Zohar iii. 195*b*, which says that there is no need for a man to confess all the sins he has committed; when he confesses those of which he knows he is pardoned for all his sins.

the sages say Ber. 12*b*.

And they said further Ber. 7*a*.

***Raya mehemna*, 'Naso'** Zohar iii. 122*a*, 123*a*.

Malkhut ... is ... verbal confession because Malkhut, the final stage in the sefirotic process, represents God giving expression to His will. Malkhut, represented by the second *hé* of the Tetragrammaton, is the divine 'speech'.

'Take with you words' i.e. Malkhut, 'and return unto the Lord', i.e. to Tiferet.

supernal repentance Binah.

lower repentance Malkhut.

letter *vav* Tiferet.

the son of *yod* and *hé*, called Binah Tiferet is born of Ḥokhmah, represented by *yod*, and Binah, represented by *hé*. *Yod* and *hé* together form YH, or *yah*; 'the son of *yah*' is *ben yah*, which can be rearranged in Hebrew to form Binah.

vav* returns to *hé Tiferet returns to Malkhut, representing the unification of the *sefirot*.

The main thing is for you to let your soul cleave to religious works so that you observe what your duty is to the Creator of all worlds, especially to the Zohar, the main principle of all, and this will inflame your heart with flaming fire. The Zohar is that which opens and that which closes.*

V

A person should guard himself against anger and pride, see on this the *Sha'ar hakedushah*.* However, when Hayim Vital says, in connection with pride: 'and especially in matters of *halakhah*',* this does not refer to enjoyment of learning, although this also stems from the hold exercised by the evil inclination, as it is stated in the *Midrash hane'elam*,* section 'Toledot', p. 138. And of Jehoshaphat it is said: 'And his heart was lifted up in the ways of the Lord' [2 Chron. 17: 6].

The main thing in connection with pride is that a person should not feel superior to others and to his companion because his heart tells him that he has greater learning (see the tale of the man who was judged because he wished to put his neighbour to shame in matters of *halakhah*; Zohar, 'Shelaḥ',* p. 167), and he feels superior to his companion who is less learned. Especially with regard to this science, comprehension is frustrated when a man imagines that he has grasped and understood it. It is certain that if he has a sense of superiority over his companion who does not know as he does, he can be sure that he has not even touched it and has comprehended nothing at all. The reason why he feels superior is because he has comprehended in some corporeal sense. He has made corporeal (in his own mind and thought), Heaven forfend, the supernal qualities and channels, and it is from this that his pride stems. For he sought to attain by his thinking a place where no thought whatsoever can reach. He must know that repentance is called for, to unify the truly One, in a spirit of self-sacrifice, to elevate the Female Waters* and to unify them by means of the

that which opens and that which closes the Zohar is the alpha and the omega.

Sha'ar hakedushah Vital's *Sha'arei kedushah*, II. iv. 12*a–b*.

matters of *halakhah* study of the legal side of Judaism.

Midrash hane'elam a section of the Zohar; the reference is to Zohar i. 138*a*: 'The evil inclination extends into the world, for without it there would be no joy in study'—of *shematata*, meaning halakhic studies.

Zohar, 'Shelaḥ' Zohar iii, 167*a–b*. E. understands Vital's reference to pride in matters of *halakhah* to mean vaunting oneself over people who are less learned but not finding joy in the study itself.

Female Waters the Female Principle (Nukba or Malkhut) is assisted in Her 'copulation' with the Male Principle (Ze'ir or Tiferet) by the souls of the righteous and the deeds of the righteous on earth; these provide Her with the 'Female Waters' (*mayin nukbin*) that

unification mentioned in the *Sha'ar hayihudim*, in the *tikun* for the sin of pride,* and by means of the unification explained at the end of the [*tikun* of the] Holy Beard so that the Outside Ones can have no hold over him. He should have in mind twice the name Elohim with their ten letters,* which is explained by us in the name of R. Akiba, who entered in safety and emerged in safety. Akiba's very name points to this unification, for *a, k, b** is equivalent to twice Elohim; the *yod* represents the ten letters, for the *yod* is always in the mystery of: 'The reward* of humility is the fear of the Lord' [Prov. 22: 4]. And the *alef* represents* the all-embracing Lord of the world (see chapter 7 of the gate 'Counting of the Omer'*), who helped him* so that the ministering angels should not push him out.

However, if a man delights and takes joy in his learning, from the novel interpretations and the inner aspects of this science, this is certainly permitted. As it is stated in the *Raya mehemna* and the *Tikunim*,* the companions have no greater joy than when they are able to discover new ideas in the Torah. This is a great *mitzvah* by means of which comprehension is attained. Nothing helps comprehension more than joy in the *mitzvah*; see *Sefer hagilgulim*.* The special quality of joy is that it then brings

cause the Waters of the Male Principle (*mayin dikhrin*) to flow. A *tikun* is a putting right of flaws in the sefirotic realm. *Yihudim*, 'unifications', are meditative exercises involving various combinations of divine names. One of these is the *tikun* of the Holy Beard, representing the flow of grace from the highest, 'the strands of the Holy Beard'.

in the *tikun* for the sin of pride a *tikun* ('rectification') is a spiritual exercise by means of which a sin can be put right. Z.E.'s note provides this *tikun* in brief: one guilty of pride should have in mind the name YAH, which has the numerical value of 15: *yod* (10) + *hé* (5). This has the same numerical value as *ga'avah*, 'pride': *gimmel* (3) + *alef* (1) + *vav* (6) + *hé* (5) = 15.

twice the name Elohim with their ten letters the five letters of Elohim are: *alef* (1) + *lamed* (30) + *hé* (5) + *yod* (10) + *mem* (40) = 86. Twice 86 = 172. Adding a further 10, to represent twice the number of letters in the word (i.e. 5 × 2), gives 172 plus 10, for a total of 182.

a, k, b the name Akiba is made up of the consonants *ayin*, *kof*, *bet* and the vowels *yod*, and *alef*. *Ayin* (70) + *kof* (100) + *bet* (2) = 172, whereas Elohim = 86 (see previous note). Adding *yod* for the ten letters gives 182. The *yod*, which represents Ḥokhmah, is also the smallest of the letters, and hence it also represents humility.

The reward Hebrew *ekev*, formed of the same three letters.

the *alef* represents the final *alef* of the name Akiba is not counted because it represents the *aluf*, 'Lord' of the world, i.e. Ein Sof who embraces all the *sefirot*.

'Counting of the Omer' In *Peri etz hayim*, ch. 7, pp. 107*d*–110*b*.

who helped him who helped R. Akiba when he entered Paradise.

As it is stated in the *Raya mehemna* and the *Tikunim* E. possibly refers to Zohar iii. 27*b*–28*a* (*Raya mehemna*) and *Tikunim*, Introd., p. 126, but the main passage on original ideas is Zohar i. 4*b*; E. is probably quoting from memory.

Sefer hagilgulim a work on metempsychosis by R. Hayim Vital. E. probably refers to the account of the life of the Ari at the beginning of this work, according to which the Ari rejoiced greatly when he studied.

down Male Waters to draw down beneficent influences to the House of Israel. And so peace.

VI

'A person must sanctify himself when he has marital relations so that he has no pleasure in the act.' Thus writes R. Hayim Vital. Now the truth is that no man can observe the sanctity of intercourse if he has not studied this science* so as to be aware of the channels of unification and strip coarse materialism from his thought and to sanctify himself in his mind with the unifications of His blessed name in the source of intercourse, all in a spirit of self-sacrifice, truly for the sake of the Lord.

And I have heard my master* say that the main principle of sanctifying the act of intercourse is before the act, that is, a person should direct his thoughts to bind himself to the Creator, blessed be He and blessed be His name, may He be exalted, as it is stated in the books on holiness. But during the act it is quite impossible for him to have no pleasure. His proof of this is from the saying of the rabbis, of blessed memory, in *Midrash shoḥer tov*,* on the verse: 'Behold, I was brought forth in iniquity' [Ps. 51: 7]. 'Did Jesse have the intention of bringing me into the world? ... His intention was for his own pleasure.' And David's father was Jesse, who died only as a result of the machinations of the serpent.* In the holy work *No'am elimelekh*,* it is stated that the reason why the rabbis did not ordain that a blessing be recited before intercourse is because the act is impossible without a mixture of the inclination.*

For all that, I train my disciples that even though no blessing with the divine name and a reference to Sovereignty has been ordained, a God-fearing man will offer praise and thanksgiving for the pleasure that the Creator, blessed be He and blessed be His name, has in His abundant mercy and great goodness afforded him, giving help to one who is helped to

studied this science according to kabbalah, the marital act mirrors the unification of the Male and Female Principles on high—'the unification of the Holy one, blessed be He (= Tiferet) and His Shekhinah (= Malkhut)'. Consequently, for the kabbalists, the act is to be engaged in purely as a religious duty, without pleasure or passion.

my master the Seer of Lublin.

Midrash shoḥer tov This is found neither in Mid. Ps. nor in Mid. Prov. but in Lev. R. 14: 5, pp. 308–9.

the machinations of the serpent Shab. 55*b*, i.e. he was sinless and suffered death only because it had been so decreed through Adam's sin.

No'am elimelekh by R. Elimelekh of Lyzhansk (1717–87). The statement occurs in the comment on Gen. 32: 25 ('Vayigash') (ed. Nigal, p. 95).

the act is impossible without a mixture of the inclination there is bound to be something of the evil inclination even when the motivation for sex is otherwise pure.

be strong.* Nevertheless, whatever a man can do in order to distance himself from having pleasure he should certainly do, in the way I have heard in the name of the holy rabbi, our master, Dov Baer,* of blessed memory, in a comment on the words of our holy master:* 'I have enjoyed no pleasure even from my little finger.' This refers to sanctity in the act of intercourse,* in the manner the rabbis say:* 'Not all fingers are the same.' Yet if you do experience pleasure you must give thanks to the Creator of all worlds for your portion, in any language that you understand and speak. In this way you will restore the pleasure to its Owner and will not trespass on the sacred.*

VII

'Purification and immersion at all times,* or at least when it is necessary.'* There, in the *mikveh*,* you should have in mind that it hints at the foundation of the Mother, the foundation of repentance, since it is She who purifies the Delightful Son, following the mystery of 'Let the mother come and wipe ...' As it is stated in the Zohar, 'Bereshit',* p. 33: 'R. Hiyya said: "the gathering of the waters" [Gen. 1: 10] this refers to the *tzadik** of whom it is said, when he reaches the waters: "And God saw that it was

giving help to one who is helped to be strong one who is strong is one who is firm; E. probably means by this the help given to the pure man to have an erection.

Dov Baer the Maggid of Mezhirech (d. 1772).

our holy master Rabbi Judah the Prince; in Ket. 104*a*.

This refers to sanctity in the act of intercourse because the 'little finger' represents the penis.

the rabbis say Pes. 112*b*, where 'finger' means the penis.

will not trespass on the sacred referring to Ber. 35*a–b*, which says that everything in the world belongs to God, so that the benediction thanking Him is akin to the redemption of sacred things for profane use.

Purification ... at all times this is not an exact quote from Vital but a paraphrase of his conditions.

at least when it is necessary i.e. after an emission of semen.

mikveh the ritual bath; kabbalists and Hasidim attach great significance to regular immersions in the *mikveh* and regard it as having powers of purification. The imagery in this passage is complex and relates to Rashi's commentary on the rite of the red heifer, whereby after Israel had sinned by worshipping the golden calf, the purification rites had to be performed with the ashes of the cow, the mother of the calf (Num. 19: 2). Rashi quotes the midrash of R. Moshe Hadarshan that when an infant soiled the floor of the king's palace, the king ordered the mother of the child to wipe up the mess. The kabbalistic application, to which E. refers, is that all this represents the sefirotic processes. Human sin sends baneful influences on high that affect Tiferet (the Delightful Son, Ze'ir Anpin). Binah, the Mother, 'purifies' her Son since She represents repentance. The waters of the *mikveh*, the purifying agent, are thus a representation of Binah.

Zohar, 'Bereshit' Zohar i. 33*a*.

tzadik 'righteous', *tzadik*, representing Yesod, the sixth of the lower *sefirot* around Tiferet.

good" [Gen. 1: 10], and elsewhere it is said: "Say ye of the righteous that he is good" [Isa. 3: 10].' I have explained this passage at length in a responsum. The waters of the *mikveh* are the waters of knowledge,* as Rambam* says at the end of 'The Laws of *Mikvaot*'.* And in the same passage in the Zohar it is stated: 'R. José said: "the gathering of the waters" refers to Israel, as it is said: "The Lord is the *mikveh* of Israel"* [Jer. 17: 12].' This is the Foundation of the Father,* the supernal Wisdom, which is the Knowledge* of the Lesser Countenance* and called Israel and is drawn from the Supernal Brook,* the supernal *mazala*,* *notzer ḥesed la'alafim** (the initial letters forming the word *naḥal*).* And one should have in mind the intentions of the unifications of the *mikveh*. In that responsum I have treated at length the subject of the intentions to be had while in the *mikveh*; may the Lord be with me that I may publish it, for in it I have explained the great principle of the source of living waters. Immersion after a seminal emission should be in cold water,* according to the mystery of: 'As cold waters to a faint soul so is good news from a far country' [Prov. 25: 25]. 'A far country' is the name given to the foundation of repentance. For the foundation of Father is called 'far': 'from afar the Lord appeared unto me' [Jer. 31: 3]; 'and he saw the place afar off' [Gen. 22: 4], as is explained in the *Siddur*.* 'A far country' is the name given to the foundation of Mother, Repentance ('far' denoting Binah, as in: 'She bringeth forth her food from afar'* [Prov. 31: 14]), which is the essence of the *mitzvah*, and on the basis

the waters of knowledge Da'at, 'Knowledge', is the intermediary between Ḥokhmah and Binah.

Rambam Maimonides (1135–1204).

'The Laws of *Mikvaot*' ch. 11: 12 in Maimonides' *Mishneh torah*. Maimonides remarks that just as the *mikveh* removes bodily contamination, the waters of knowledge, i.e. the sinner's proper intention to sin no more, remove spiritual contamination from the soul. E. uses this for his interpretation of the kabbalistic terms.

The Lord is the *mikveh* of Israel in the verse the word means 'hope', but in the Mishnah (Yom. 8: 9) the verse is interpreted to mean that God purifies Israel as a *mikveh* does. E.'s interpretation on the basis of kabbalah, is: 'The Lord (= Malkhut) is the *mikveh* of Israel' (=Tiferet). Malkhut is called the *mikveh* of Israel because as the waters flow into the *mikveh*, so the *sefirot* flow into Malkhut.

of the Father Abba, Ḥokhmah.

Knowledge Da'at.

the Lesser Countenance Ze'ir Anpin.

Supernal Brook Binah.

mazala here understood as the 'flow', i.e. of the *sefirot*.

notzer ḥesed la'alafim Hebrew for 'keeping mercy unto the thousandth generation' (Exod. 34: 7).

naḥal 'brook'.

seminal emission ... cold water a seminal emission is *keri*; E. here plays on the words *keri* and *karim*, the latter meaning 'cold'.

Siddur the reference here is to the Lurianic prayer-book; see 1894 edn. by Jacob Koppel of Mezhirech.

'She bringeth forth her food from afar' the 'woman of worth' of Prov. 31 who brings her food from afar is Malkhut, whose 'flow' stems from Binah.

of this it is called 'the dry land* earth' [Gen. 1: 10]. And the mystery of 'cold waters' is that its numerical value is that of *m–t*.* This is the mystery mentioned, in the name of the Baal Shem Tov, that the *tzadik* is released from the death due to him because of emission, according to the mystery of: 'Precious [*yakar**] in the sight of the Lord is the death of His saints' [Ps. 116: 15]. (For the *tzadik** suffers more when he has a seminal emission [*keri*] than the sufferings of death, and as a result he is released from death. And from this you can understand the saying at the end of *Yoma** that he who has a seminal emission on Yom Kippur will see seed* and live long. Note this well.) *Yakar* is formed of the same letters as *keri*,* and it is as cold waters to a faint soul. And waters belong to the mystery of self-sacrifice, as in falling on the face,* and the sin is erased by the cold waters. As a result he will have the merit of comprehending, according to the mystery of good news: 'and God saw the light,* that it was good' [Gen. 1: 4], as stated above from the Zohar. Elsewhere I shall expound on this at length; here I have referred to it only incidentally in connection with comprehension of this science. And so I have it as a tradition from my teachers.

VIII

'No night should be allowed to pass ... And he should reflect each night on his deeds during the day.' Thus far his words. The Zohar refers to this in the expression 'the masters of reckoning'.* This is a great principle for the attainment of this science. And it is said, 'that in the night they may be *mishmar* [a guard] to us, and may labour in the day' [Neh. 4: 16]. *Mishmar*

dry land Malkhut.

m–t the root letters of 'death' have a numerical value equivalent to that of 'cold waters', *mayim karim*. For *m,t* = 'death': *mem* (40) + *tav* (400) = 440. *Mayim karim* = 'cold waters' = *mem* (40) + *yod* (10) + *mem* (40) + *kof* (100) + *resh* (200) + *yod* (10) + *mem* (40) = 440.

yakar the point here is that *yakar*, 'precious', is formed of the same letters as *keri*. Thus, the saint is so remorseful for having an emission that it is for him as bitter as death, and in this he finds the 'precious' gift of atonement.

the *tzadik* the saint on earth (used in Hasidism for the Hasidic master), of whom Yesod, the *tzadik* on high, is the counterpart. In the bodily representation of the *sefirot*, Yesod is the organ of generation.

Yoma 88*a*.

see seed a play on the word *zera*, 'offspring', but also meaning 'semen', i.e. one who has had a seminal emission and expresses extreme remorse for it will 'live long'.

Yakar* ... *keri as above, *keri* is formed of the letters *k,r,y*.

falling on the face The prayer of supplication (*Taḥanun*) recited while 'falling on the face' (in practice, only symbolically, by placing the head on the arm) as a representation of death.

the light i.e. the light of knowledge, of compassion.

'the masters of reckoning' i.e. men who count their sins and repent of them; Zohar iii. 178*a*.

is connected with the word *meshameret*, the vessel through which wine is filtered. For the day is for worship, and during worship it is impossible for a man to reflect deeply on his own unworthiness and to engage in self-abasement since that might cause him to be in a state of misery and melancholia, Heaven forbid, whereas at night he is not engaged in worship.

It is also stated in the *Zohar ḥadash** (on the verse: 'And the Lord God planted a garden eastward, in Eden' [Gen. 2: 8]; study it carefully there) that one should not even study the Torah before midnight for the gates are closed,* except during winter when the night borrows from the day* so that one can then study the Torah. And the Ari, of blessed memory, decreed that one should not sleep for the first three hours of the night, and at that time a person is obviously obliged to study the Torah. For what else should he do? Should he sit doing nothing, Heaven forfend? That is surely impossible. But so that you have no difficulty in understanding the matter, you must know that both in winter and in summer we have the same way of counting time,* that is, midnight is twelve o'clock, and the time for sleep is six o'clock. This is explained in the books, not as it appears from the work *Sha'arei tzion*;* and see the work *Tevuot shor*,* at the end, and the work *Leḥem min hashamayim*.*

Now, my brother, sleeping should not be as the beast sleeps. But for the purpose of sleep you must study the 'Intentions while Reciting the *Shema* before Retiring,'* how to elevate the Female Waters* to the foundation of Mother,* the foundation of repentance, offering up the self as if in death, lying on your left side where death is bound up.* Then you should examine and reflect on all that you have done during the day; you must confess your sins and beg for mercy, speaking in your heart like a son who entreats his

Zohar ḥadash 18*a*; that one should not study the Torah until midnight since only then do the angels in Heaven begin to sing their songs of praise.

the gates are closed the heavenly gates.

during winter when the night borrows from the day when the nights are long and the days short, part of the night is treated as the day for this purpose.

the same way of counting time i.e. not following the opinion that the night is divided into twelve equal portions and that midnight lies at the half-way point.

Sha'arei tzion collection of prayers by Nathan of Chelma, of the school of R. Hayim Vital; see ibid. pp. 6–7 on the long nights. On this question of reckoning the time of the midnight visit see Y. D. Harfenes, *Yisrael vehazemanim*, chs. 18–19, pp. 167–76.

Tevuot shor by Ephraim Zalman Schor (Lublin, 1716).

Leḥem min hashamayim by Jacob Zemah; a variant of his *Nagid umetzaveh*.

'Intentions while Reciting the *Shema* before Retiring' in *Peri etz ḥayim*, gate 15, pp. 68*a*–72*a*.

Female Waters of Malkhut, the Shekhinah, as above.

Mother Binah, Imma.

left side where death is bound up the *sefirot* on the left—Binah, Gevurah, Hod—are the source of judgement and death.

father to forgive him. Weep if you can, and let your heart break within you. Then you will cause all the forces of judgement in the darkness to be diminished by means of *sheinah*,* which has the numerical value of 365, that is, thrice the 120 numbers of the combination of Elohim plus the five root letters,* as is explained in the 'Intentions of *Pitum haketoret*'.* All judgements will then be sweetened and you will have no fear when you sleep, and your sleep will be sweet after you have elevated your soul to deposit it in the foundation of Mother, and She will watch over you.

Verily, my brother: the Ari, of blessed memory, has many intentions to be borne in mind while reciting 'Into Thy hand I commend my spirit'; see the 'Intentions while Reciting the *Shema* before Retiring'. And if this impossible for you to do, you must not make the ascent.* For the basic principle here is that a man should not fool himself. It is essential for an intelligent person who really desires to attain the pillar of worship* to prepare himself correctly, readying his instrument* by every movement of complete worship to be worthy for the great thing. And if you are aware that you are incapable of performing the unification by surrendering yourself to death and by summoning up the Female Waters to deposit your soul in the supernal foundation when you recite: 'Into Thy hand I commend my spirit', you must not then dwell overmuch on your own lowliness so that you do not go to sleep in a spirit of misery and melancholia, Heaven forfend. And you must not look too closely into the deeds you have performed during the day so that, Heaven forfend, judgement should not prevail against you as a result of misery and melancholia. And there is even greater danger that the depths of the sea* should challenge you, Heaven forfend. (And you must not, Heaven forfend, weep in a spirit of misery, for a downcast spirit brings about judgements and reinforces them, and you will then be incapable of sweetening them and, Heaven forfend, your power will be diminished.) Concerning this David said: 'And see if there be

sheinah Hebrew for 'sleep': *shin* (300) + *yod* (10) + *nun* (50) + *hé* (5) = 365.

365, that is thrice the 120 numbers of the combination of Elohim plus the five root letters There are 120 possible permutations of the five Hebrew letters that make up Elohim (i.e. ELHYM, EHLYM, etc.), and 3 × 120 = 360. Adding 1 for each of the five letters of Elohim (i.e. 5) gives 360 + 5 = 365.

'Intentions of *Pitum haketoret*' *Peri etz ḥayim*, III. v. 12 *c–d*.

must not make the ascent if you feel unable to achieve the correct intentions it is better not to try to do so.

pillar of worship rabbinic literature sees Judaism as having three central 'pillars': worship, Torah, and benevolence; see Avot 1: 2.

readying his instrument E. means that the worshipper should use his mind—his 'instrument'—with the proper intentions to the extent that he possibly can.

depths of the sea the *kelipot*.

any way in me that is grievous,* and lead me in the way everlasting'* [Ps. 139: 24]; that is, in the way of simple folk who have no comprehension of this science to be able to ascend the ascents of the *tzadik* (and the ladder with its feet on the ground ...* with self-sacrifice for the Lord's sake; because of melancholia). David requested that his power should not be diminished, Heaven forfend, at a time when was unable to perform the unification (and see Rashi's comment on this verse) in order not to reinforce the judgement through worship in a melancholy state, Heaven forfend.

In all this you must have a well-thought-out assessment to the best of your ability and in accordance with the power of the instrument you have prepared* during the day; for with regard to holy sacrifices, the night follows on the day.* And if you are unable to make the assessment you should not be aggrieved. As I have explained in a comment on the translation (in the Targum)* of the verse: 'One such day, he came into the house to do his work' [Gen. 39: 11], translated as 'to examine the accounts',* that is, to render an account of the temptation of his inclination,* and he was then in a state of grief and misery. And for the reason it says *vayehi*,* an expression of grief; see the Zohar, 'Vayeshev',* p. 190*b*. Because he examined his accounts, this caused her to seize hold of his garment* [v. 12]; that is, she was able to get hold of his garment, and the depths of the sea overcame him, Heaven forfend, until he saw the image of his father,*

any way in me that is grievous the Heb. *derekh otzev* is understood by E. as denoting *atzvut*, 'melancholia', 'sadness', a miserable state of mind, so he imagines Rashi's comment to be in this vein.

in the way everlasting the Hebrew for 'everlasting' is *olam*, which can also mean 'world'. Hence 'the way of the world', the way of the ordinary folk. In Hasidism, the term *olam* represents the Hasidim as opposed to the master, the *tzadik*.

and the ladder with its feet on the ground Jacob's ladder (Gen. 28: 12), with its feet on the ground and its head reaching to heaven, is interpreted in the moralistic literature as referring to prayer.

the power of the instrument you have prepared the preparation of the mind to concentrate adequately.

the night follows on the day usually in Judaism (with regard to the sabbaths and festivals, for example), the day follows the night, e.g. the sabbath begins at nightfall on Friday and ends at nightfall on Saturday. The pattern with regard to the Temple was different in that the holy sacrifices were offered by day and the meat eaten until daybreak the next day or, in connection with some sacrifices, the daybreak after that.

Targum the Aramaic translation of the Torah by Onkelos.

to examine the accounts the plain meaning of the Targum is literally that Joseph went in to do his book-keeping, but E. understands it to mean that Joseph went in to render an account of his deeds, to engage in self-scrutiny.

temptation of his inclination to sin with Potiphar's wife.

vayehi 'and it came to pass', interpreted as *vai yeḥi*, 'Woe there was'.

Zohar, 'Vayeshev' Zohar i. 190*b*.

caused her to seize hold of his garment the 'her' refers to Potiphar's wife. 'His garment' is understood as the 'cloak' of the evil inclination.

the image of his father Midrash Gen. Rab. 87: 7. 'R. Huna said in the name of R. Mattena: "He saw his father's image, at which

namely, the mystery of *avir Ya'akov* (the letters of which form the name Rabbi Akiba) and he was able thereby to cast all the Outside Ones into the depths of the sea so he 'got away and fled outside'. This, as stated above, is a great principle.

And then, at least, you must make the assessment after midnight when you rise from your bed. This is what R. Hayim Vital means when he says that the whole night should not pass ... namely, when he observes that a person who has not repented before going to sleep should repent after midnight. The general principle is that the main effort of rendering an account—repenting, confession, and remorse—is 'the night of vigil for all the children of Israel throughout the ages' [Exod. 12: 42]. This is the reason why night and darkness have been created: so that the Outside Ones should not draw sustenance from the copulation of the King* so that the wicked are deprived of light, and the arm of the wicked* is broken. The sleep of the wicked* is beneficial ... but the righteous rejoice and exult before the Lord.

R. Hayim Vital's admonition to rise at midnight encompasses this. Consult it there. A person should weep with many tears, crying out to the mountains. And he should perform the *tikun* referred to in the work *Mishnat ḥasidim.** He should weep bitterly over the verses recited then, which bring weeping to the sensitive soul. Afterwards he should see to it that he follows the order of studies laid down by the disciples of the Ari, of blessed memory, mainly the study of the Zohar, which at that time greatly assists comprehension, as is well known from the sacred books. Especially, he should study the writings of the Ari, of blessed memory. Then he will be wise and successful, and speed safely on his way. What can I say, what can I speak, O my brother? The Zohar is full of this, how they did everything to encourage rising at midnight, which is when the Holy One, blessed be He, takes delight with the saints in the Garden of Eden. The main nature of this delight is stated in the Zohar, 'Balak', p. 193. Consult it there, and its completion* in the *Zohar ḥadash* on this section. 'R. Eleazar and R. Abba

his blood cooled, for it says: 'By the head of the mighty one of Jacob' (*avir ya'akov*, Gen. 49: 24)".' E. sees *avir Ya'akov* as a reference to R. Akiba (the two are acronyms in Hebrew, who was able to withstand the Outside Ones).

copulation of the King of Tiferet with Malkhut.

arm of the wicked based on Ps. 10: 15.

sleep of the wicked Mishnah Sanh. 8: 5: 'Wine and sleep for the wicked is beneficial to them and beneficial to the world', i.e. when they are in a drunken stupor or when they sleep they do no harm. E. applies 'the wicked' to the *kelipot*.

Mishnat ḥasidim by the Italian kabbalist Immanuel Hai Ricchi (1688–1742), pt. iii, pp. 40*b*–51*a*.

Zohar, 'Balak', p. 193 ... and its completion Zohar iii. 193*a*–*b*; *Zohar ḥadash*, 53*a*–*b*. The passage E. quotes first is from the Zohar, not the *Zohar ḥadash*.

went to visit R. José ben R. Simeon ben Lakunia, the father-in-law of R. Eleazar. They arose at midnight ... R. Eleazar said: "Now is the time and the occasion when the Holy One, blessed be He, enters the Garden of Eden to take delight with the saints therein." What is this delight and how does He take delight with them? Said R. Eleazar: "This was a wondrous mystery, a secret I did not know." Said R. Abba: "Were they, the great men of former times, relying on an empty fantasy, and did they not seek to understand on what they were established in this world, and what they were to expect in the next?" (He meant this as an expression of surprise.) So R. Eleazar then began to expound the verse: "O Lord, thou art my God ...".' See the completion in the above-mentioned *Zohar ḥadash*: 'We learn from this that whoever rises at night at the time when the Holy One, blessed be He, takes delight with the saints, should recite this verse with deep feeling and with full intention. After this verse: "O Lord, Thou art my God, I will exalt Thee, I will praise Thy name, for Thou hast done wonderful things" [Isa. 25: 1], he should recite the verse: "I will give thanks unto Thee, for I am fearfully and wonderfully made" [Ps. 139: 14], and this was the praise offered by the saints of old.' Consult the whole of the passage and you will see how great is the joy and how great the reward of those who rise at midnight. It is a peg and cornerstone for attaining the true wisdom of the Torah, and a door that opens to those who knock in repentance. Especially in this generation, how many activities should one who wishes to attain to Torah and worship engage in so that he should be able to rise at midnight to be among the companions in the Garden!

My brethren, my friends, it is not sufficient to do what many devout folk do, driving sleep away and remaining awake until after midnight, when they perform the *tikun* and then go to sleep. For [in doing so] they invert and change the channels, Heaven forfend. For until midnight is the time for sleep, an act of divine worship in itself, and afterwards one should rise, at the time of compassion and acceptance after midnight. They invert the order. So do not be contrary and sleep after midnight, the time when the Holy One, blessed be He, goes to take delight with the saints in the garden of Eden.

This does not apply to one who wishes to remain awake all night as a means of penance and mortification, concerning whom the Ari, of blessed memory, writes that this frees him from the punishment of *karet*.* But even here care must be taken that a person does not forfeit his own life,* as it is

karet 'extirpation', being 'cut off' from the people—the divine punishment for certain sins.

forfeit his own life by tormenting himself without studying the Torah.

stated in the Mishnah:* 'One who remains awake at night . . .'; see there the comment in *Tosafot yom tov*.* If a person reckons that his mind will not be clear for the morning prayer, he is allowed to sleep a little before daybreak. As stated in the religious works and the work *Reshit ḥokhmah*.* Of this there is more to speak and investigate, but here is not the place.

But for the person who does not wish to remain awake all night, the main *mitzvah* is to rise at midnight. He should drive sleep from his eyes in the true longing of his soul for God, to bestir the love until the desire is awakened to perform the *mitzvah*. As it is stated in the Zohar, 'Aḥarei', p. 68:* 'Come and see perfect worship . . . As we have learnt: "And thou shalt love the Lord thy God" [Deut. 6: 5]. A man must love the Holy One, blessed be He, with his very soul. This is perfect love, the love of his soul and spirit. Just as these are attached to the body and the body loves them, so should man be attached to the Holy One, blessed be He, with all the love of his soul. Hence the verse says: "My soul hath desired Thee in the night" [Isa. 26: 9]. In his love for the Holy One, blessed be He, a man should rise each night to strive in His worship until the dawn breaks to draw down upon himself a thread of mercy.' Consult the whole of the passage on this verse.

So it is stated clearly that the main thing is for a person to rise at midnight in loving desire to give satisfaction to his Maker and Creator. He should fulfil the verse: 'and when thou liest down and when thou risest up' [Deut. 6: 7], referring to 'and thou shalt love' at the beginning of the chapter, sleeping being a form of worship in its own right and rising likewise, according to the mystery of the *komah*,* so as to be counted among the companions in the Garden.* There is no better time of the day than after midnight for a person to be in solitude and engage in repentance, remorse, and confession, to speak words of love and supplication in private to his Maker, to offer supplication for his soul and to be drawn to his Beloved with the delights of love. He should beg pardon, forgiveness,

in the Mishnah Av. 3: 4. 'He that wakes in the night . . . and turns his heart to vanity, is guilty of his own life.'

Tosafot yom tov commentary to the Mishnah by R. Yom Tov Lippmann Heller (1579–1654), E.'s ancestor. Heller, in his comment on this Mishnah, interprets the saying to mean that even if one does not intentionally stay awake in order to turn one's heart to vanity, one is still guilty.

Reshit ḥokhmah by Elijah de Vidas (16th cent.), a disciple of Cordovero; the reference is to 'Sha'ar hakedushah', ch. 7.

Zohar, 'Aḥarei', p. 68 Zohar iii. 68*a*.

mystery of the *komah* the *shiur komah*, according to which every human act has its counterpart on high.

the companions in the Garden the 'companions' are the mystical adepts who escort the Shekhinah in the Garden of Eden.

and atonement for what has transpired during the day if he has not conducted himself in the abstemious manner fitting for those who serve God.

And it is impossible for him to have walked on the way and to have had conversations with others without offending against: 'Happy is the man who forgetteth Thee not.' It is well known that remembering the unity of God is a permanent obligation from which a man is never released for a single moment, as the *Sefer ḥaredim** states. Let him, at least, remember it at night. Let him recall all that he has done during the day that has past, at every hour and every moment, and recall literally every word he has spoken, at least in general, how he has spoken and conversed with his friend and members of his family and how he has behaved. And he should recall whether he has fulfilled the verse 'when thou liest down and when thou risest up', as it is stated in the Zohar, 'Va'etḥanan', p. 269;* see that passage on the qualities contained in the first paragraph of the *Shema*. And he should consider thoroughly all his deeds, begging his Maker to pardon him. And he should request the Creator to help him in the coming day to be attached to the essence of the unifications of the wisdom of the Torah and its pleasant ways of conduct, and that no mishap at all should befall him, Heaven forfend; rather, he should be bound to the Creator and His Torah and to the mercy of God all the time, and be saved from strange thoughts and from strange fire, and only be in fear of the Lord all the day.

IX

'A person should be engaged as little as possible in business activities. If he has no other means of sustenance, let him devote to it Tuesday and Wednesday.' Thus his words.

Now, my brother, it may be impossible for him to devote so little time to his business that he can only engage in it on Tuesday and Wednesday. Moreover, there may be a person whose business activity is considerable, lending and borrowing, paying his debts and behaving generously, especially in this generation when earning a living is exceedingly difficult. Concerning this the Zohar, 'Ekev', p. 273*b*,* states: 'Because of this quality they will be redeemed, as it is written, "and the afflicted people Thou dost

Sefer ḥaredim by Eleazar Azikri (1533–1600), Safed kabbalist. The reference is to ch. 1: 1 (Jerusalem edn., 1966, p. 49) and ch. 4: 40 (ibid. 63).

Zohar, 'Va'etḥanan', p. 269 Zohar iii. 269*a*.

Zohar, 'Ekev', p. 273*b* Zohar iii. 273*b*.

save" [2 Sam. 22: 28]. "Afflicted" is an expression denoting poverty.' Consult the passage. And it is forbidden for a businessman to give up his activities, for he can do many *mitzvot* with his wealth by giving to those who have not, especially in this generation where we have to bear the yoke of heavy taxation, the severe yoke of Exile in this generation of the Heels of the Messiah,* when the people of the land are increasingly in decline; upon whom can we lean?*

Yet, my brother, you are not free to desist from the study of this science, Heaven forfend, because you are heavily engaged in business, whether in wealth or, Heaven forfend, in direst poverty. For why else do you enjoy life? And why else did the Lord send the Ari, of blessed memory, to reveal unto us that which has been revealed to no other generation except those of R. Akiba and R. Simeon ben Yohai and his companions? In this generation the vast majority of people need to seek out a means of earning a living, from the great to the small. Even the saints of the generation,* whose sole aim is to detach themselves in a spirit of self-sacrifice for the worship of God at every hour and every moment, have no rest, because of the extremely severe need for sustenance on the part of the Lord's people who are increasingly on the decline, poor, afflicted, and crushed, literally every head is sick . . . and yet by this quality they will be redeemed. And what are the simple of our people, the people of God, to do? And why were the writings of the Ari, of blessed memory, explaining the Zohar, only revealed in such a time?

But it is obvious that even a person unable to go to such lengths in decreasing his business activities (and the truth is that he is, indeed, obliged to do all that is in his power and even more so), yet afterwards he is obviously not exempt from engaging in the study of this hidden science. On the contrary, he should seek to know this science as he searches for treasures, to search for it, to wear out his legs going from strength to strength, from *yeshivah* to *yeshivah* of the great men of Israel, and to do all in his power at all times to engage in its study in his own house, to set aside a definite period for the study of this science. There is enough room in the head* and enough time to study for one who so desires and is careful not to let it go by default. You will obviously learn according to your ability, at first

Heels of the Messiah a talmudic expression (Sot. 49*b*) referring to the period just before the coming of the Messiah when his footsteps are heard.

upon whom can we lean? the passage in Sot. 49*b* continues: 'on whom can we lean except on our Father in Heaven'.

saints of the generation the Hasidic *tzadikim*.

enough room in the head based on the talmudic saying (Eruv. 95*b*): 'There is enough room on the head to wear two *tefillin*.'

the simple rules and Talmud and Codes. You must never abandon regular courses of study to which you have become accustomed. This, however, is what you should do. If you have acquired the habit of studying, say, five pages of Gemara or five chapters of the Mishnah, you can study a little less,* say, one or two pages, as you are able. (In the Midrash on *Shir hashirim** it is said: 'R. Levi said: in former times pennies were frequently to be found and a man had a longing to hear some *mitzvah* or law or Talmud. But now that pennies are not frequently to be found,* and especially since they are all sick because of the severe bondage, they only want to hear words of blessing and consolation'. 'And in *Midrash ruth** it is stated: 'R. Isaac said: "In former times when pennies were frequently to be found, a man would say to his neighbour: Tell me such-and-such a law." But now that pennies are not frequently to be found, a man says to his neighbour: "Tell me such-and-such an Aggadah" '.) And the *Sifre*, 'Re'eh'* states: 'R. José said: "If it is your desire to recognize your Maker, engage in Aggadah." Do this so that you will find time to engage in the study of the science. For this is the foundation of the Torah and the main topic of religion. On it hinge the doors of the Torah and divine worship. Without it you cannot know the meaning of Torah for its own sake, for you will have no knowledge of the roots of the forms of the divine names, blessed be He and blessed be His name. You are not free to desist from it because of your engagement in business, just as you are not free to desist from studying the plain things of the Torah, even if the business load is heavy and required in order to earn a living. For it is concerning this that one is asked:* "Did you set aside time for the study of the Torah?" How much more are you not free to desist from the study of the inner secrets of the Torah, for without this science a man is like the beast, like an ox eating grass, as mentioned above from the *tikunim* on the verse: "All flesh is grass" [Isa. 40: 6].'

X

The words of R. Hayim Vital, 'A person should take care to utter no word unless it be for the sake of a *mitzvah* or for something essential, and at the

you can study a little less so as to have more time for kabbalistic studies.

Shir hashirim Mid. Song Rab. 2: 5. Cf. Sof. 16: 14.

now that pennies are not frequently to be found now that times are more difficult economically.

Midrash ruth the passage is not in Mid. Rab. Ruth.

'Re'eh' E. paraphrases here; the passage is not in Sif. Deut. 'Re'eh' but in Sif. Deut. 'Ekev', 49.

one is asked on Judgement Day; Shab. 31*a*.

time of prayer he should take care not to utter even a word of *mitzvah*.' Thus far his words.

In what follows, I shall explain how when you gain comprehension in this science your utterances can be holy, for you will combine your words with your thoughts and there will be a unification. For every sound that comes out of your mouth, have in mind that it is in the mystery of HVYH,* and every word in the mystery of Adonai.* Keep this constantly in your thoughts, HVYH and Adonai, until you have become accustomed to it as if it were second nature. It is to this that the rabbis, of blessed memory, say,* 'Whoever engages in Torah for its own name* merits many words.' The meaning is that with every word uttered by the mouth a unification is achieved; this will be explained in what follows, with the help of God. A man will then have the merit of uttering many words in order to unite His name, blessed be He and blessed be His name. For in every word there is a copulation,* as in the expression, 'If they saw her speaking ...'*

I have heard the following in the name of my master,* his name is for a blessing, when we examine the expression, 'merits many words'. Since it goes on to say, 'And not only this ...',* what are the many words mentioned earlier? He remarked that the word *zokheh** is connected with the word for victory, as in the expression,* 'with this R. Eliezer won a victory over the sages'. The 'many things' are the Outside Ones, the *kelipot*, called 'many' as in the mystery of the verse, 'the people of the land are many' [Exod. 5: 5], which hints at the mystery of the breaking of the vessels* mentioned in

every sound ... is in the mystery of HVYH the Tetragrammaton is usually formulated HVYH out of reverence for the sacred name. E.'s claim that every word uttered is divine refers to the kabbalistic idea that the sound represents Tiferet and the actual words represent Malkhut. Hence in every word there is a unification of 'the Holy One, blessed be He (Tiferet), and His Shekhinah (Malkhut)'.

Adonai the traditional way of pronouncing the Tetragrammaton and representing Malkhut; usually translated 'the Lord'.

the rabbis ... say Av. 6: 1.

for its own name Hebrew *lishemah*, usually translated as 'for its own sake', but E. puns on the word to mean 'for its name'. In the passage the expression used is 'many things', *devarim*, but E. takes it to mean 'words'.

copulation of Tiferet and Malkhut.

'If they saw her speaking ...' the Talmud (Ket. 13*a*) understands the statement in the Mishnah about witnesses who observed a woman 'speaking' to a man to mean that she had intercourse with him.

my master the Seer of Lublin.

'And not only this ...' the Mishnah first says that he merits many things and then goes on to say 'and not only this' and lists many other things. What, then, are the first-mentioned 'many things' or, rather, the 'many words'?

zokheh the Seer interprets 'merits' to mean 'he gains the victory', as in the statement about R. Eliezer, where the word denotes 'victory'.

as in the expression in Nid. 38*b*.

breaking of the vessels so that the sparks from the *sefirot* went outside the divine unity into the 'many', the domain of the *kelipot*. Thus the one who studies *lishemah* wins the victory over the 'many', the *kelipot*.

the *Tree of Life*. This is what he says, and the words of the wise are gracious, to be kissed by the lips.* But I would interpret 'merits many words' to mean that when a person speaks of worldly matters, of things clothed in the garments of worldly concerns, his thoughts are bound and attached to the Creator;* he thereby effects the unification of sound and speech, of HVYH and Adonai, as stated in the *Tikunim*, and so he has the merit of uttering many words. This is the mystery of 'I will greatly multiply thy seed' [Gen. 16: 10] and the mystery of 'Raise up many disciples.'* And the mind is also engaged, since there are higher worlds in every letter.* He thus elevates the letters to their Source to unite them with the One, so that many are derived from the One.

This is also the significance of studying those matters and laws of the Torah which will apparently never have any application. For instance, a man who has no business dealings, who neither buys nor sells, yet studies the laws of property and how this is acquired, and so forth; or we study *Kodashim** and *Tohorot*,* but why should we toil to know whether this authority or that is followed?* And among the laws of the Talmud many very unusual cases are recorded, cases with which we will never be faced, as I shall explain briefly. However, as a result of Torah study and the words spoken in this activity, things are bound and united to the Source of the Torah since the world is an impression of the Torah. By this means we infuse all things with vital power. When, for instance, a man studies tractate *Kelim** and, in the process, reads the names of many different kinds of vessels, his words and his study are the vital power that keeps the vessels in being. Because he has found the sanctity of unification in his study of the Torah, he succeeds in drawing down the vital power from the Source of the Torah, the Tree of Life and the elixir of life.* As he declares that this [thing] is unclean and this clean, he removes from them their external aspects, sifting the good from the bad. Another illustration: a man studies

the words of the wise are gracious, to be kissed by the lips a customary expression of commendation, based on Prov. 24: 26.

his thoughts are bound and attached to the Creator because he makes a practice of performing the unifications he can speak of all sorts of things, secular as well as sacred, which then all become elevated.

'Raise up many disciples' Av. 1: 1.

higher worlds in every letter the letters of the Hebrew alphabet hint at the lofty worlds on high, so that the mind is engaged in reflecting on them.

Kodashim order of the Mishnah dealing with the sacrificial cult in the Temple.

Tohorot order of the Mishnah dealing with ritual contamination in Temple times.

whether this authority or that is followed since now there is no Temple the ruling has no practical consequences.

Kelim 'Vessels', a tractate of the Mishnah dealing with the ritual contamination of vessels.

elixir of life The Talmud (Kid. 30*b*) refers to the Torah as an elixir of life.

the chapter on selling a ship with its accessories, or the chapter on selling a house together with its contents,* or the laws regarding the purchase of trees, or all the things in the world that are mentioned in detail in the Torah—heaven and earth; the act of ploughing and sowing ... trees, herbiage, and grass; beast, fowl, and cattle. And by means of his study of the Torah and his speaking of it, he elevates all things to their Source since his study is for the sake of the Name. And so, too, the word *osek** has the numerical value of 236, and this belongs to the mystery of the *shiur komah** of the Creator, as is known from the work 'The Letters of Rabbi Akiba';* and see chapter 7 of the gate 'Divine Names'.* When a man refers in his study of the Torah to all the things in the world, he draws down the Torah unifications of His blessed name to all things and all that happens under the sun and helps them to continue to be. The unification of His blessed name fills all worlds* and surrounds all worlds* ... (From this you can understand the power of this inner science which speaks of the supernal *sefirot*, qualities, and illuminations. How great will the clarity and purity of your soul be if you delve into it profoundly, in order to live thereby. You will have the merit of having the traits of your character merge together to do the will of your Creator. And you will attain full comprehension, understand, and be wise, eye to eye and soul to soul.)

And so it is with regard to every simple word spoken by the perfect man who cleaves to the Creator: 'The casual speech of a scholar requires study.'* That is to say, one needs to study how to speak and how to engage in refined speech. Every word the scholar utters certainly contains the way

the chapter on selling a house together with its contents chs. 4 and 5 in *BB* (but E. gives ch. 5 first).

osek the term *osek* ('engaging')—one talks about being engaged in the study of the Torah—has a numerical value of 236: *Ayin* (70) + *vav* (6) + *samekh* (60) + *kof* (100) = 236, paralleling the height of the Creator, which according to R. Akiba and R. Ishmael is 236 parasangs (see below).

mystery of the *shiur komah* the mystical dimensions of the deity.

'The Letters of Rabbi Akiba' a late Midrash, but there is nothing there about the measurements. E. is probably referring to another Midrash attributed to R. Akiba and R. Ishmael, the *Shiur komah*, in S. Musiaoff's *Merkavah shelemah*, 30*a*: 'The height of the Creator, blessed be He, is two hundred and thirty six parasangs.'

'Divine Names' in the *Etz ḥayim*, ii. 201, where the number 236 is arrived at by a complicated *gematria*.

fills all worlds a Zoharic expression for the divine immanence. Zohar iii. 225*a*.

surrounds all worlds a Zoharic expression for the divine transcendence; ibid.

'the casual speech of a scholar requires study' a Talmudic saying from Suk. 21*b*. The plain meaning of this is that even the casual words of a scholar, that is, not only words of Torah, should be studied carefully as they are bound to contain wisdom. E. applies the saying to mean that the scholar himself is required to study the kabbalah so that even his 'casual speech' will become endowed with cosmic significance.

of the Torah, and as he speaks he recalls many things, and creatures are visited by him to remember them for life.* When it is said, 'In the multitude of words* there wanteth not transgression' [Prov. 10: 19], this refers to where a man's words exceed his thoughts, that is, where, in proportion to his thoughts, they are in the majority (and they are not uttered in the manner of unification and are consequently a 'multitude of words'). If a man speaks without performing the unification, Heaven forfend, transgression is certainly not wanting. For he then wastes his words, and it is well known that the covenant of the tongue* corresponds ... as stated in the *Sefer ḥaredim*.* Furthermore, a man is obviously obliged to control his speech since silence is an aid to wisdom,* as R. Hayim Vital writes in his introduction. (And in the *Sha'arei hayiḥudim* he writes that it is a highly effective means of achieving comprehension in this science.) For all that, if a scholar talks a great deal, one can be sure that his intention is for the sake of Heaven, as mentioned above, so that even though, Heaven forfend, transgression is not wanting, he will see to it that he repents immediately so as to convert *pesha* into *shefa*.* With God's help I shall elaborate on this later on.

creatures are visited ... to remember them for life from the *musaf* of Rosh Hashanah, referring there to God's judging His creatures.

multitude of words that is, without the unifications the words are separated from the divine unity so that they are a 'multitude' of words instead of forming a unity.

covenant of the tongue a kabbalistic saying according to which the tongue (speech) corresponds to the 'covenant' of circumcision, and just as a seminal emission involves the sin of 'wasting seed' so the other involves the sin of 'wasting words'. Moreover, through vain and wasteful speech man is led to wasting seed; hence, 'a multitude of words brings about sin'.

Sefer ḥaredim the saying is not found in this work but in de Vidas's *Reshit ḥokhmah*, in 'Sha'ar hakedushah', 11: 6, with which E. has evidently confused it. The saying goes back ultimately to *Sefer yetzirah*, 1: 3 and 6: 4.

silence is an aid to wisdom Av. 31: 3, applied by E. to the wisdom of kabbalah.

pesha ... shefa the word used for 'transgression' in the verse quoted is *pesha*, the letters of which transposed form the word *shefa*, 'flow'; that is, the sinner's repentance brings about the flow of the divine grace and he thus converts *pesha* into *shefa*.

AND DO GOOD

I

'TO RISE AT MIDNIGHT* and to carry out the order with sackcloth and ashes and with great weeping and with full concentration on that which he utters with his lips. And then to study the Torah ...'

Now, my brother, I have mentioned previously the subject of the midnight vigil. Here I speak of the value of this vigil, for which you should consult the words of the Ari, of blessed memory. Yet it is desirable that you make the preparations for the midnight vigil before going to sleep by reciting the night prayer, the benediction of *Hashkivenu*; and when reciting the benediction *Hamapil*, you must offer supplication to your Creator, the One who has formed you, your Maker, the King of kings, that He should send His angel to accompany you with gracious favour when you sleep so that you will wake up in time with the proper intention for the vigil. This is found in the printed *Siddur* of the Ari, of blessed memory.

My brother, you should know, moreover—I have this as a tradition from my teachers—that a time of acceptance is bestirred at the midnight vigil to pardon any sin whatsoever in a far better way than the pardon offered as a result of many fasts and self-torments. In this generation, there is no man on earth capable of self-mortification through fasting. For fasting requires great separation, a departure into deserts, forests, and caves, as we find the heroes of the Zohar going out to the deserts of the dark mountains, places in which no man had trod; and they were as hermits of the desert, like the Old Man mentioned in 'Tetzaveh'.* The whole of the Zohar is full of this. Such and such a *tanna** would go into the desert, into a cave, and there in the desert he would strip off from himself all worldly concerns and draw

'To rise at midnight ...' this and subsequent quotations that appear at the start of sections are quotations from the work of R. Hayim Vital that E. is expounding.

'Tetzaveh' Zohar ii. 183*b*–187*b*, where there is a lengthy account of the old man of the desert.

Such and such a *tanna* a member of the group of scholars teaching in Palestine in the first and second centuries known as *tannaim*.

down the holy spirit by means of the songs and praises of King David. And by means of the inner Torah* they would proceed from world to world as stated in the *Sha'arei kedushah.** Go and see how R. Simeon ben Yohai and his son R. Eleazar acquired, through their separation from the world, their profound clarity of perfection in the cave in which they were hidden for thirteen years.* Here R. Simeon acquired a greater degree of comprehension than all the companions; thus he became the master of R. Judah bar Ilai, first to speak* on every occasion, and of R. Pineḥas ben Yair, his father-in-law, a holy man of the highest degree, as stated in tractate *Shabbat.** And the story of the Ari, of blessed memory—he separated himself from the world, as is well known from the work *Emek hamelekh.** And in our own day, our fathers have told the stories of the Baal Shem Tov, of blessed memory, how he separated himself in the wild mountains from human haunts before he revealed himself to others. The whole of the Zohar was literally composed in the wilderness.*

The conclusion to be drawn from all this is that, in reality, comprehension in this science is not achieved only by means of fasting and mortification, and that fasting is not so essential. What is essential is separation and solitude, fasting being only an incidental means of self-control in order to weaken the power of evil in a man's nature that stems from his physical desires, Heaven help us. By fasting, a man demonstrates a great spirit of self-sacrifice in the act of separation from physical appetites, and he offers his soul as a sacrifice to the Lord, as stated in the Zohar, 'Shemot'.* But the main aid to comprehension is separation, and the same applies to repentance, not as those devoid of all wisdom imagine.

Now if a man fasts without going away to a place where no one can see him and without any association in word or deed with others and he engages in self-torment, he will certainly bring on himself more evil traits

the inner Torah kabbalists speak of their doctrines as an 'inner Torah', in contradistinction to the surface meaning of the Torah.

Sha'arei kedushah of R. Hayim Vital; Part iii. 5 (p. 29).

hidden for thirteen years R. Simeon and his son spent thirteen years hidden from the Roman government officials.

first to speak he is so described in the passage E. quotes.

tractate *Shabbat* Shab. 33*b*, where the account of R. Simeon in the cave is given. Here and elsewhere in the Talmud, R. Pineḥas ben Yair is actually R. Simeon's son-in-law, but in the Zoharic literature he is, as E. states, R. Simeon's father-in-law.

Emek hamelekh by Naftali Bacharach (first half of the 17th cent.). E. refers to the account of the Ari's life in the Third Introduction to this work (pp. 10*a*–15*a*, esp. 10*a*–*c*).

composed in the wilderness reflecting the belief that the substance of the Zohar comprises the reflections of R. Simeon b. Yohai and his sons during the thirteen years they took refuge in a cave.

Zohar, 'Shemot' Zohar ii. 20*b*.

since the fast will arouse judgements upon him,* Heaven forfend. See in the 'Intentions of Fasting',* that fasting stems from the Small Minds,* according to the mystery of the backfilling of the letters of Elohim.* It is well known that the hold exercised by the evil inclination stems from the powers of the small aspect of Elohim,* and one must not use fasting as if it were in itself repentance so that sins may be forgiven. Unless one fasts with the proper intention, as if it were a sacrifice on the altar, the fast will cause more sinfulness; for one thus bestirs on oneself the forces of judgement, Heaven forfend.

Now in this weak generation, when it is obvious that only one in a million million will be found who separates himself from the world in the desert, when lust prevails higher than the head, as R. Zemah* remarks in his Introduction to the *Tree of Life*, later to be quoted, fasting certainly involves a far greater risk of producing severe defects of character, sadness, melancholia, bad temper, anger, and pride, Heaven forfend and Heaven help us. I myself have seen many renowned people who went in this way, only to make themselves stupid, Heaven help us. For they did not forsake the haunts of men to be on their own in solitude and to sweeten the judgements with the intellectual exercises and unifications known to those who are expert in the science, with the result that the judgements prevailed over them to an even greater extent, Heaven save us.

Come and I will show you what the *Sefer ḥaredim** has to say on the subject of the type of repentance which does not require fasting and mortification of the flesh. It writes as follows: 'In a manuscript attributed to the Ari, of blessed memory, in the book *Beit midot* (this is not the same work at the *Beit midot* in print)* I have found that all the early teachers have

the fast will arouse judgements upon him God will judge him adversely for making public demonstration of his piety.

'Intentions of Fasting' in *Sha'ar hakavanot*, 277–9.

Small Minds *moḥin dekatnut*, the stage when the 'mind' of Ze'ir Anpin is still undeveloped.

the backfilling of the letters of Elohim 'backfilling' (Heb. *aḥarayim*) is a complicated method of *gematria* based on 'going back' over the word and infilling the spaces between the letters with particular combinations of those letters; Z.E. gives a complicated note on how applying this method to Elohim can increase its value from 86 [*alef* (1) + *lamed* (30) + *hé* (5) + *yod* (10) + *mem* (40) = 86] to 930, equivalent both to the years of Adam's life and to the *gematria* of the word for a fast, *ta'anit* [*tav* (400) + *ayin* (70) + *nun* (50) + *yod* (10) + *tav* (400) = 930].

the powers of the small aspect of Elohim the 'small aspect' of Elohim is where the divine judgement that Elohim represents is present but somehow muted or implicit.

R. Zemah Jacob Zemah (d. after 1665).

Sefer ḥaredim 'Mitzvat hateshuvah', ch. 3, p. 203.

***Beit midot* in print** the phrase in parentheses is not E.'s but is in Eleazar Azikri's *Sefer ḥaredim*; for the *Beit midot* see I. A. Ben-Jacob, *Otzar hasefarim* (Vilna, 1880).

said with regard to penances for sin—mortification of the flesh, self-torture by rolling in snow and being stung by nettles, and fasting for uninterrupted periods—only apply to one who does not toil in the study of the Torah. But one for whom Torah is a constant occupation, who has knowledge and fears the Lord, his remedy is not to weaken himself and thereby be compelled to give up his studies. This is what he should do: he should choose a day when he can forsake the haunts of men to be alone with his Maker. He should bind himself to Him as if he were standing in His presence on Judgement Day and should converse gently with God, blessed be He, as a slave speaks to his master and a son to his father.' Consult this holy work for many other remedies for the soul. It is also stated that the Ari, of blessed memory, gave penitents fasts in a number corresponding with the flaws each had brought about, and gave each a special unification of those names in which he had by sinning brought about a flaw. And this is the main idea of repentance, as with God's help I shall expound further. It follows that repentance depends mainly on separation and solitude.

Now, my brother, there is no better time for separation and solitude, when there are no distractions from the thoughts of other human beings, than this time (that is, midnight). Then a man can offer supplication for his unfortunate soul which for its sins has become remote from the source of life, pure life, and been made coarse by the material body whose foundation is dust. As the saint says,* 'Behold I am before Thee like a vessel full of shame and contempt.' At this hour he should review all his past life; speaking like a slave in the presence of his master, bending the knee and prostrating himself with outstretched arms and legs, he should utter gentle words from the heart, humbling himself while reciting words of supplication. He should offer his prayers in the vernacular that he speaks and understands, in order that they might flow easily from his soul's anguish at his sins and iniquities, and, as mentioned earlier, he should beg for forgiveness, as I have mentioned from the words of the Zohar, 'Naso',* 'As for us, all we have is confession'; consult the passage. And he should accept this upon himself. He should offer supplication to God who made him, formed him, and created him, the true God, the Lord, to help him to serve Him and to fear Him with a perfect heart in truth. Let him linger at length on this. My brother, this is certainly far better than all the fasts, which only confuse and distract the human mind. This is the aim of rising to repent at

as the saint says the Babylonian teacher Rava, in Ber. 17*a*.

Zohar, 'Naso' in *Raya mehemna*, Zohar iii. 122*a*, quoted by E. earlier.

midnight. It is the resurrection of the dead,* for sleep is a sixtieth part of death.* All impure deeds are known as death, Heaven forfend, as it is said: 'The soul that sinneth it shall die' [Ezek. 18: 4], so that when a person rises from sleep and speaks from his heart to his Creator, he certainly resurrects the dead. His very sins are thereby turned into merit for Torah and for prayer, endowing him with the vital energy and joy he should have in the performance of the *mitzvot* and good deeds. Now if you will reflect on this before you go to sleep and request help from Heaven, it is certain that when you sleep you will have no fear and be at peace.

Hence, my brother, use various skilful devices in your battle against sleep so that it should not prevent you from rising at midnight, since that is the time for true repentance, for you to be bound to your Maker in separation and solitude. For all that, you can take it a little easier, not to rise actually at midnight, on occasions when it is beyond your control; when, for instance, you have just returned from a journey and are worn out, or when you require immersion in a *mikveh** and none is available. Even though the holy book *Reshit ḥokhmah** does allow study after midnight without prior immersion, yet for repentance and for the attachment of your soul to your Creator you certainly cannot proceed with an unpurified soul; you must do all you can to get to a *mikveh*. Now if it happens that you are prevented from rising at midnight you must repent for this as well, and you must give alms to the best of your ability. And if you cannot rise from your bed, at least see to it that you lie awake on your bed, uttering loin-breaking groans at the mishap, and take care to scrutinize your deeds. Concerning such matters the rabbis say,* 'Whether one does much or does little ...' More will be said of this later with God's help. May God give me the merit of serving Him with a sincere heart.

II

'To be among the first ten in the synagogue. And he should proceed to the synagogue before dawn, before the time of the obligation to put on the *tallit* and the *tefillin*.' Now in this matter all depends on the heart's intention, and the act should be within your ability to carry it out. The main thing is to be zealous in your deeds all your days, as it is stated in the *baraita* of

It is the resurrection of the dead i.e. in the category of the resurrection of the dead.

a sixtieth part of death Ber. 57*b*.

when you require immersion in a *mikveh* after marital relations.

Reshit ḥokhmah in 'Sha'ar ha'ahavah', ch. 11, p. 35.

the rabbis say in Ber. 5*b*, quoting Mish. *Menaḥot* xiii. 11.

R. Pineḥas ben Yair:* 'Torah brings to watchfulness and watchfulness brings to zeal.' Yet even for zeal it is necessary to offer supplication that one should not be, Heaven forbid, one who is zealous and loses therewith, as the rabbis say,* but one who is zealous and gains therewith.

The reason why one should be among the first ten appears to my humble mind to be this. The rabbis derive the rule that there must be a quorum of ten for all sacred matters* from the verse, 'and I will be hallowed among the children of Israel' [Lev. 22: 32]. Now there are ten sanctities (*Idra rabba*,* p. 134*a*) and a hundred benedictions, since each sanctity requires a benedictory blessing, and a blessing denotes multiplication, as Rashi, of blessed memory, remarks.* The sanctity has to be increased by the benedictions we recite (as stated in *Bava metzia*, chapter 'Hamekabel', p. 114*a*), so that each sanctity constitutes ten sanctities.*

Now the first sanctity* is called the *sefirah* of our Holy Creator, the sanctity of Keter. The first sanctity is for the time and for the future.* We know from the 'Gate of Abya'* that Keter occupies the middle ground between the Ein Sof, blessed be He and blessed be His name, and all the other *sefirot* and worlds, and is known as hylic matter;* just as there is a middle, salt, between minerals and plants; a middle, stones of the field, between plants and animals; and a middle, the ape, between animals and humans. Now the first ten hint at the sanctity of Keter. This is considered to be Nothing.* It is the source of nothingness and its function is to be Nothing, void and empty. So as a result of being among the first ten, a man attaches himself to the quality of Nothing and he is able to pour out his soul and his speech before the Lord because he proceeds with the greatness of

***baraita* of R. Pineḥas ben Yair** Av. Zar. 22*b*.

as the rabbis say in Pes. 50*b*.

The rabbis derive the rule that there must be a quorum of ten for all sacred matters see Ber. 21*b*.

Idra rabba Zohar iii. 134*a*.

as Rashi ... remarks in his commentary on Num. 6: 24 that *berakhah*, 'blessing', means 'increase'.

ten sanctities the ten *sefirot* are multiplied by ten through the 'blessing'.

the first sanctity a talmudic saying with regard to the Land of Israel (Meg. 10*a*). E. applies it to Keter, sanctified for itself and for that which emerges from it, the *sefirot*.

for the time and for the future the Mishnah (Ed. 8: 6) states this with reference to the sanctification of the first temple, but E. applies the saying to Keter, i.e. that the sanctity of Keter endows the other *sefirot* with sanctity.

'Gate of Abya' in the *Etz ḥayim*. Abya stands for the four worlds Atzilut (Emanation), Beriyah (Creation), Yetzirah (Formation), and Asiyah (Action).

hylic matter the hylic matter (from the Greek) of mediaeval Jewish philosophy is, for the kabbalists, Keter, the stage at which the *sefirot* have not yet emerged from it.

Nothing because it is incomprehensible and nothing can be said of it; it is also in a suspended state since, at this stage, nothing has emerged.

Ein Sof,* blessed be He, and he unites all the *sefirot* and all the sanctities with the truly One, the Ein Sof, blessed be He and blessed be His name. And he becomes the intermediary between them and the Creator of all worlds, as a result of which energy is drawn down to all those who have been emanated, created, formed, and made. This is a wondrous means with regard to the root of God's unity to elevate* the Female Waters* to form One together with the source of the First Sanctity. This sanctity was for the time when it was emanated, and it is the Source of unification in which its sanctity extends to the future, to all those emanated after it. The First Sanctity is composed of all ten, and it unites all that is emanated with the One from whom they are emanated. We are in possession of another mystery* regarding this topic, but here is not the place to expound it.

This is why the Ari, of blessed memory, put an end to the practice of going to the synagogue while wrapped in the *tallit* and *tefillin*. He did it so that a man should strive to be among the first ten in the synagogue and even though to walk to the synagogue wearing *tallit* and *tefillin* is also mentioned in the Zohar 'Va'etḥanan'* (the subject of the first ten is in the Zohar, 'Naso', p. 126),* since the special function of all the other *mitzvot* is to influence the other *sefirot*, while the function of this one is to perform the tremendous and awesome unification of the attachment, relatively speaking, of the First Sanctity to Ein Sof.

III

'Before a person enters the synagogue he should take to heart: "Love thy neighbour as thyself" [Lev. 19: 18].'

Now in *Torat kohanim*,* R. Akiba observes of this *mitzvah*, 'This is a great principle of the Torah.' See *Likutei torah*, 'Kedoshim'; in brief, this is what he says there: 'Know that all Israel belong in the mystery of a single entity of souls, as is well known to us, according to the mystery of: "a time

with the greatness of Ein Sof since he is there among the first ten he represents Keter, which produces the other *sefirot*, and hence, like Keter, he makes himself as naught and thereby reaches to Ein Sof.

This is a wondrous means ... to elevate in the mind of the mystic, the sanctity of the other *sefirot* is elevated to that of Keter.

Female Waters the impulse from below, human effort, makes the *sefirot* unite in Keter.

another mystery E. does not tell us what this is.

Zohar, 'Va'etḥanan' Zohar iii. 265*a*.

Zohar, 'Naso', p. 126 Zohar iii. 126*a*.

Torat kohanim *Sifra* 'Kedoshim', 2: 12) on Lev. 19: 18.

when one man had power ..."* [Eccles. 8: 9]. And each Israelite is a particular limb ... For each man is a surety* for his neighbour ... This is why my master, of blessed memory, used to recite all the confessions even though he personally was not guilty of those sins.' This is the secret behind the saying in *Torat kohanim** on this verse where Ben Azzai says: 'This is the book of the generations of man'* [Gen. 5: 1], to imply an even greater *principle** of the Torah. For the command to love thy neighbour is derived from: 'This is the book of the generations of man.' For all creatures are a single man composed of all souls. And the wise will understand.

Now, my brother, how great is the lesson to be derived from this! This is the ultimate aim of the first ten of Israel,* that the name of the Holy One, blessed be He, should be sanctified and blessed, and the ten become one and the Holy One, blessed be He, associates His name with them. But if there is, Heaven forfend, a division of heart among them, although the Holy One, blessed be He, does not despise the prayers of the many* (that is to say, even though they are many, Heaven forfend, and are not perfectly united as one), as it is said, 'Behold mighty God does not despise' [Job 36: 5], yet it seems that even though he does not despise it, it is still not really worthy.

Now this *mitzvah* can only be comprehended through the study of this profound science of the root of God's unity with all one's heart and soul and with self-sacrifice to the Lord as if one had departed this life. Only then does a person become capable of fulfilling this *mitzvah*, of which the expression 'thy neighbour' is used. This is sufficient for the wise. For he will know that his own soul is at stake and he will not fuss over his neighbour when he sees that the latter is far from perfect. And so have I heard it said in the name of the Baal Shem Tov that when a man sees some slight fault in his neighbour, he should imagine that he is looking into a mirror and seeing his own face (in the polished mirror) and not the face of

one man had power that is, each individual is part of all others—all Israel is as a single person.

each man is a surety based on Shev. 39*a*: 'All Israel are sureties (*arevin*) one for the other', but E. seems to understand *arevin* in its alternative meaning of 'mingled', such that all the souls of Israel are mingled to form a single unit.

Torat kohanim *Sifra*, 'Kedoshim', 2: 12.

of man that is, all the souls were contained in the soul of Adam, the first 'man', from whom all are generated.

principle italics mine. E. takes *kelal gadol*, 'great principle', to mean 'a great inclusion': all human beings are embraced in one great inclusion, forming a single large entity.

the first ten of Israel the first ten men in the synagogue.

does not despise the prayers of the many based on Ber. 7*b*, where the verse is taken to mean that God does not despise the 'many', i.e. communal prayer; E. takes this to mean 'even though they are many', though in the context the passage means *because* they are many.

his neighbour. Thus far his words. These words are in full accord with those of the Ari, of blessed memory. This is because he perceives, through the study of the science of the unifications of the Life of Worlds, how all souls form a single entity. Apart from this, when an idiot gazes into a mirror, he imagines, lacking in intellect, that he sees someone else. Know, therefore, my dear brethren, that this is a great principle of the Torah upon which every detail depends. For this is man's purpose: to know his own lowly state, and that there is none inferior to him anywhere in the world, once he has perceived through his study of this science (how sanctity) ascends from effect to cause and from cause to higher cause until it reaches Ein Sof, blessed be He and blessed be His name, the Cause of all causes.

It is this, the all-encompassing knowledge, that is the ultimate intention in the performance of all the *mitzvot*. The root and source of love is in knowledge, as implied in the verse, 'You only have I known ...' [Amos 3:2]. Now when a man is whole in his knowledge, the unification is complete; but when, Heaven forfend, each person hates his fellow and is envious of him, seeing his fellow in a less than generous light and imagining that he is superior to him and wiser than he, concerning such a one it is said in the *Tikunim*, *Tikun* 1:* 'Whoever separates one from the others,* it is as if he has caused a division in Thee.' Such a person, Heaven help us, is like one who cuts off the shoots,* the unifications of the Creator, blessed be He and blessed be His name.

Now a man may love his neighbour, yet may still see himself as superior to his neighbour. To be sure, there are superior degrees of grasping the greatness of the Creator, as we certainly observe in our experience. For although a man is a single body, so that when a particular limb is in a state of joy this joy extends to the whole body, the stage of the head is superior to that of the legs. In the same way, a man may say: 'To be sure I love my neighbour, but I am the head whereas he is in a lower stage, like the leg in relation to the head', and there are many different stages here. It would seem that such an attitude is no way contrary to love, yet it is still imperfect. For the reason why the head is superior to the leg is really because it is in the head that knowledge resides, the knowledge that if something is lacking in the leg it is man's head that aches. The mind is then

***Tikun* 1** this is actually in the Introduction to the *Tikunim*; E. quotes from memory.

Whoever separates one from the others whoever separates one of the *sefirot* from the others, instead of treating them as a unity.

cuts off the shoots used in Ḥag. 14*b* of Elisha ben Abuyah when he entered Paradise. In kabbalah, to 'cut off the shoots' means the mystical heresy in which the *sefirot* are divided in the mind from their Root and treated as if they are separate entities.

confused and seems useless, so that the leg is actually the same as the head since it is the leg that makes the mind whole. How, then, can the head exalt itself over the leg, since both belong to the same single body? (This is the reason why the sacrifices were offered up on the altar with the head and the leg together, in the second chapter of *Yoma*,* to unite and connect the end with the beginning.) So that where there is a lack in some other limb it affects, so to speak, the head. And this extends from cause to cause, reaching, as it were, to the First Cause, blessed be He and blessed be His name. As the rabbis, of blessed memory, say in tractates *Eruvin** and *Sanhedrin*:* 'When a man suffers, what does the Shekhinah say? "I am light in my head and light in my arm".' All this is when a man's gaze is directed downwards, seeing himself as superior to his neighbour. But when his heart gazes upwards, seeing by means of the wisdom implanted in the heart of every wise man, the pure, great, exaltedness of our God, he will see that he is inferior to every man on earth, since the load is in accordance with the capacity of the camel.* He will then see that he is responsible for every fault in the whole world, for if only he were the one to turn sincerely to God he would cure all the world's pain. (Especially in relation to his neighbour, if he really believes that he is good and, Heaven forfend, his neighbour not so good, then he is obliged to train him and encourage him to be better through well-meaning rebuke, as is stated in the Zohar, 'Kedoshim'.)* As it is said in tractate *Yoma*:* 'Resh Lakish said: "Even if a single person repents of his sins the whole world is pardoned for his sake" ', and he would succeed in removing all the evil from the world. And how did the leg come to have pain? It may be that the head was not perfect and the mind wandered so that the leg tripped over a stone, Heaven forfend. There is no need to elaborate on this for the wise. If a man really imagines himself to be so perfect, why did he not save the world and his companions from folly and the spread of evil? So it was he who caused harm to his neighbour, and he is consequently inferior to his neighbour. See what is said in tractate *Makkot*,* chapter 'These Go in Exile', on the reason why an accidental

Yoma Mish. *Yoma*, 2: 7: the head of a burnt-offering is brought to the altar together with the animal's leg. E. understands this as symbolically representing the unity of head and leg in humans.

Eruvin this is in fact found not in *Eruvin* but in Ḥag. 15*b*.

Sanhedrin Sanh. 45*a*.

the load is in accordance with the capacity of the camel Sot. 13*b*; i.e. the greater the man, the greater his responsibility.

Zohar, 'Kedoshim' Zohar iii. 85*b*–86*a*, in *Raya mehemna*.

Yoma 86*b*; Resh Lakish is mentioned in the passage, but in fact the actual saying is attributed to R. Meir.

Makkot Mak. 11*a*. The High Priest is held responsible because his merit should have been so great that such a thing could not have happened; and so in the matter of the lion.

homicide is obliged to remain in the city of refuge until the death of the High Priest, and the story of R. Joshua ben Levi, to whom Elijah failed to appear because a lion had eaten a man within three parasangs of his residence. The wise man will appreciate that I am unable to discourse on this topic at length for it is profound, and it all turns on the idea of a single entity.

This is the mystery behind the idea of loving one's companions, the great principle of the whole Torah. From whence does evil come? It is derived from the Primordial Kings,* who died because there was no friendship and love among them; hence it follows that all lusts and waste products are derived from pride, the grandfather of impurity, [from the view that] 'I shall be the ruler'*—this is why they embody the qualities of breaking and annihilation and flaw, as is known from the words of the Ari, of blessed memory, and from R. Hayim Vital's *Sha'arei kedushah*. But if a man who desires life and loves mercy loves his neighbour, his companion in the Torah, with real unity, with a love that cannot be exceeded, by this quality he brings about the repair of the channels and vessels in which there had been division and the cutting off of shoots [and which were] 'separating a familiar friend' [Prov. 16: 28], the *alufo** of the world. Now this (namely, the breaking of the vessels) is the root of all evil traits, and the root of all the evil in the world, like the unclean animals and birds to which the evil is attached; the diseased animal the like of which cannot live; carcasses, creeping and crawling creatures; and the loathsome, uncircumcised thing to which are attached all who offend against the laws regarding illicit sexual unions; see *Likutei torah*, 'Shemini' and 'Kedoshim'. But from the love of Israel, the love of companions who serve the Lord with all their heart, with all their soul, and with all their might, in accordance with the service of the house of our God, as ordained in our holy Torah, it follows that this aspect of brotherly love brings about love among the supernal channels and vessels. And when the channels are whole they cause all goodness to flow to the whole world. The vessels are whole and the channels flow with pure, clear water, directly receiving and giving one to the other. It follows that all repentance and the whole of the Torah revolves around this idea. See the Zohar, 'Naso',* p. 122, on the verse, 'When a man or woman shall commit any sin' [Num. 5: 6], where the following is said: 'It is written: "Now Heber

the Primordial Kings at this stage the seven lower *sefirot*, separate from one other, were unable to sustain one another to receive the light streaming into them from above and they were shattered.

I shall be the ruler E. refers to the over-ambitious Hasidim who wanted to 'rule', i.e. to become Hasidic masters rather than mere followers.

alufo translated as 'friend'; can mean the *alef* of the Lord, i.e. the *alpha* and *omega*; furthermore *aluf* can mean 'Lord'.

Zohar, 'Naso' Zohar iii. 122*b*–123*a*.

the Kenite had severed himself from the Kenites, even from the children of Hobab the father-in-law of Moses" [Judg. 4: 11] ... He made a nest for himself in the wilderness like a bird in order to study the Torah ... Happy the man ... he brings about a flaw to the whole world. It can be compared to sailors on a ship. A stupid man wanted to bore a hole ...' See the whole passage. This ancient parable is well known. Before the hole has been stopped up it is impossible to save the ship from going under by pouring out the water, but once the hole has been stopped up it is easy to save the ship. So it is here. Once you have repaired the broken vessel and the loss that results from it, you are able to put right that which has become crooked. Through companions loving one another, love is awakened among the supernal qualities and we are thereby able to remove all evil and to draw down all good. In a responsum on the subject of a pure *mikveh* I have also expounded this topic at length, and I have written to colleagues on the many ideas and moral lessons contained in this quality, since the ultimate aim of worship is to repair the source and root from which comes all that has been perverted. This quality is essential for repentance and the performance of good deeds in order to stop up the hole through which the presumptuous waters of the waves of the sea enter; see *Tikun* 19, p. 39.*

Therefore, my friends and brothers, know that the Outside Ones attack this quality especially to create divisions among the more immature companions and these among the mature and among the *tzadikim** and the servants of God. The Gentiles are in a state of tranquillity, the Sitra Aḥara* promoting harmony and peace among them so that in this generation they are more united than they have ever been. And yet the Sitra Aḥara attacks the companions and the servants of God, Heaven help us, and causes separation in the *aluf*. Every person to whom the Lord has given intelligence and good sense must be strong in seeing to it that there is love, brotherly feeling, peace, and friendship in the Jewish soul for the sake of this quality; that there should be even more love of Israel and the companions.

Believe me, my friends, after all this lengthy exposition and weariness of the flesh, I have not said even as much as when one puts a reed into the sea. I recall that when I was a kid* and the light of the disciples of the Baal Shem Tov began to sparkle,* how great was my desire and longing to take

***Tikun* 19, p. 39** *Tikunei zohar*, 39*a*.

to create divisions among the ... *tzadikim* referring to the quarrels among the various Hasidic groups.

Sitra Aḥara 'The Other Side', the demonic forces.

when I was a kid 'kid' (*talya*) is used idiomatically here to mean a very young man.

began to sparkle E. became attached to the circle of the Seer of Lublin, the disciple of the Maggid of Mezhirech who was in turn a disciple of the Baal Shem Tov.

delight and to become attached to them when I witnessed their limitless love for one another and their spirit of unity! And this has been stated, too, in the *Sefer hagilgulim*,* how the disciples of the Ari, of blessed memory, loved one another as is proper. And see how the heroes of the Zohar, the *tannaim*, the high mountains* for the climbers, kissed one another with flaming kisses and were proud of one another. It is not necessary to state this at any length. See the Zohar, 'Vayikra',* 'We are united to Him'; see there on p. 7*a*.* There is no need to state at length what everyone knows. At this time the Sitra Aḥara has begun to wage war to create division and controversy among the companions in order to make a division in the *aluf*. And yet it makes peace among the nations, the wicked and the atheists. For our sins, we still behave foolishly, holding back the Redemption. What shall we say! What shall we speak!

Truly, my friends and brethren, all this sprouts from the absence of truth, as the rabbis say:* 'This teaches that the truth is divided like flocks of sheep', with different ideas and divisions. Each flock is on its own.* It alone possesses the truth and no other grasps the truth. I can find some slight excuse in that it is the result of the great poverty which prevails and the hardships which have sprung up in this generation, as the wise and discerning know full well. Yet I will speak the truth, Sovereign of the universe, that it is really due to the lack of wisdom and knowledge of the ways of the unity of God and the God of our fathers that our fathers, enticed by the evil inclination, closed and bolted the door against engagement in the inner science,* giving it a bad name by declaring that whoever engages in it becomes an easy-going and wicked person, Heaven forfend, as with the one of whom the tale is told.* But, brother, you should know that at the age of 20 approximately I began to study this science, and I do not know who was responsible for the bad report that has gone out against it. Behold, the Zohar is absolutely full of the fear of Heaven and moral lessons on the *shiur*

Sefer hagilgulim the work on metempsychosis by R. Hayim Vital.

the high mountains (Ps. 104: 18) i.e. the *tannaim* are those who scale the high mountains of the *sefirot*.

Zohar, 'Vayikra' Zohar iii. 7*b*.

Zohar, 'Vayikra' ... 7*a* should be 7*b*.

the rabbis say in Sanh. 97*a*.

Each flock is on its own each Hasidic group believes that it alone is in possession of the truth.

our fathers ... bolted the door against engagement in the inner science after the débâcle of the false Messiah Shabbetai Zevi in the seventeenth century, the study of kabbalah (the 'inner science') was frowned upon since his ideas had been based on the Lurianic system.

the one of whom the tale is told probably referring to the legend of Joseph Della Reina, who sought to gain victory over Satan but became corrupt in the process; see *EJ* x. 241–2.

komah, how to dedicate each limb and literally each hair to the service of the Creator, blessed be He and blessed be His name; regard especially the writings of the Ari, of blessed memory. It is hair-raising to see how he investigates and seeks to grasp the word of the Lord in connection with each and every movement. How can this be, as the stupid imagine in the enticement of the evil inclination, to keep them remote from belonging to the Lord's inheritance? Such drippings of the honeycomb, such pleasant words! If all the seas* were of ink it would not be sufficient to explain ... how it could have been possible to write all that is in space, so many delightful things! Moreover, they do not know the roots of the unification of the Creator, with the result that controversies arise among the companions who serve the Lord, for they do not unite properly the God of truth, blessed be He and blessed be His name, with His names. The result is that the flow of grace is decreased. It is indeed true that the controversies are the result of poverty, oppression, and hardships, but ultimately it is due to the absence of the wisdom that revives those who possess it. Because of this the foundations have been corrupted, and the evil inclination is seductive in declaring that it is this science which is corrupting, Heaven forfend. Is there any greater libel, brother, than this? And as for that tale, this has always been the case, as that saint prayed that our company should not be like ...* So we see that in former generations whoever wished to go out* could do so (in his free choice). Therefore, my brother, 'taste and see that the Lord is good. Happy the *gever* that trusteth in him' [Ps. 34: 9]—the *gever* and *a fortiori* the *ish*.* The Lord is good to those who hope for Him, seeking Him with all their heart and soul. Be strong and firm and all will be well.

So far as the other conditions to which R. Hayim Vital refers under the heading 'Do Good', these are appropriate for every spiritually-minded

If all the seas ... Shab. 11*a*: 'If all the seas were ink ... they would not suffice to record the space of government', i.e. the Roman government; but for E. here the meaning is the divine government of the world.

company should not be like ... see Ber. 17*b*, where the prayer is uttered (E. refers to its author as 'that saint') that our company (i.e. group or association) should not be like that of David, from which Ahitophel came, or like other groups in ancient times from which wicked men came; i.e. kabbalah must not be seen as tainted because it led astray one who ought not to have been in the company of kabbalists in the first place.

whoever wished to go out i.e. from the realm of the holy—there is freedom of choice to leave the Jewish way.

the *gever* and *a fortiori* the *ish* the word *gever*, used for 'man' in Ps. 34, denotes a type inferior to that of *ish*, meaning a man of stature; hence E.'s *a fortiori* argument. If God helps those who have the lowly stage of *gever*, how much more so will He help those who have attained the stage of *ish*.

person, quite apart from the question of their advantage for the study of this science. We need only add that when he states 'to have *kavanah** in prayer', he is not referring particularly to the *kavanot** stated in 'The Pillar of the Amidah'.* For, believe me, even if a man spends all day on this form of *kavanah*, reflecting on it all the time, he will be unsuccessful in completing a single prayer in the proper manner, since its length is as the length of the earth; the exception is those people of the highest degree of sanctity, those separate from all worldly concerns, apart from ordinary humans, those whose being is in the high places of the world. In this generation there is no mind that can bear it. No one today is able to float through the lengthy exposition stated there, namely, the basic means of perfecting the supernal illuminations of the copulations of the *sefirot* and the *partzufim* as they ascend from world to world, in order to assist them to copulate face to face.

Verily, the chief *kavanah* required in prayer is for a man to sacrifice himself to the Lord, delving deeply in the recesses of his thought to pour out his soul to the Lord until he reaches the stage of self-annihilation. This is the stage of the stripping away of corporeality* referred to in the *Shulḥan arukh*.* See especially 'The Gate of Prayer',* chapter 7, that the main purpose of prayer is to engage in the process of selection. This means that a man should cast away the evil and elevate the good in the root of his soul in his attachment to God, to elevate the Female Waters by pouring out his soul to the Lord in a spirit of self-sacrifice with all his strength and with more than his strength, binding himself with the most powerful attachment during the recitation of the *Shema* and the Prayer* so that the One who knows all secrets will be able to testify on his behalf that his desire and will, with all his soul, is for the good, like the saints who serve God in truth. He should offer supplication on behalf of the Lord and the people of the Lord, that the name of the Holy One, blessed be He, and blessed be His name, should be hallowed by every single movement and every single limb of the body. And he should dwell deeply on this idea with all his might.

To be sure, he should study the order of the *kavanot* stated in *Peri etz*

kavanah 'intention', 'concentration'.

kavanot plural of *kavanah*, here referring to the elaborate intentions in the Lurianic writings which the kabbalist has in mind when reciting his prayers.

'The Pillar of the *Amidah*' in *Peri etz ḥayim*, 41*b*–56*c*.

stripping away of corporeality a trance-like state.

Shulḥan arukh *Oraḥ ḥayim*, 98: 1.

Gate of Prayer in *Peri etz ḥayim*, 6*c*–8*b*.

the Prayer the *Amidah*, the central prayer recited after the *Shema*.

ḥayim* and toil over them in order to discover in them the ways in which the Lord is to be worshipped, for it is a tremendous thing: how to elevate his *nefesh*, *ruaḥ*, and *neshamah** inwardly and outwardly, the innermost and the surrounding illuminations, the sparks of his soul's instrument, to the root and source from whence they were hewn. He will learn the roots of the qualities, the *sefirot* and the *partzufim*, of the subtle hidden illuminations, concealed and not revealed, and how these extend from stage to stage, to his Maker, to the One who formed him, the One who created him, the One from whom he was emanated,* to the Ein Sof, blessed be He, all in accordance with the capacity of his intellect and the spiritual stage he has attained; thus we have it as a tradition from our teachers. But at the time of prayer itself, the main thing is for him to pour out his *nefesh*, *ruaḥ*, and *neshamah* to the Lord, like a son who entreats his father. Enough said. See the Zohar, 'Beshalaḥ', the passage beginning with the words: 'See the Lord hath given you the Sabbath', p. 63*b*:* 'R. Hiyya began his discourse: "*Shir hama'alot mima'amakim*" . . .' Consult the passage and you will see the ways of prayer in general.

Also when R. Hayim Vital says 'to perform, in accordance with the mystery of the *tzadik*, 90 amens, 4 *kedushot*, 10 *kadishim*, 100 benedictions', this includes, to my humble mind, that he should attach himself in every prayer, and when he studies the Torah, especially the study of this science, that it should all be for the sake of attaching himself and uniting himself according to the mystery of the *tzadik*. And he should chase after charity* and deeds of lovingkindness, and love the *tzadikim*,* going from strength to strength, from one *tzadik* to another.* Let the wise hear it and take it to heart.

We must speak with our companions further lessons regarding study. These are based on the rabbinic comment* on the verse: 'And there shall

Peri etz ḥayim this work gives all the detailed *kavanot* for prayer and other Jewish rituals.

nefesh*, *ruaḥ*, and *neshamah different elements of the soul.

Maker . . . formed him . . . created him . . . emanated referring to the four worlds of Asiyah, Yetzirah, Beriah, and Atzilut.

p. 63*b* Zohar ii. 63*b*.

mystery of the *tzadik* the word *tzadik*, meaning a righteous person (and also an appellation given to Yesod).

charity Heb. *tzedakah*, hence the association with *tzadik*.

the *tzadikim* the Hasidic masters, a further association with *tzadik*.

from one *tzadik* to another in order to learn the way in which each serves the Lord.

rabbinic comment this and the other quotes from the Talmud around which E.'s argument is here developed is in Shab. 31*a*: 'Resh Lakish said: "What is meant by the verse, 'And there shall be faith in thy times, strength, salvation, wisdom, and knowledge'? (Isa. 33: 6). 'Faith' refers to the Order of *Zeraim*; 'thy times' to Order *Mo'ed*; 'strength' Order *Nashim*; 'salvation' Order *Nezikin*; 'wisdom' Order *Kodashim*; 'knowledge'

be faith in thy times ... the fear of the Lord is his treasure' [Isa. 33: 6]—that is, the aim of study is for the fear of the Lord to be one's treasure, that this science should lead to the awe which stems from the realization of God's majesty, as stated above in the name of R. Hayim Vital. The words 'and there shall be' denote joy,* as the rabbis always remark, and, indeed, the main preparation for comprehension is to be in a state of joy, as implied in the verse 'And it came to pass, when the minstrel played, that the hand of the Lord came upon him' [2 Kgs. 3: 15], and in the saying that a harp hung above David's bed,* all for the purpose of awakening the holy spirit and the prophetic spirit. See Rambam, 'The Laws of the Foundation of the Torah',* ch. 7. And Scripture also says: 'Serve the Lord with gladness' [Ps. 100: 2]. Much is said of this topic in the Zohar, especially in 'Vayeḥi', p. 229*b** 'Joy in the morning and song in the evening'. The truth of the matter is that, after the midnight vigil, to which reference has already been made, which has to be conducted with a broken and contrite heart, a man must at once seek to draw down joy upon himself and he should sing some joy-producing melody, as I have quoted previously from the *Zohar ḥadash*, 'Balak', 'to rejoice in the delights of the King'. He should give thanks to the Lord who has given him the merit of belonging to the company of those who stand at night in the House of the Lord to serve Him and bless His name, and for all the goodness He has bestowed upon him to allow him to know his lowliness and recognize that which he lacks, and to confess his sins before Him and offer supplication for his poor soul tainted by his sins. After this he should study with great joy the order of studies laid down by the Ari, of blessed memory, until the time of prayer arrives. He should study especially the Mishnah and the Zohar and the writings of the Ari, of blessed memory. Especially, he should study the Zohar at that time, with powerful concentration. Then his knowledge will be increased and he will rejoice in his portion. 'Who is rich?* He who rejoices in his portion', referring to knowledge; the only people who should be called poor are

Order *Tohorot*. Yet even so: 'the wisdom of the Lord is his treasure' [end of verse]." Rava said: "When a man is led in to be judged he is asked: 'Did you conduct your affairs in faith; did you fix times for the Torah; did you engage in procreation; did you hope for salvation; did you engage in the dialectics of wisdom; did you understand one thing from another?' Yet even so, if "the fear of the Lord is his treasure" yes; otherwise no.'

joy the Hebrew for 'and there shall be' is *vehayah*, which expression, according to the talmudic rabbis, denotes joy; perhaps onomatopoeically, like 'ha ha'.

a harp hung above David's bed Ber. 3*b*.

'The Laws of ... Torah' *Mishneh torah, Yesodei hatorah*, 7: 4, where Maimonides declares that joy is essential for the attainment of the prophetic state.

Zohar ... 'Vayeḥi', p. 229*b* Zohar i. 229*b*.

'Who is rich?' Av. 4: 1, interpreted by E. in terms of spiritual riches.

those who are poor in knowledge.* And he should remain literally for the whole of the day in a constantly joyous frame of mind, and especially when carrying out the *mitzvot*. All this has been well explained in the holy books.

Implied in 'and there shall be' is the obligation for a man to depict constantly before his eyes the name HVYH,* as stated by R. Hayim Vital in the above-mentioned conditions.

Note. This does not mean that you should have before your eyes the name HVYH written with ink on paper or parchment. The meaning is rather that in your mind's eye you should constantly be bound and attached to His name, blessed be He, and as if there were letters flying before you in the air. You should depict these according to your understanding, that is, sometimes white fiery letters, or black, or green, or red, in accordance with the qualities of the Chariot.* In this, too, Heaven forfend that you have a corporeal concept. For there is a fire that burns and one that cools, as stated in the *Berit menuḥah*.* Concerning this it is said, 'And thou shalt fear thy God'. The eyes of the sage will be in his head. Enough said for the intelligent and for the one who walks uprightly. Not, as is the widespread practice,* of actually writing down the name HVYH on paper or parchment and then looking at it, for a great catastrophe is the result. He who does so thinks that he has fulfilled the verse: 'And he gazed at the likeness of the Lord', whereas, in reality, he has offended against: 'for ye saw no likeness'. The truth is that the wise man, even when he reads the Torah, depicts for himself black fire on white fire in order to dread and fear His name, blessed be He, as it is said, 'and was afraid of My name' [Mal. 2: 5]. There is another widespread practice in which the holy names are written in red or green. And they paint near to the name animals and ugly pictures and they call this a menorah.* And they write down the name not in accordance with its true likeness, to which the Zohar, 'Aḥarei', p. 65,* applies the verse: 'Because he hath despised the word of the Lord ...' [Num. 15: 31],

the only people who should be called poor are those who are poor in knowledge based in Ned. 40*a*.

HVYH the Tetragrammaton; because of the reluctance to write or pronounce the letters of the Name in the proper order (YHVH) it is usually written in this form.

the qualities of the Chariot i.e. according to the *sefirot*, each of which has its own special colour, e.g. white for Ḥesed, red for Gevurah, green for Tiferet.

Berit menuḥah a work attributed to the Spanish kabbalist Abraham of Granada (15th cent.).

widespread practice this practice appears to have sprung up in the circle of some pre-Hasidic kabbalists but it is not mentioned in the Lurianic writings.

a menorah Ps. 67 is often presented in the form of a menorah, a seven-branched candelabrum, representing the seven lower *sefirot*.

Zohar, 'Aḥarei', p. 65 Zohar iii. 65*a*.

Heaven save us. There are some who carve the name in front of the reading desk in the synagogue on wood or stone and fill it in with gold or silver paint. Woe to them for they have no concern for the honour of the holy name. Consequently, it is right for every spiritually-minded person to abolish that inferior practice, widely spread in this generation out of ignorance, in that they have no one to guide them. It is astonishing that all the great men have not protested against this, since the ordinary folk come very close to real error and to lopping off the branches, Heaven forfend. If the Ari, of blessed memory, ordered those who know to depict the name HVYH, where did he order them to write down the verse, '*Shiviti* ...'*? This is nowhere found attributed to the Ari, of blessed memory. One of the disciples later pointed out to me that the wise author of the *Penei yehoshua*,* of blessed memory, in tractate *Gittin*, p. 6*b*, protested vigorously at this, stating that it is contrary to the Gemara in chapter 'Hanezikin'* that one must not write a scroll* for a child. See it there. And see the *Taz** on *Yoreh de'ah*,* p. 283. And I was pleased when this was pointed out. I have dwelt on this at length because my heart grieves to witness this scandal that no one takes to heart. May the All Merciful pardon and forgive those who are ignorant.

AND THERE SHALL BE is spelled with the same letters* as those of which the holy name is composed, as the Zohar* states in a comment on the verse: 'Come up to Me into the mountain and be there' [Exod. 24: 12], for 'and be' refers to constant Being* that never ceases. This will be effective for you whenever you suffer some anguish, Heaven forfend; for instance, when you have done something, or when you have had some impure thought, or when you have associated yourself with the pain of Israel, witnessing how great is their distress and their oppression. The power of this name will prevent you from falling, from your spiritual stage, Heaven forfend, into a stage of smallness of soul, Heaven forfend, to bestir

the verse '*Shiviti* ...' 'I have set (*shiviti*) the Lord always before me' (Ps. 16: 8) is often written on a parchment or plaque and placed before the reading desk in the synagogue.

Penei yehoshua a commentary on the Talmud by R. Jacob Joshua Falk (1680–1756).

'Hanezikin' Git. 60*a*.

one must not write a scroll i.e. it is forbidden to write out a biblical verse except as part of a complete Torah scroll.

Taz the standard abbreviation for *Turei zahav*, a commentary on the *Shulḥan arukh* by David ben Samuel ha-Levi (1586–1667).

Yoreh de'ah *Shulḥan arukh, Yoreh de'ah*, 283. The *Taz* (see above) frowns on the practice of inscribing biblical verses on the walls of synagogues and such like.

'And there shall be' is spelled with the same letters Heb. *vehayah*—the letters of the Tetragrammaton transposed.

Zohar ii. 125*b*.

constant Being *veheyeh*, 'and *be*'.

the judgements, and you will remain as you are, like R. Akiba who laughed* when he saw a fox coming out of the place of the Holy of Holies. A hint is sufficient to the wise. Hence 'and be', you will always retain your present state of being. However, the first manifestations of joy should be at the time when you are in solitude, when you should rejoice in the portion that the Lord has graciously given you—knowledge to rejoice in the Torah and worship, in performing *mitzvot* and doing good deeds. Especially you should rejoice in the love of companions so that when you are in their company you will experience pleasure and joy of which there is none greater. The experience of such joy should not be, however, in anything but a serene spirit,* and you should converse with your companions in matters of Torah and true wisdom, drawing counsel from the depths of the heart for the ways of divine worship, and you should be remote from foreign joy, strange fire,* Heaven forfend.

FAITH, which the rabbis, in the chapter *Bameh madlikin*,* interpret to mean that on Judgement Day man is asked: 'Did you conduct your business affairs in faith?' Apart from its plain meaning, this saying hints that every intelligent person should conduct his affairs with *faith* [*emunah*], that is to say, that everything one does should be according to the mystery of *emunah*, the quality of Malkhut on high that is known as *emunah*: 'And he was *omen* to Hadassah'* [Est. 2: 7], referring to *emunah* of *omen*, as is well known. Whatever one does, speaks, sees, hears, and engages in should all be in the mystery of faith.* As the nursing father carries the sucking child, not allowing it to be absent from his mind for a single moment, so should man, the God-fearing man, conduct all his affairs with faith. It would appear that the reason this is referred to as *nosé* and *noten** is because *nosé* refers to the mystery of Yesod, *tzadik*,* as in the statement 'the living

who laughed see Mak. 24*b*. R. Akiba laughed because he had faith that although the Temple was destroyed, it would be rebuilt; seeing a fox in the holy place did not cause him to lose faith.

serene spirit evidently a critique of Hasidic gatherings, at which there was a good deal of hilarity and frivolity.

strange fire a reference to the incorrect practices that lead to the death of Aaron's sons, Nadav and Avihu (Lev. 10: 1–7).

Bameh madlikin the passage in Shab. 31*b* on which E. comments in this section.

***omen* to Hadassah** 'he was foster father (*omen*) to Hadassah'. *Emunah omen* is in Isa. 25: 1, the verse E. quotes at the beginning of his tract. In the kabbalistic interpretation, *omen* is Tiferet and Hadassah is Malkhut; hence *emunah* is Malkhut.

should all be in the mystery of faith all man's efforts should be devoted to bringing about the unification of the *sefirot*.

nosé* and *noten in the passage quoted from *Bameh madlikin* the term for 'business affairs' is *nosé*, 'taking', and *noten*, 'giving'; hence E.'s explanation revolves around these terms.

nosé* refers to the mystery of Yesod, *tzadik *nosé* can also mean 'to carry'. The rabbis

carries itself'. And *noten* refers to Da'at,* since it is Da'at which gives—'Who giveth bread to all flesh' [Ps. 136: 25]; and the mystery of bread is that it refers to the Female* as it is said: 'aught save the bread which he did eat' [Gen. 39: 6] and 'all flesh' is Yesod,* and Da'at is the one which unites them, after the mystery of Yesod and Malkhut. Or it can be said, 'food' is the mystery of the three brains,* the three *havayot*, and 'all flesh' refers to Yesod and Malkhut since 'all' is Yesod and 'flesh' is Malkhut. Now the *tzadik** functions as an intermediary between one world and another. At first he is *nosé*,* that is, he elevates all his deeds to Heaven and as a result of this gives strength and draws down vitality to all creatures; and this is the meaning of 'with Faith'. For the letters *e, m, n** of the word *emunah* represent HVYH and Adonai and the letters *vav* and *hé* of the word *emunah* are roots of the name in general, as is well known.

Furthermore, it belongs to the mystery of faith that the matter should not be in such doubt that difficulties and uncertainties reverberate through a man's heart with regard to belief. The word *emunah* is connected with 'And I will fasten him as a peg in a sure place'* [Isa. 22: 23] and with 'But he that is of faithful spirit* concealeth a matter' [Prov. 11: 13]. That is to say, the matter should be a certainty and it will belong to him alone, with no strangers* plundering that over which he has toiled. As it is said at the beginning of *Idra rabba*:* 'R. Simeon began his discourse: "He that goeth

say (Shab. 94*a*) that 'the living carries itself' (i.e. to carry a living creature on the Sabbath is not really 'carrying' since the living creature carries itself), and Yesod, which is called the *tzadik*, is known as the 'living' because it carries down the life of the *sefirot* into Malkhut. Hence 'the living' is called *nosé*, 'the one who carries', and *nosé* is Yesod, the *tzadik*.

noten refers to Da'at Da'at is an intermediary between the *sefirot* of Ḥokhmah and Binah. Through them, Da'at 'gives' to the lower *sefirot*, hence it is *noten*, 'the giver'.

the mystery of bread is that it refers to the Female the Female is Malkhut. In the rabbinic interpretation of the passage quoted (Gen. Rab. 70: 4), the 'bread' is understood as referring to Potiphar's wife.

'all flesh' is Yesod Yesod is called 'all' because it is the channel through which all the *sefirot* flow to Malkhut; and 'flesh' is sometimes a euphemism for the penis, which Yesod also represents.

three brains or aspects of the divine Mind, namely, Ḥokhmah, Binah, Da'at, each represented by HVYH.

tzadik the Hasidic master on earth who represents the Tzadik (God) on high.

nosé *nosé* meaning also 'to raise', 'to lift up'; and he 'gives', *noten*.

the letters e, m, n *emunah* is spelt *alef, mem, vav, nun, hé*. If *vav* and *hé*, two of the letters of the Tetragrammaton, are taken away, we are left with *alef* (1) + *mem* (40) + *nun* (50) = 91. The Tetragrammaton, representing Tiferet, has a numerical value of 26 [*yod* (10) + *hé* (5) + *vav* (6) + *hé* (5) = 26. ADNY (Adonai), 'Lord', representing Malkhut, has a numerical value of 65 [*alef* (1) + *dalet* (4) + *nun* (50) + *yod* (10) = 65]. Adding 26 and 65 gives a total of 91.

sure place 'sure' is Heb. *ne'eman*, from the same root as *emunah*.

of faithful spirit Heb. *ne'eman ruaḥ*.

strangers the *kelipot*.

beginning of *Idra rabba* Zohar iii. 128*a*.

about as a tale-bearer revealeth secrets; but he that is of a faithful spirit concealeth a matter" [Prov. 11: 13]. The verse is difficult. It should have said "a tale-bearer". Why does it say "He that goeth about as a tale-bearer"? But whoever is not serene in spirit and has no faith, the word he hears enters into him like a thorn into water until it is pushed out. Why is this so? Because he is not firm of spirit. But of one whose spirit is firm it is said: "But he that is of a faithful spirit concealeth a matter". The one who is of a faithful spirit is one whose spirit is firm, as in the verse: "And I will fasten him as a peg in a sure place".' When he says that the word heard enters like a thorn into water, he means that the thing is uncertain to the hearer and he is in doubt all the time, constantly seeking to grasp the matter with his intellect. Anything his mind cannot grasp he does not believe with perfect faith; and because of this he goes about as a tale-bearer, for in his uncertainty the matter goes around and around in his mind until he pushes it out. Consequently he reveals the secret, like uncovering the nakedness* of those forbidden to him, Heaven forfend. But the faithful of spirit—the firm of spirit, he who believes even though he cannot grasp it in the mind, which is the purpose of the mystery and the aim of knowledge—does not reveal the secret, since he knows that he does not know and has nothing to sell. He is a full vessel* that holds its contents since his mind has been completely emptied. For, 'What have you sought out? What have you found?'*

Behold, my brother, the great principle of this science is to know that one does not know. For the true aim of the science is the practice of repentance and good deeds and the fear of the Lord all the day. This is the aim of knowledge: to come to the knowledge that because of one's lowly state and the majesty of the Creator of all worlds, one does not know.

I have explained how to derive the fear of God and moral lessons from the accounts of the *partzufim* in the Zohar, in the two *Idrot*, and in the words of the Ari, of blessed memory. Take, for example, the statement that the *partzuf* called Abba is wisdom and the *partzuf* called Imma is understanding, the supernal returning; as explained in a comment on the verse: 'Behold, the fear of the Lord, that is wisdom' [Job 28: 28]. (This refers to

uncovering the nakedness i.e. he lays bare the secret, he violates the mystical doctrine. Since he believes that he really knows the secret lore he is eager to impart it to others.

a full vessel according to kabbalistic teaching, only a full vessel can absorb more of the divine light; an empty vessel can absorb nothing.

What have you sought out? What have you found? a Zoharic saying: after seeking to grasp the mystery of the *sefirot*, what can you really be said to have found since it is all incomprehensible. See Zohar i. 1*b*.

awe in the presence of the divine majesty.) And 'turn aside from evil' represents understanding. Consequently, when we read that the *partzuf* called Abba is wisdom, we mean the inner fear of God; and when we read that the *partzuf* called Binah is understanding, we mean turning aside from evil, namely, the supernal returning. And similarly, it is stated in the *Raya mehemna*, 'Naso',* that Torah and *mitzvah* are the Male and Female,* Son and Daughter.* You may ask, why should we refer to this as a *partzuf*?* You should know that any account such as wisdom is the fear of God, understanding, returning, a departure from evil, needs to be represented by the human form, complete with all its 248 limbs and 365 sinews, so that the fear should be adequately mingled and should not be in an unformed state, as it is written: 'They had the likeness of a man' [Ezek. 1: 5], and so that it should not be as a mere point,* since a point is in an unfinished state. Fear requires for its expression a complete form, with a brain, with right and left, with a body and the sign of the covenant, and with thighs and calves. There are various stages in each category, known to those who are familiar with this science. For instance, 'the head of Abba represents fear' means that the elevated majesty of the divine should be sought out by means of the science in which the supernal worlds are depicted—the subtle pictures of the Tabernacle, the pictures of Solomon's wisdom in the building of the Temple, and the pictures in Ezekiel's vision of the future Temple, all of which is for the purpose of knowing how to be in awe of God's majesty, blessed be He, and blessed be His name. The same applies to the hands of fear, right and left, for example. The right hand of fear means that a man should rebuke himself in an intelligent manner so that he comes to love God with all his might. And the left hand means to rebuke himself with thoughts of how the divine power chastises him, as a father chastises his son. One can draw similar conclusions for repentance and good deeds from this kind of deep reflection with regard to all the other *partzufim*. Now all the various stages depend on His unique name, blessed be He, and blessed be His name. Thus, the upper point of the letter *yod* hints at the *partzuf* Arikh,* the mystery of nothingness concealed from every living creature. (For the purpose of divine worship the stage of nothingness

***Raya mehemna*, 'Naso'** Zohar iii. 122*b*.

Male and Female Tiferet and Malkhut.

Son and Daughter of Abba ('Father'), or Ḥokhmah, and Imma ('Mother') or Binah.

why should we refer to this as a *partzuf*? why not use simple terms like 'fear' and 'repentance'?

mere point before the *sefirot* were differentiated they were mere 'points' in Adam Kadmon.

Arikh the highest of the five *partzufim*, corresponding to Keter in the *sefirot*.

represents utter abasement. As it is stated in the *Tikunim*, 'The supernal crown, though it is the primordial light, bright and brilliant, yet, in relation to the Cause of causes,* It is black . . .'.) The letter *yod* itself represents the *partzuf* Abba (the higher fear). The first letter *hé* represents Imma (supernal returning), and *vav* and *hé* represent Son and Daughter (Torah and *mitzvot*). All worlds and all souls depend on these, as you will see, brother, when you enter the gates.* You will then enjoy boundless desires.* How great are the means of worship and the seeking for God that you will discover in the wonderful ideas of the *partzufim*, all for the purpose of acquiring the skills of divine worship. And you will grasp it all with full comprehension and in a willing spirit. And so, too, with regard to the matter of copulations. It is all for the purpose of divine worship, in order to sweeten the judgements by means of the mingling and copulations of the qualities and channels of the unifications of His names, blessed be He, and blessed be His name, to unite each of them in the One, the Lord is One and His name One.

You might ask, why use terms like *partzuf* and copulation since it is all metaphorical, referring to the stages in divine worship? Why not use the idea which each stage is said to represent in the writings of the Ari, of blessed memory? You should know that without the use of such substitute terms, the human mind, even if a man lived for a thousand years, would be capable of grasping neither in words nor in thought the ways of the divine thoughts: to serve God, blessed be He, and blessed be His name, with a warm heart, the heart of the wise. All the substitute terms we use are figurative, like the tiny marks and figures made on a royal crown to represent the greatness of the king, his glory, and his deeds. Similarly, when we used expressions such as *partzuf* or copulation, it is all in order to compare the form to the One who formed it. (As it is stated in *Midrash shoḥer tov* on the verse: 'For the Lord God is a sun and a shield' [Ps. 84: 12]: 'R. Hezekiah said in the name of R. Hiyya: "Happy are the righteous, for they compare the form to the One who formed it and the plant to the One who planted it" '; see the passage.) Each form hints at many thousands of stages which the mouth is incapable of expressing and the mind of comprehending. (See the book *Ḥovot ḥalevavot*,* chapter 10 of the 'Gate of

the Cause of causes Ein Sof.

when you enter the gates when you understand R. Hayim Vital's works with their references to the various gates of the supernal worlds.

you will then enjoy boundless desires you will then enjoy having boundless desires fulfilled.

Ḥovot halevavot. The reference is to ch. 1 of gate 10, the 'Gate of Unification', which discusses the question of the divine attributes.

Unification'.) Every stage and every *sefirah* is allotted a complete human form, all for the purpose of divine worship. There is no need to say more since you will understand it for yourself when you study this tremendous science.

Now, brother, all the intellectual perceptions you will have of the supernal forms in order to serve God (see Rambam,* chapter 2 of 'The Laws of the Foundations of the Torah'), if you have the merit that the Lord will help you to enter in peace and to emerge in peace, know that above all these ideas you grasp in your mind for the purpose of divine worship are millions of worlds you are quite incapable of comprehending and which no thought whatsoever can ever grasp. There are supernal configurations of HVYH, blessed be He, and blessed be His name, spiritual entities in the highest bound up with the divine names, blessed be He, and blessed be His name. Their main aspects are not those you are able to grasp with your mind for the purpose of worship; they exist as extremely subtle spiritual entities unknown to you and of which you can have no idea. This is the final aim of knowledge: 'Reflect on that which you are allowed to reflect. Have no engagement with secret things'* that no creature can possibly comprehend. You should know that once you have confined the divine to the grasp of your mind, it is akin to having a corporeal conception of divinity. Anything you can grasp and depict for yourself—for example, when you say that the *partzuf* Abba is the higher fear; once you have comprehended it so that it has been grasped and confined by your intellect, limits have been imposed on it; and Heaven forfend that limits be placed on the divine qualities. But when you appreciate and acknowledge that these are spiritual, hidden entities, whose being is beyond the comprehension of any creature—this notion, too, has a more elevated notion of which you can have no comprehension, depths which you cannot possibly penetrate. This is the mystery of 'And ye shall eat old store long kept' [Lev. 26: 10], which the Targum translates as *Atika de'atikin*, with *atika* having the meaning it has in the verse, 'And he removed* from thence' [Gen. 12: 6], namely, it is removed from every human comprehension. And the comprehension of this, too, is also infinitely beyond any comprehension reaching to Ein Sof, blessed be He, and blessed be His name. If you reflect profoundly on this topic you will be successful and your intellect will soar ever higher and higher. This is the mystery of faith. For that which the mind grasps is not a matter of belief but of fact; that which the mind cannot grasp is called faith, belief in

see Rambam ... This is the part of *Mishneh torah* where Maimonides discusses the disembodied intelligences.

'Reflect on ...' a Talmudic quote (Ḥag. 13*a*) from the Book of Ben Sira.

and he removed Heb. *vaya'atek*.

the truth of that which one does not know and of which one has no understanding. Rather, I believe that the Nothing is Something in relation to the Nothing above It, as it is said in Elijah's Prayer* at the beginning of the *Tikunim*: 'Thou didst prepare many bodies for them;* called bodies in relation to the garments by which they are covered'. This is the meaning of: 'Did you conduct your affairs in faith?' That is, you must not say: Since it is impossible to comprehend anything at all except by the mystery of faith, and since after all the effort, you know that you do not know, why should you bother to engage in it at all? Just believe without any engagement in this science. Hence the author of this saying seeks to reject this opinion. Why? Because after you have made the effort and have toiled, it will be pleasing to you. For: 'If anyone says: "I have not laboured and still have found",* do not believe him.' I have explained that although we see many who have found things without making any effort to do so, and although it is said 'Happy is the man who findeth wisdom' [Prov. 3: 13], you should believe that it is easy to lose it since no effort has been expended on its acquisition. (And once it has been lost, it is as if it had never been found.) And this is why it says: 'Do not believe him', as in the verse: 'And I will fasten him as a peg in a sure place'* [Isa. 22: 23]. Enough said. From this you will understand how deep and wide is the higher faith. Everything rests on it, and the righteous person shall live by his faith, by the unifications of the divine names. Amen.

I have gone to great lengths in this matter because I see that some contemporary sages* take and expound all the words of the Zohar and the *Idrot* and the Ari, of blessed memory, which speak of the *partzufim* of Abya,* in a figurative sense, as a parable, a riddle and skill for divine worship. They seek to explain these topics by means of illustrations taken from the processes of the human mind and they take the topics in other than their actual meaning in order to bring everything closer to matters of

Elijah's Prayer *Tikunei zohar*, 2nd Introd. The implication of Elijah's Prayer is that the *sefirot* have 'garments' that conceal their 'bodies'. The garments can be comprehended, so reason as well as faith can be applied; belief and inquiry are not incomparable.

for them for the *sefirot*.

I have not laboured and still have found *Meg.* 6*b*: 'If someone says to you: "I have laboured but have not found", do not believe him. [If he says] "I have not laboured and still have found", do not believe him. [But if he says] "I have laboured and I have found", believe him.'

in a sure place Heb. *ne'eman*, with the same root as *ta'amin*, 'believe', i.e. he may have found it now but it will not last; do not be *sure* that it will last.

some contemporary sages E. obviously refers here to the Habad school in Hasidism, which he attacks in a later note (see p. 116).

Abya E. uses an acronym to represent the four worlds of Atzilut, Beri'ah, Yetzirah, and Asiyah.

sense-perception, as I have seen someone write* on the subject of the Head that Does Not Know* and the like, in order to make seem reasonable matters which belong to the Highest. This is not our way.

I have a tradition from my master, rest his soul, that one must reject the approach in which the topics are taken out of their actual, literal meaning in order to make them intelligible to the human intellect. One who does this is guilty of entertaining a corporeal notion of deity that is close, Heaven forfend, to that stated in the story of Aher,* Heaven spare us. Rather, as stated above, it is essential to believe that all the accounts in the *Idrot*, the *Book of Concealment*, and the Ari, of blessed memory, are all of subtle, spiritual illuminations perceived in the form of a Chariot by those whose gaze is pure, those possessed of the holy spirit, and the prophets, as Rambam, of blessed memory, states.* It is accepted by us that there are numerous illuminations, inaccessible to any prophet or seer, which are abstract and incomprehensible to any thought, hidden in one concealment to another more elevated and more internal. As it is said: 'Seeing it is hid from the eyes of all living, and kept closed from the fowls of the air' [Job 28: 21]. Is that which the master* has taught so unacceptable? (On the topic of the Head that Does Not Know, and that it means that we do not know which process It selects from the World of Points* and from which categories of MAH and BEN* It chooses for Itself, see 'The Gate of

as I have seen someone write the reference is probably to someone of the Habad school but I have been unable to locate it.

Head that Does Not Know *resha de lo'ityada*—a stage of the *partzuf* Arikh, meaning something like the unknowing mind of the deity. The sages to whom E. refers were evidently puzzled by the notion of an 'unconscious mind' in the deity and tried to explain the matter philosophically.

Aher Elisha ben Abuyah, called Aher, 'The Other One', Ḥag. 14*b*–15*b*, referred to above.

Rambam ... states *Mishneh torah, Yesodei hatorah*, ch. 7, on prophecy.

the master the Ari.

World of Points the stage at which the *sefirot* are mere points and have not yet assumed differentiated form.

MAH and BEN there are different ways of 'filling' the letters of the Tetragrammaton, giving different totals for the numerical value of the expression. Thus, spelling out the individual letters and filling the *vav* with an additional *yod* gives a total value of 72 [*yod* = *yod* (10) + *vav* (6) + *dalet* (4) = 20; *hé* = *hé* (5) + *yod* (10) = 15; *vav* = *vav* (6) + *yod* (10) [the 'extra' *vav*] + *vav* (6) = 22; *hé* = *hé* (5) + *yod* (10) = 15, giving a total of 20 + 15 + 22 + 15 = 72, corresponding to the numerical value of the combination *ayin-bet*, pronounced *av*, which in turn corresponds to the *partzuf* Abba. If the *vav* is filled not with a *yod* but with an *alef*, the total numerical value of the expression is 9 less, or 63, corresponding to the letters *samekh–gimel*, pronounced *sag*, which in turn corresponds to the *partzuf* Imma. If the two *hés* are filled with *alefs* instead of *yods*, the total is 2 × 9 = 18 less, or 45, corresponding to the letters *mem–hé*, pronounced *mah*, corresponding in turn to the *partzuf* Ze'ir. Finally, if the two *hés* are filled not with *hés* but with *alefs* and the *alef* previously 'filling' the *vav* is also deleted, we get 53 + 5 + 5 [for the two *hés*]—3 [for the 3 *alefs*] = 45 + 10 − 3 = 52, corresponding to the letters *bet–nun*, pronounced *ben*, corresponding to the *partzuf* Nukba. See further in my Introduction.

Atik'.* And the root of MAH and BEN provides an unimpeded thoroughfare for the worship of God by the mingling of the qualities and channels of the sacred for the sake of the unifications of the divine names, blessed be He, and blessed be His name.) Why need we invent it out of our own minds?

Come and see that the Ari, of blessed memory, strongly advised against the study of kabbalistic works composed after Ramban,* of blessed memory, because these are constructs of the human mind. I have explained that when a man grasps an idea in this science with his intellect, that idea possesses the limits imposed on it by the human mind and it comes close to entertaining a corporeal notion of deity. Therefore, brother, take good care not to engage in speculation or in the use of illustrations in divine matters, explaining them by human intellect. In the study of this science, have for your teacher only a master you know has himself been taught, mouth to mouth, by Elijah or by the souls of the other saints. But keep away from other people who use illustrations, whoever they might be, for their teaching is based on human intellect and is thus prone to error. Solomon in his wisdom states: 'As a thorn that cometh from the hand of a drunkard, so is the parable in the mouth of fools' [Prov. 26: 9]. And when the Gemara at times uses analogies, it often says, 'this is not to be compared with this but with that'. How, then, can you use an analogy you have invented in your own mind? It may well be that the analogy is inexact since with regard to the supernal illuminations it is essential to hit the target within a hair's breadth. Therefore, take care not to accept any theory based on analogy or speculation. Accept only that which comes from those endowed with the holy spirit, those who received the teaching mouth to mouth like our rabbis of the Midrash and the Baal Shem Tov, rest his soul, and the disciples of our master R. Dov Baer and his companions, who are acknowledged as belonging in the ranks of those who enter and come out again (see the remarks of R. Hayim Vital* on those who enter and come out again), not in the way, widespread in this generation, of clever theorizing by analogy. So do I have it as a tradition from my master. Discussions of this kind by the human mind come close to confusing thought. So, now, you must know this and keep far away from it lest your mind be disturbed so that you become like one who flounders in the deep sea. But the main thing is to proceed to comprehend the mystery of the unification and the combination

'The Gate of Atik' *Etz ḥayim*, 'Sha'ar atik', 56 f.

Ramban Nahmanides. The Ari's statement on this is in Vital's Introd. to the *Etz ḥayim*, 19–20, 21.

remarks of R. Hayim Vital Introd. to *Etz ḥayim*, 23–4.

of the divine names, blessed be He, and blessed be His name. For this is the purpose behind the knowledge of this science: to unify His name, blessed be He, and blessed be His name, as it is stated in the 'Gate of Unification' that the Shekhinah in exile has pleasure only through the unifications.

Brother, a further idea contained in the question 'Did you give and take* in matters of faith?' is that you should not behave as a credulous fool even in respect of an expert and renowned rabbi. Even if he is like an angel of the Lord of Hosts,* do not follow blindly any of his practices* until you have weighed them up carefully for yourself, examining thoroughly every movement you observe. You must argue it out to see what reason the master has when he makes this movement. (Do not seek to refute my argument by quoting the rabbinic saying,* 'You can only have the judge of your own day.' This only applies to a case of doubt that can be determined by the use of theory and the balancing of arguments. It does not apply to a rule clearly laid down in the Talmud and the Codes.) This is so even if the particular movement and mode of worship of your master finds favour in your eyes, so that you enjoy it since it seems gracious to you. Even then, it is said in the *No'am elimelekh** that it is like a graven image; it refers to copying some movement made by your master. This is well known to Hasidim and men of deeds.* But if you do argue it out and you see that the particular movement can be justified by the Torah, and that the intention is in accord with the Torah, then you will prosper; as it is said: 'that ye may prosper in all that you do' [Deut. 29: 8]. This applies especially when you see your master doing something that is not in accord with the Torah, for example, if he postpones the time for saying his prayers, or if he changes the times the sages have set aside for something, even for the meal of the scholar.* Although the rabbi is a renowned *tzadik* you must not offend

Did you give and take *nosé venoten* is now understood in the sense: 'Did you argue it out?' E. holds that matters of faith must not be taken simply on trust.

like an angel of the Lord of Hosts see Ḥag. 15*b*: 'If the master is like an angel of the Lord of hosts seek Torah from his mouth, otherwise, do not seek Torah from his mouth.'

do not follow blindly any of his practices some of the early Hasidic masters were accused by the Mitnaggedim of letting their pursuit of *devekut*—attachment to God—through performance of bizarre movements in prayer take preference over the performance of the deeds required by the *halakhah*. E. urges caution in this matter.

rabbinic saying *Rosh hashanah*, 25*b*. The saying implies that one must be satisfied with the master one has and not seek to have an infallible teacher.

No'am elimelekh On the verse: 'Turn ye not unto the idols' (Lev. 19: 4); see *No'am elimelekh*, 61*d*; ed. Nigal, 330–1.

Hasidim and men of deeds a talmudic expression commonly used to refer to saintly men who were renowned for their acts of benevolence.

against the words of the Torah or the words of the sages, Heaven forfend, even with regard to a single movement. As for the master, the *tzadik*, it may be he does it as a temporary measure, perhaps because of the state of his health and his particular capacity. You should judge him on the scale of merit, and Heaven forfend that you should entertain bad thoughts of him; yet you must not behave as he does in contradiction to the Torah until you argue it out with him to discover what his reasoning and intention are. If he then demonstrates to you that he has a reason for it that is in accord with the Torah, explaining it to you in a convincing manner after you have investigated it, then believe; but otherwise do not believe. Even if he tells you that he has received it from Elijah, do not believe him and do not obey him. Our sages have said: 'If Elijah comes and says that *ḥalitzah* can be performed ... we do not listen to him.'* And you must not listen to him, even if he tells you to do something in contradiction to the ordinances of the sages. Thanks be to God, blessed be He, the true recipients of the appearance of Elijah—such as the teachers of the Talmud, the heroes of the Zohar, Ramban and his colleagues, the Ari, of blessed memory, and the Baal Shem Tov—never said the slightest thing in contradiction to the Talmud. Therefore, brother, take care. This is the purpose of discussion on matters of faith, and with this peace be with you. It serves as a great introduction into this science that you should weigh everything on the scales, that there should be nothing against the Talmud and the Codes. If you find something in the Zohar, it is obvious that the Zohar will never say anything contrary to the Talmud, Heaven forfend. (As it is explained in the work *Matzref leḥokhmah* by R. Joseph of Candia.)* And if there is a debate on the matter in the Codes, the decision of the Zohar is final and you must follow it. Anyone who refuses to follow the Zohar in such matters will be brought to account. If you do this, having faith in this science and finding words of wisdom built on the foundations of the Talmud and the *halakhah*, you will proceed in safety and will not make a fool of yourself, Heaven forfend, but will find grace and good favour in the eyes of God and man.

It follows *a fortiori* that you should not believe in a master who has not been ordained by an expert master himself ordained by a master, and so on up to a master who has been ordained by Elijah, one who is acknowledged

the meal of the scholar on that the scholar takes his morning meal at the fourth hour of the day, see Pes. 12*b*.

'If Elijah comes ...' Yev. 102*a*: 'If Elijah comes and says that *ḥalitzah* may not be performed with a sandal, we do not listen to him.'

R. Joseph of Candia: 'Joseph of Candia' was Joseph Solomon Delmedigo (1591–1655). The point he made was that if the Talmud is correctly understood there is in fact no debate (Warsaw edn., 1924, pp. 86 ff).

as a master by the vast majority of the *tzadikim* of the generation; in such a one believe. But do not believe in anyone else, not even if the rabbi prophesies or conveys things to you by means of the holy spirit, for who knows what kind of spirit it is, as I shall quote later on from R. Hayim Vital's *Sha'arei kedushah*. There are many proofs for this from the ways of the Torah. My master, of blessed memory, said that one who believes in anyone who has not been ordained is not a believer at all and comes close to real idolatry, Heaven forfend. And it is said: 'according to the law which they shall teach thee' [Deut. 17: 11]—only if it is 'according to the law'. And see Rambam,* end of 'The Laws of Kings', on the means of identifying King Messiah.

THY TIMES.* On this it is stated in the Gemara that a man is asked on Judgement Day: 'Did you set aside times for the study of the Torah?' In truth there is a great principle here, for how good is a thing in its season; each period has a function peculiar to it. For instance, after midnight is the special period for the study of this science; the morning is the special period for the morning prayer with the *tefillin*, whereas night is not the time to wear *tefillin*. Even if a man's mind is clear, serene, strong, and healthy at night, the Torah still states that it is not the time for *tefillin*. A thing that is not in its season is not good; for there are channels through which the divine qualities flow, and each has its special time allotted to it by the will of the Creator. The quality of the day is one thing, the quality of the night another. (See the Zohar, 'Koraḥ',* on the verse: 'In the morning the Lord will show ...' [Num. 16: 5].) Therefore, my brethren, take great care to observe the times and the periods set aside by the sages for the recitation of the *Shema*, morning and evening, blessed be He who has chosen them and their teaching. The same applies to the time for eating, the time to sleep, and the time to get up; for each there is something corresponding to it in the mystery of the way the channels of the qualities are distributed, in accordance with the special function of each. Behold, there are three watches in the night.* One would have been sufficient, but that is how the divine wisdom has apportioned it, giving each a rule and a time, and the function of each is not to be changed for another. Anyone who changes a period to one different from that fixed by the Torah inverts the channels,

Rambam *Mishneh torah*, *Melakhim*, ch. 11, that the Messiah must act in accordance with the Torah, otherwise he cannot be identified as the true Messiah.

Thy times continuation of the passage in Shab. 31*a*.

Zohar, 'Koraḥ' Zohar iii. 176*b*.

three watches in the night Ber. 3*a*.

Heaven forfend, and spoils the foundations. I shall now quote to you the language of the Zohar, 'Pikudei', p. 223*a*:* 'He began his discourse: "And there shall be faith in thy times ..." Our companions have established the meaning of this verse. But he who devotes himself to the study of the Torah in this world and appoints set times for it must do so in faithfulness. He must direct his mind to the Holy One, blessed be He, and study for the sake of Heaven. "Strength of salvation", means that judgement be infused with mercy.* "Wisdom and knowledge", these two must rest one on the other, the one that is hidden* and concealed to rest on the other.* "The fear of the Lord is his treasure"*—the treasure of all these qualities because it takes all these channels and becomes a treasure store for them all.'

I have explained a profound mystery contained in the statement about studying the Torah in this world, representing the unification of Tiferet, which is the Torah, with Malkhut, which is 'this world'.* By means of his study of the Torah, a man causes influences to flow from the channels of Ze'ir to the Female of Ze'ir,* known as 'this world'. He has the merit of 'setting aside a time for the Torah',* namely, the setting aside of a time for the unification of Ze'ir and the Female. For in the whole of the Zohar, 'a time' represents the quality of Malkhut, see Zohar, 'Vayetzé'.* And the mystery of 'setting aside' is the mystery of Ya'akov,* the mystery of the Sabbath,* which is fixed and established,* the mystery of Ya'akov Yosef,* called 'established' (*kayam*),* since *kayam* has the numerical value of Yosef. Setting a fixed time means that they are never separated;* you should have in mind that the fixing of the time for the Torah is so that the Male and

Zohar, 'Pikudei', p. 223*a* Zohar ii. 223*a*.

judgement be infused with mercy 'strength' is 'judgement'; 'salvation' is 'mercy'.

the one that is hidden to rest on the other Ḥokhmah, 'wisdom', becomes known or revealed through Da'at, 'knowledge'.

the fear of the Lord is his treasure Malkhut is the 'treasury' of all the *sefirot*.

'this world' in contradistinction to Binah, 'The World to Come'.

Female of Ze'ir the *partzuf* Nukba.

setting aside a time for the Torah E. understands the Zoharic passage to mean that the student of the Torah causes 'this world' to be united at the proper time.

Zohar, 'Vayetzé' Zohar i. 153*a*.

Ya'akov Jacob = Tiferet.

the Sabbath the Sabbath *day*, as opposed to the Sabbath night, corresponds to Yesod.

fixed and established the time of the Sabbath has been fixed from the seventh day of the Creation; see Pes. 117*b*: 'The Sabbath is fixed and established.'

Ya'akov Yosef Ya'akov = Jacob = Tiferet; Yosef = Joseph = Yesod.

called established (*kayam*) the numerical equivalent of *kayam* is: *kof* (100) + *yod* (10) + *mem* (40) = 150. The numerical equivalent of Yosef is: *yod* (10) + *samekh* (60) + *pé* (80) = 150.

never separated they are 'fixed' together.

Female are never separated one from the other. This is the meaning of 'in faithfulness he should willingly intend it for the sake of the Holy One, blessed be He, for the sake of Heaven'. For the mystery of the will and the intention hints at the category of Yah*, since will is formed in Binah and intention is in Ḥokhmah: 'windows were opened',* and 'with wisdom He opens'.* And 'to intend it for the Holy One, blessed be He'* represents the mystery of Tiferet, while 'he should intend it for the sake of Heaven' represents the mystery of Malkhut, referred to there as faith.

I have written in many places that this is the mystery of *amen*, *vav* and *hé*:* the mystery of *amen* is that it represents HVYH, Adonai,* Male and Female, the mystery of *vav* and *hé*. However, it is necessary to draw to them 'strength and salvation' so as to infuse judgement with mercy. Strength and salvation are the two *hé*s of the divine name, blessed be He. Strength represents Binah. She it is who endows Her pleasant Son with all the brains, from the root meaning of *ḥas*, according to the mystery of life,* the mystery of the *tefillin*. And it is the mystery of the straight *nun*,* which extends to the Male and Female as stated in the Zohar, 'Vayelekh',* p. 285. Consult that passage. Salvation refers to the Female, as stated in the Zohar, 'Bereshit',* p. 1. Wisdom and knowledge are the letters *yod* and *vav* of the [divine] name, for 'the two rest one on the other'. For strength and salvation represent mercy and judgement, the two *hé*s. For the first *hé** represents mercy, and the second *hé** judgement. For the root of Binah is mercy even though judgements bestir themselves from there, as it is stated [Zohar, 'Aḥarei',* p. 65]. And Malkhut is salvation, according to the

Yah a divine name made up of *yod*, representing Ḥokhmah and *hé*, representing Binah.

'windows were opened' Dan. 6: 11: 'now his windows (*vekhavin*) were opened'. E. plays on the words *khavin* and *kavanah*, 'intention'.

'with wisdom He opens' from the evening prayer: 'with wisdom He openeth the gates'.

the Holy One, blessed be He Tiferet.

vav* and *hé Tiferet and Malkhut.

HVYH, Adonai the numerical equivalent of *amen* [*alef* (1) + *mem* (40) + *nun* (50) = 91] is equivalent to that of HVYH [*hé* (5) + *vav* (6) + *yod* (10) + *hé* (5) = 26] plus Adonai [*alef* (1) + *dalet* (4) + *nun* (50) + *yod* (10) = 65]; 65 + 26 = 91.

strength ... from the root meaning of *ḥas* ... according to the mystery of life *ḥosen*, 'strength', is derived from the root *ḥas*, 'pity', which is spelled: *het* (8) + *samekh* (60) = 68. *Ḥayim*, 'life', is spelled: *ḥet* (8) + *yod* (10) + *yod* (10) + *mem* (40) = 68.

straight *nun* there are 50 gates to Binah, 'understanding', and *nun* has a numerical value of 50. The straight *nun* is the elongated final *nun* that is the last letter of *amen*, and this represents the extension from Binah.

Zohar, 'Vayelekh' Zohar iii. 285*b*.

Zohar, 'Bereshit' Zohar i. 1*a*.

yod* and *vav Ḥokhmah and Tiferet.

first *hé* ... second *hé* Binah and Malkhut.

Zohar, 'Aḥarei' Zohar iii. 65*a–b*.

mystery of 'the cup of salvation',* and it is 'the law of the government'.* Now the man who studies in faithfulness unites Male and Female, *vav* and *hé*. And *amen* is the mystery of Yah in its full spelling, as follows:* YVD, HY, YVD, HA, YVD, HH, having the numerical value of *amen*, as stated in the 'Intentions of the Kaddishim'. Through this the name HVYH is united to make one rest on the other,* namely, the Hidden One,* Abba and Imma, and also through this Ze'ir and the Female. (See what is said in the Zohar, 'Balak',* p. 133*b*, on the mystery of wisdom and knowledge, the Males, on strength and salvation, the Females. The name HVYH, blessed be He, and blessed be His name, is unified. 'The fear of the Lord is his treasure ... It becomes a treasure store for all of them.' This is what is written there. Reflect well on this, for it contains a great mystery.) You, brother, reflect on this and be wise. Although much more can be said about this, I shall not go to any greater lengths; one who wishes to enter the secret of the Lord is obliged to fulfil all that is written in the book. It is a statute never to be transgressed.

In brief, the word 'times' refers to the Sabbaths and festivals, that these should be kept with the utmost degree of clarity in the worship of the true God, to remember them and to keep them. This is effective for the comprehension of this science (something out of nothing).* Further on, 'thy times', this is Keter, as stated in the *kavanot* of 'from Thee comes their rest'. Included in this is that the God-fearing man must watch over his times and his very moments, not to waste them in the pursuit of worldly vanities, Heaven forfend, as is stated in the Zohar on the verse: 'And Abraham was old, well advanced in days' [Gen. 24: 1]. Consult the passage in the Zohar, 'Ḥayei',* p. 129, and 'Beshalaḥ',* p. 63*b*: 'R. Judah said: "Every day the world is blessed through that Supernal Day".' (This means that on

'the cup of salvation' in Zohar i. 1*a*, Malkhut is the 'cup of salvation' because it is the 'cup' into which the wine of the *sefirot* is poured.

'the law of the government' *dina demalkhuta dina*, 'The law of the government is law', a talmudic ruling, Git. 10*b*. In the kabbalah this is interpreted as 'the law (i.e. the judgement, *dina*), is of the government', or Malkhut.

And *amen* is the mystery of Yah in its full spelling, as follows i.e. when the *hé* of Yah is spelled first with *yod* then with *alef* then with *hé* thus: 10 + 6 + 4 = 20 for the *yod*, of which there are three = 60. The *hé* has a numerical value of 5; 3 times 5 = 15, giving a total of 75. Add the *yod* of the first *hé* = 10; the *alef* of the second *hé* = 1; the *hé* of the third *hé* = 5; = 16 + 75 + 91. As shown above, this is equivalent to the numerical value of *amen*.

the name HVVH is united to make one rest on the other the letters of the Tetragrammaton represent the *sefirot* resting on one another, i.e. in unison.

the Hidden One Keter.

Zohar, 'Balak' Zohar iii. 133*b*.

something out of nothing *creatio ex nihilo*.

Zohar, 'Ḥayei' Zohar i. 129*a–b*.

'Beshalaḥ' Zohar ii. 63*b*.

each day the sustaining influence of that day is drawn down to it. On the first day the quality of Ḥesed, and so on each day.) Consult the passage. 'This is why Moses said: "Let no man leave of it* until the morning" [Exod. 16: 19]. What is the reason? Because one day neither gives nor lends to another day, but each day rules on its own, for one does not rule over the others.' (And so do the rabbis say:* Once the day is over its particular sacrifice is abolished. See the 'Expositions on the Form' and the 'Gate of the Form', chapter 1, the great lesson to be derived from this. And you will then understand the remark of the Yanuka in the Zohar, 'Balak':* 'I knew it from the odour of your garments* when I came near to you', even though, according to the strict law, they were exempt from the obligation to recite the *Shema*. There is much to say on this, but here is not the place for it.) Yet it is stated there that although all the other days are blessed because of the Sabbath, yet the weekdays are the preparation for the Sabbath. If a man does not prepare himself for the Sabbath, even though he may still acquire through much toil an experience of intense enthusiasm on the Sabbath, this will be 'a change of habit ...',* as is well known. Every Hasid* must pray for this acceptable time, and who knows if at that time he will reach Malkhut.* Consequently, every spiritual person should take wise care of his times and his very moments to examine them, as it is said: 'And try him every moment' [Job 7: 18]. (And consult further the unifications of the divine names, blessed be He, applicable to each day, as explained in the words of our master.)

STRENGTH.* 'Did you engage in procreation?' Now it does not say: 'Did you fulfil the command to procreate?' I seem to recall that Maharsha,* in his *Novellae on the Aggadot*,* raises this question, but I do not recall his

Let no man leave of it of the Paschal lamb eaten on the night before the Exodus from Egypt.

And so do the rabbis say Ber. 28*a*.

Zohar, 'Balak' Zohar iii. 186*a*. The Yanuka ('holy child') is an infant who spouts mystical teachings.

I knew it from the odour of your garments the Yanuka had the mystical power of detecting sin from the smell of their garments and therefore knew that they had not recited the *Shema*.

change of habit Ket. 110*b*, in connection with a poor man who is not used to eating good food but does so on the Sabbath.

Every Hasid Ps. 32: 6: 'for this let every Ḥasid pray ... in the time of finding'.

Malkhut a pun on the verse: 'and who knoweth whether thou art come to reach estate (*malkhut*) for such a time as this' (Est. 4: 14).

Strength continuing the exposition of Shab. 31*a*.

Maharsha R. Samuel Edels (1555–1631), author of a standard commentary on the Talmud.

Novellae on the Aggadot The Maharsha's *Novellae* are on both the *halakhah* and on the Aggadah of the Talmud. His solution is that the reference is to a person who 'engages in procreation' by helping poor boys and girls to marry by giving them dowries.

solution. But to my mind the meaning is that each person should be engaged in conversation with a companion in order to encourage him to increase his own knowledge, as it is said: 'that thou mayest tell in the ears of thy son, and thy son's son ... that ye may know that I am the Lord' [Exod. 10: 2]. That is to say, in telling it you thereby engage in the procreation of knowledge and you encourage your companion (as stated in the Zohar, 'Terumah',* p. 181), and by raising many disciples your own knowledge is increased. One should engage in this with a good companion and with a good disciple and should delve deeply into the subject for the purpose of divine worship, as the rabbis say:* 'Much have I received from my teachers, more from my companions, and most of all from my disciples', who are called 'children'.* There is no greater activity of procreation than this, that the honour of Heaven be increased. In the *Hilkhot derekh eretz vetalmud torah*, by R. Meir Poppers,* it is said that one must not be barren in the Torah but should have a mind prolific in discovering new ideas in the Torah. In truth, this is a great principle with regard to wisdom, to discover new ideas. You will then experience great joy and comprehension.

SALVATION.* He is asked: 'Did you hope for salvation?' It seems to me that this means that a man should retain his self-confidence at times when he is in a state of small-mindedness, when the Outside Ones, who attack those whose engage in this study, seek to seduce him, as stated above in the name of the Ari, of blessed memory. There are times when a man falls from his high spiritual stage, and then he should hope for salvation and not relinquish that which he has attained, as I have written above in my discussion of the fourth condition in the name of my master, of blessed memory. One's heart should be firm in its trust that the Lord will not forsake His pious ones. They will always enjoy His protection, and salvation is from the Lord. And if at times a man has dominion over another it is bad for him since he takes out of his mouth all that he had swallowed,* all the sparks that have been absorbed by him. But when a man who worships falls from his higher state and then truly repents, through the pouring out of his heart to the Lord, he elevates many souls and sparks unable to rise

Zohar, 'Terumah' Zohar ii. 181 is 'Tetzaveh', not 'Terumah'.

as the rabbis say Ta'an. 7*a*.

called 'children' Sif. Deut., 'Vaethanan' 34, on Deut. 6: 7.

Meir Poppers Jerusalem kabbalist (d. 1662).

Salvation continuing the exposition of Shab. 31*a*.

takes out of his mouth all that he had swallowed one who lords it over another loses all the holy sparks he has swallowed, i.e. through the sin of pride he loses his merits.

and sunk in the *kelipot*. Brother, how profound the thoughts of the Holy One, blessed be He, and blessed be His name.

And so it is according to Resh Lakish,* who says that salvation denotes *nezikin*.* Verily, Scripture says: 'I will lift up the cup of salvation'* [Ps. 116: 13]. For they obtain* their nourishment from *kos*,* which has the numerical value of Elohim, the mystery of powers,* but they are sweetened 'with the mighty acts of His saving right hand'* [Ps. 20: 7]. For this is the cup of blessing, which is taken with both hands* and then put into the right hand. Now, the Outside Ones obtain their nourishment from the powers and the judgements. More than one person has risen against us to destroy us, yet the Holy One, blessed be He, saves us from their hand.* This is what is said on the Zohar, on the section 'Saba of Mishpatim', on the reason it is called *nezikin** and not *mazikin** (as the *Tosafot yom tov** notes). The answer given is that one who harms another becomes himself the victim, since the verse says: 'When one man had power over another to his hurt' [Eccles. 8: 9], meaning 'to his own detriment'.* (For then he himself becomes a victim, since all that he has absorbed of extra blessing and sanctity is taken away from him. See there for this delightful idea.) Hence it says, 'Did you hope for salvation?' That is the mystery of 'He looks at it', said of the cup of blessing,* called 'the cup of salvation', which rests on the five fingers, representing the five powers,* as stated in the introduction to the Zohar on 'Bereshit',* and in many other places. I shall not go to any greater lengths to convey the many sweetmeats we have, thank God, on this topic. For my

Resh Lakish in the passage in Shab. 31*a*.

nezikin the fourth Order of the Mishnah is called *Nezikin* ('Damages'), meaning the avoidance of damages; here it hints at the *kelipot*, which cause damage.

the cup of salvation the Hebrew for 'cup' is *kos*, and E. goes on to explain the significance of this word.

they obtain: 'they' is the demonic forces, the *kelipot*.

***kos* has the numerical value of Elohim** *kos* is spelled *kaf* (20) + *vav* (6) + *samekh* (60) = 86; Elohim is spelled *alef* (1) + *lamed* (30) + *hé* (5) + *yod* (10) + *mem* (40) = 86.

powers Gevurah, the aspect of the divine represented by the name Elohim.

right hand Ḥesed, mercy, love.

with both hands the cup is taken in both hands, the ten fingers representing the ten *sefirot* as a whole. But then it is taken in the right hand so that the *sefirot* on the right side, the *sefirot* of mercy, will dominate.

More than one person has risen against us ... a quotation from the Passover Haggadah.

nezikin meaning victims of damages.

mazikin meaning the perpetrators of the damages.

Tosafot yom tov on BK 1: 1.

'to his own detriment' the perpetrator of violence harms himself more than his victim.

said of the cup of blessing Ber. 31*a*, where it is said that the cup of blessing, i.e. over which benedictions are recited, must be taken up with both hands and then transferred to the right hand, and that the eyes must gaze at it.

five powers five *sefirot*.

Zohar, 'Bereshit' Zohar i. 1*a*.

aim here is to expound only that which is necessary for one who studies this science: that when, as sometimes happens, he falls from his higher stage, he should not give up. This [tendency] is especially prevalent among those who study this science or the Torah or who worship, since the Outside Ones attack them, as I have already quoted the Ari, of blessed memory, as saying. Therefore, my son, be firm and courageous. As I have said, be not afraid. 'Rejoice not against me, O mine enemy; Though I am fallen, I shall arise' [Mic. 7: 8]. Let him revert to his full stature in divine worship, to engage in Torah, worship, and prayer even more than his former custom. For this descent is for the purpose of a greater ascent;* once the poor man has risen from the dust he raises up sparks with him, and his intentional sins are turned to virtues. This is sufficient for those who desire the true wisdom and engage in it for its own sake.

Included in 'hoping for salvation' is the idea that a person should hope to be saved by the merits of an even greater stage than that he has currently attained. Even though he sees himself as having fallen from grace, he should not be deterred thereby from drawing near to the holy. He should not say 'Who am I [to merit salvation]?', but should hope to be saved.

WISDOM.* The rabbis, of blessed memory, say on this that they ask,* 'Did you engage in the dialectics of wisdom?' Now why do they not ask, 'Did you engage in the dialectics of the Torah?' From this we learn that the dialectics should chiefly be in matters of wisdom, not in vain dialectics. And this is stated [in the commentary] by Maharsha. Therefore, my brethren, keep far away from dialectics that have no practical consequences, and do not waste your time and your life on these. The truth is that when the *magid* said to the Beit Yosef* that the Holy One, blessed be He, rejoices in your dialectics, he referred to dialectics in the true science. Believe me, my brethren, we have keen dialectics and much expertise in the give and take of the doctrine of the Ari, of blessed memory, in his exposition of the Zohar. It is very profound. Who can find it? Happy is the man who has found wisdom.

descent is for the purpose of ... ascent a Talmudic expression (from Mak. 7*b*), applied by E. to spiritual descent and ascent, i.e. sometimes one must descend spiritually in order to rise later to even greater heights.

Wisdom continuing the exposition of Shab. 31*a*.

they ask the Court on High asks.

when the *magid* said to the Beit Yosef the Beit Yosef is R. Joseph Karo (1488–1575), author of the *Shulḥan arukh*, who also wrote a commentary by this name on the *Tur*. Karo kept a mystical diary (*Magid meisharim*) in which he recorded the communications he received from a heavenly visitor, the *magid*.

Already in my youth, I served great scholars in Israel, thank God, and I engaged myself much in dialectics and discovered many new things. I spoke before kings,* thank God, by means of questions and answers, with sharpness and expertise, and the drawing of distinctions in the study of the Talmud and the Codes. Behold, when God gave me the merit to enter within, according to my capacity, not, Heaven forfend, into that too great and too difficult for me, in the studies of the Ari, of blessed memory, how sweet the honey and how great the illumination of the eyes that I found in the dialectics of this science, and how my eyes were illumined in the mysteries of the Zohar which have been revealed in this generation. How many wondrous things did I observe in the Zohar through engaging in dialectics and theorizing by means of the introduction of our master, the Ari, of blessed memory, to understand and be wise, to keep and to practise. Whoever possesses a Jewish soul will seek the truth of the innermost reasons of the Torah's channels, will certainly see to it that his yearning soul will engage in the dialectics of this science, the soul root of the House of Israel.

Now the one who engages in it must agree with what I say: there is not as much delight and true joy in the dialectics of the Talmud (in its simple form) as in the dialectics of the innermost science. 'And out of the midst thereof as the appearance of the *ḥashmal*' [Ezek. 1: 4] *ḥash** and *mal** become revealed. From the things that are uttered quietly, the mystery of *mal* becomes revealed (that is, the foreskin is cut away from the otherwise obscure details of many of the marvellous things our rabbis have said in connection with the plain meanings of the Torah), so that the words of our rabbis are made to refer openly* to the supernal worlds, according to the wondrous ways of our rabbis in the Talmud, so sweet to the taste. When, thank God, we come to investigate the reasons for the laws or some puzzling topic or some verse, our souls are sated and our bones become fat in the great joy and delight we experience in our holy Torah, that we have been given the merit to understand slightly the fear of the Lord and the profound thoughts of the Lord our God. How mighty is Thy name in all the earth!

Furthermore, to engage in dialectics means to delve deeply into the

before kings meaning here 'rabbis', based on Git. 62*a*.

ḥash 'quiet'.

mal circumcision; the things hidden, kept quiet, by the rabbis are 'circumcised', i.e. become revealed in their true meaning.

so that the words of our rabbis are made to refer openly meaning that kabbalah helps us to have an appreciation of what the rabbis of the Talmud really mean.

halakhah, the eternal ways, the thing itself,* to know how to unify the divine name, blessed be He, and blessed be His name, in every word and every letter, not, Heaven forfend, to waste one's days, one's years, and one's mind on mere after-courses of wisdom, that is, on the working out of *gematriot*. To be sure, these are very effective and concerning them it is said in the *Tikunim* and the Zohar, 'Pineḥas', p. 220,* that 'there is no work, nor device, nor knowledge, nor wisdom, in the grave, whither thou goest' [Eccles. 9: 10]; and see the *Zohar ḥadash*, p. 98*b*, where it is said: 'Because a man possesses this power it is said that whoever does not know how to work out *gematriot* and calculations is destined to descend to Sheol.'* However, these are only after-courses,* and the main thing is to engage in dialectics of this science and to unify the holy name by means of its own power. Note it well and consult the passage. (And see the end of this tract where I have quoted my exposition of the passage in the Zohar, 'Pikudei', p. 225*b*.)*

Now the mystery of engaging in the dialectics of this science is in order to put right the sin of Massah and Meribah,* 'because they tried the Lord saying "Is the Lord among us or not?"' [Exod. 17: 7]; 'whether there is wood therein or not' [Num. 13: 20]; those who proceed in doubt and bring about a separation between Ḥokhmah called, as is well known, Yesh,* and Keter, called Ayin.* As it is said in the Zohar, 'Beshalaḥ'.* And in the *Idra rabba*, p. 129:* 'Israel desired in their hearts to perform the unification, as it is written, "Is the Lord among us", between Ze'ir Anpin,* called the Lord, and Arikh Anpin,* called Ayin. Why, then, were they punished? Because they did not do it with love but as a test, as it is written "because they tried the Lord".' And consult the Zohar, 'Shelaḥ', p. 158*b*.* Now to expound this topic as a hint for the ways of divine worship. A man must not make any division between Something and Nothing, but he should make Nothing out of Something and Something out of Nothing. For in relation to the Creator's great majesty all are as Nothing and are considered as void and empty, from which he draws down Something, namely blessing and har-

the thing itself i.e. to put it to work in practice, not to engage in mere theoretical dialectics.

Zohar, 'Pineḥas', p. 220 Zohar iii. 220*b*.

Sheol the biblical name for the realms of the dead, interpreted as meaning Hell.

after-courses based on Av. 3: 18: '*Gematriot* are the after-courses of wisdom'—in the sense that they follow on from wisdom, or must be preceded by it.

Zohar, 'Pikudei', p. 225*b* Zohar ii. 225*b*.

Massah and Meribah 'Testing' and 'Trying'.

Yesh that which is.

Ayin that which is not.

Zohar, 'Beshalaḥ' Zohar ii. 64*a*–*b*.

***Idra rabba*, p. 129** Zohar iii. 129*a*.

Ze'ir Anpin corresponding to Tiferet.

Arikh Anpin corresponding to Keter.

Zohar, 'Shelaḥ', p. 158*b* Zohar iii. 158*b*.

mony. To those who are wise in worship this will be pleasant. And so it is in the dialectical process. First a man raises objections to refute a particular law so that it becomes Nothing. And then he provides the solution, and so the law becomes Something. This is the final aim, to remove the thorns from the vineyard. Know, my brother, that unless one who worships has problems at first when studying this science, investigating each matter thoroughly, he will never enjoy a sweet taste in his study of the Torah since he has not toiled over it. As it is said: 'If ye walk in My statutes' [Lev. 26: 3], which means, to toil in the study of the Torah* in order to arrive at the correct conclusion for practice, to produce that which is precious from that which is cheap.* For the word *amel** is connected in form to *amelan** of the cooks, that by which they remove the scum from the dish. So, too, as a result of the student's toil, the Torah of the Lord becomes perfect, without any dross, and it will then endure for him. This is the final aim in the matter of dialectics. They say in the name of the Ari, of blessed memory, that when he raised an objection he would do so energetically in order to break the power of the *kelipot*. These are humbled through the study of the Torah for its own sake by those who are wise. This is the mystery behind the expression *pilpalta** in wisdom, with the same numerical value as Keter,* called Nothing in its incomprehensibility. And the expression, '*pilpalta*' can also have the meaning it has in the chapter 'Get pashut':* '*s, p, l** above, *k, p, l* below, *samekh* in one half, *kof* n one half', from which we see that the two letters *p, l* denote a half. So, too, should an intelligent person take care not to direct his mind and his reasoning to one side only, for if he does he may overlook a stone that is a hindrance and he may stumble, Heaven forfend, without being aware of it. But if his mind is directed both ways, half this way, half the other, until, in his wisdom, he decides to be abundant in mercy, that is, to decide in favour of the view that leans to mercy and justice, clarity will be the outcome. This is true knowledge, one half of mercy, the other half of power: one half to

which means to toil in the study of the Torah an explanation deriving from the Sifra on the verse; see 'Beḥukotai', beg.

to produce that which is precious from that which is cheap Jer. 15: 19.

amel toiling.

amelan Pes. 42*b*.

***pilpalta* in wisdom** did you engage in *pilpul* (dialectics) wisely?

Keter *pilpalta* has the same numerical value as Keter [*Pilpalta* = *pé* (50) + *lamed* (30) + *pé* (50) + *lamed* (30) + *tav* (400) = 620; Keter = *kaf* (20) + *tav* (400) + *resh* (200) = 620].

'Get pashut' in BB 166*b*.

s, p, l ... the reference is to a bond or legal contract where in one half (*palga*) there was the letter *samekh* and in the other half the letter *kof*. Thus *pl* can mean a half and *pilpalta* two equal halves—hence, seeing both sides of an argument.

Aaron,* who draws down mercies to the Children of Israel, direct light; the other half to his sons, who offer themselves as a sacrifice to the Lord, reflected light, representing the divine names, blessed be He, and blessed be His name, and they cause the Female Waters of Power to ascend. Knowledge is composed half of Mercy and half of Power, and through it these become united in the truly One, and this is the actual Crown* of the Torah. This is the mystery of *pilpul*, the mystery of Knowledge, the mystery of Keter in its innermost parts, as is well known from the words of the Ari, of blessed memory. Then Something and Nothing become One, united in love. *Pilpalta* is the mystery of Keter, which, in its external aspects is Knowledge. Keter is called Nothing, and Wisdom is called Something, and Wisdom is found in Nothing, for the two have become as one through dialectics, and the Holy One, blessed be He, rejoices when dialectics are engaged in with fondness for the subject. This is the mystery of 'Wisdom is with the aged, and understanding in length of days' [Job 12: 12]. This is the special quality through which Something and Nothing are made as one. Dialectics are especially suitable for it. And the wise will understand.

AND KNOWLEDGE.* 'Did you understand one thing from another?' This needs to be understood. What connection is there between understanding one thing from another and Knowledge? This is the comment of Rashi, of blessed memory, in his commentary on the Pentateuch, on the verse: 'And He hath filled him with the spirit of God in wisdom, in understanding, and in knowledge' [Exod. 35: 31]. 'Wisdom refers to that which a man hears and learns from others. Understanding means to understand one thing from another. He understands in his own mind from that which he has learned from others. Knowledge means the holy spirit.' And yet here it is said that understanding one thing from another is called knowledge. Maharsha raises this question.* See it there. However, the matter has been explained by us in a comment on: 'If there is no understanding, there is no knowledge. And if there is no knowledge there is no understanding.'* Rashi, of blessed memory, explains there that knowledge refers to the reason for something. And so did David say: 'good reason and

one half to Aaron Yoma 17*b*. The text there says that half of the shewbread was given to Aaron, the high priest, and half to his sons.

Crown Keter.

And knowledge the passage in Shab. 31*a* identifies 'knowledge' in the verse with the question: 'Did you understand one thing from another?'

Maharsha raises this question on the passage in Shab. 31*a*.

'If there is no knowledge there is no understanding.' Av. 3: 17.

knowledge' [Ps. 119: 66]. The truth is that Rashi, of blessed memory, does not contradict himself, but says the same thing. For knowledge means that one knows and senses the reason for something, the sweet good in something, and this surely is the very thing that leads to the holy spirit, which follows on saintliness, as stated in the *Baraita* of R. Pineḥas ben Yair in tractate *Avodah zarah*,* ch. 1. Once a man knows, senses, and takes delight in its pleasantness, the holy spirit immediately rests upon him. This is why Rashi, of blessed memory, in his commentary on the Pentateuch, seizes hold of the purpose of the knowledge required for the work of Heaven, the holy work. (I have more dialectics on this subject but here is not the lace for it.)

However, it is said: 'If there is no understanding there is no knowledge.' For, as is well known, understanding is the Mother* of children. 'Yes, you call understanding Mother'* [Prov. 2: 3], and the purpose of understanding is repentance, as stated above in the name of the Zohar, 'Naso'. My master, his soul is in Eden, was fond of saying that this is hinted at in the verse, 'And understanding with their heart, return, and be healed' [Isa. 6: 10]. (And so it is stated in the holy work, *Sha'arei orah*.)* This is the meaning of the Mishnah, 'If there is no understanding there is no knowledge.' This means: If a man does not engage in simple repentance—for there is repentance and repentance, as I have quoted previously in the name of the *Raya mehemna*, 'Naso', p. 123—if a person does not engage in the lower form of repentance, confessing his sins and experiencing remorse in the greatest degree of contrition, there is certainly no knowledge, he will have no taste for Torah and divine worship, since a barrier exists which causes him to taste the sweet as bitter and the bitter as sweet. 'And if there is no knowledge', that is, if he does not know the reasons for Torah and worship, eagerly seeking to know the Lord with all his might and reason, directing all his thoughts and aims only to Him, there can surely be 'no understanding', no grasping of the higher repentance. As stated in the *Raya mehemna* quoted above: 'There is a man who repents of his sins and is pardoned. He follows the way ... Such a man has the merit of attaining to the lower repentance. There is another man who, after he has repented of his sins, engages in the study of the Torah in the fear and love of the Holy One, blessed be He, without thought of reward. Such a man merits the letter

Avodah zarah as above: 'Av. Zar. 20*b*.

Mother Binah.

you call understanding Mother in the verse in question, the letters *alef* and *mem* are pointed to read *im*, 'if' ('If you call understanding ...') whereas here they are read as *em* (Mother).

Sha'arei orah a kabbalistic work by Joseph Gikatilla (1248–1325). The reference is to Gate 8 (Jerusalem edn. 1970, pp. 59–61).

vav, the son of Yah, from which it receives the name Binah. This brings about that the *vav* returns to the *hé*.' This is the meaning of: 'If there is no knowledge', that is, the mind's grasp of the reasons for things, 'there is no understanding', that is, a person will not attain to the higher repentance, the unification of the sacred illumination, that the *vav* should return to the *hé* so as to unite and to bind together His name, blessed be He, in the root of unification, and to repair the flaw he had made in the holy channel and in the force of the name flawed, Heaven forfend, in that the unification is incomplete. The highest mysteries are contained here. Hence a person is asked, 'Did you understand one thing from another?', referring to repentance in its simpler form, in which one looks to the future and repents and confesses one's sins. Through this one attains knowledge. For it is certain that there can be no knowledge without the understanding of one thing from another and without repentance. Actually, this also follows from what I have written earlier, that to engage in the dialectics of wisdom belongs to the mystery of knowledge. This is the meaning of understanding one thing from another. 'One thing' refers to the *vav* of the holy name,* the essence of knowledge, the Son of Yah. 'From another' refers to Binah. Hence, 'one thing from another'. The wise will understand, for I have no strength to say more.

However, the result is that if there is no knowledge there is no understanding. Every open-eyed person must see that it is only possible to attain the higher repentance through knowledge and through engaging in the study of the Torah, in fear and love, without thought of reward. Such a stage, my brother, can only be reached through knowledge of the reasons for the Torah and the *mitzvot*, in which a man knows what he is doing when he worships, what *tefillin* are and what a *tallit* with *tzitzit* is, with all his deeds for the sake of Heaven, all, as I shall state presently, in accordance with the teachings of the Ari, of blessed memory. Then he will attain to the higher repentance according to the mystery of the unification of the Holy Illumination.

Further remarks on why knowledge is described in terms of understanding one thing from another. Know, brother, that it is a great principle of this science that you must not draw conclusions for practice from the knowledge you have of the reasons for things; to say, for example, that where the reason does not apply, the law is such and such; or to say that since the reason for one thing applies to another, we shall do so since the

the *vav* of the holy name i.e. as above, the *vav* represents both Da'at and Tiferet since both are descended from, i.e. the 'sons' of, Binah.

same reason applies. For this is extremely dangerous. Look at the case of King Solomon.* This is enough for the wise. When you understand one thing from another you must associate it with knowledge, that is, of the reasons for it, as Rashi, of blessed memory, quoted above, says. But, in addition, one has to be gifted with the holy spirit, that is, the teaching received from Elijah, of blessed memory, to know that it is correct, according to the mystery of: 'For the priest's lips should keep knowledge' [Mal. 2: 7]. This is because, the priestly limits in the mystery of wisdom are called knowledge, as is well known from the Saba of Mishpatim.* And for this you require that which keeps knowledge, namely, the holy spirit, as stated by Rashi, of blessed memory, in his commentary on the Pentateuch, that you know for certain that what your intellect has assumed is correct. With this you will be able to proceed in safety without, Heaven forfend, stupidly relying on your own intellect in understanding the reasons for the matter. Concerning this it is said 'And do not rely on your own reasoning'* for that is extremely dangerous. Concerning this it is said, 'Lest she should walk the even path of life, her ways wander and she knoweth it not' [Prov. 5: 6], if you rely on your own intellectual assessment. This warning is enough.

Thank God, on many occasions I have taken issue with many of the earlier kabbalists who drew practical conclusions from the Zohar according to the reasons stated in the Zohar. They drew conclusions from the meaning of the Zohar, understanding one thing, the *halakhah*, from another. For example, the *Beit yosef** says, citing the *Agur**, based on the Zohar, that one should recite only one benediction over the *tefillin*. But, thank God, we have proved at length that the opinion of the Zohar is that two benedictions are to be recited, and that what the *Agur* says is not stated explicitly in the Zohar but is derived by implication from the Zoharic statement that the *tefillin* of the arm and *tefillin* of the head correspond to 'Remember' and 'Keep'.* From this stated reason he concluded: 'just as

the case of King Solomon King Solomon argued that the reason why the king was not allowed to have many wives was because they would turn his heart from God (Deut. 17: 17); since he considered himself immune to this he could safely disregard the law and take many wives. Yet eventually they did turn him away (Sanh. 21*b*).

Saba of Mishpatim Zohar ii. 95*a–b*.

'And do not rely on your own reasoning' Av. 4: 14.

Beit yosef Karo's work on the *Tur*. The reference is to *Tur, Oraḥ ḥayim*, 25.

Agur by Jacob Landau (15th cent.).

'Remember' and 'Keep' the Exod. version of the Decalogue has 'Remember the Sabbath day' (Exod. 20: 8) while the Deut. version has 'Keep the Sabbath day' (Deut. 5: 21). To 'remember' the Sabbath is to recite the Sabbath sanctification, the *kiddush*; to 'keep' the Sabbath is to refrain from work.

"Remember" and "Keep" have only one benediction* . . . The truth is that, even from the point of view of the plain meaning, there is no comparison at all, since there the two are counted as a single *mitzvah* of the 613,* whereas here there are two *mitzvot*. But, even according to the secret meaning, I have proved that the opinion of the Zohar is for two benedictions to be recited. For the Zohar does not state it explicitly. He only drew it by implication from the reason given. I have expounded this at length in a responsum. On innumerable occasions, thank God, I have similarly taken issue.

A further comment on knowledge as the holy spirit, as Rashi, of blessed memory, says in his commentary on the Pentateuch: I come now, my brother, to say a little something on that which I have written in the discussion of the first condition: that you should not study this science for the sake of gaining some mystical state such as inspiration or prophecy. Now the truth is that we do find our early sages carrying out certain exercises in order to attain to the holy spirit by means of unifications, as explained in the *Sha'ar kedushah** and in the words of Rambam,* of blessed memory. But first you must study the *Sha'ar kedushah* by R. Hayim Vital, of blessed memory, and keep it, and then you may carry out the unifications which lead to the holy spirit, as stated in 'The Gate of Unification'. The general rule here is, weigh it all in the balance of your mind, mountains hanging on a hair,* whether you are deserving of it and whether you are worthy of performing that unification. And also whether the hour requires a person to make the effort to become inspired, and discernment is needed that with every single word one utters the Lord should be before one's eyes. One should reflect on it in dread and should depict for oneself the figurative representations* of the sacred thing concealed from all that lives.

I have quoted earlier the words of the Ari, of blessed memory, on the topic of: 'into Thy hand I commend my spirit'. And so have I heard my master,* of blessed memory, say of those disciples, in the notorious event in

only one benediction i.e. there is only one Sabbath benediction, the *kiddush*, corresponding to the injunction to 'remember the Sabbath day'.

single *mitzvah* of the 613 in the list given by Maimonides and others of the 613 *mitzvot*, only one is listed for 'Remember' and 'Keep', whereas the *tefillin* of the head and that of the hand are two separate *mitzvot*, each of which requires a benediction.

Sha'ar kedushah Vital's guide to holy living and the attainment of the holy spirit.

in the words of Rambam the reference is to Maimonides' *Guide for the Perplexed*, iii. 50–1.

mountains hanging on a hair a talmudic expression (Ḥag. 1: 8) for a complex theme hanging on a single point.

should depict for oneself the figurative representations E. refers to the forms of the letters of the divine name.

my master the Seer of Lublin.

the days of the Taz,* who formed themselves into a separate sect* and profaned the divine name. He attributed it to the fact that they desired to have the mystical experiences of Elijah* and the holy spirit and prophecy by means of unifications. But they failed to preserve a proper balance and they did not humble their physical matter and remained impure. They failed to take proper care of themselves and walked in ways remote from their capacity. They performed unification ('and the donkey kicked over the lamp')* without refining their physical matter. And so they depicted for themselves the higher forms from under the Chariot, with the result that lewd and adulterous forms* got the better of them, Heaven save us, and what happened happened, Heaven spare us. This is what my master said. And he said in the name of the Baal Shem Tov, his soul is in Eden, that these fools studied this science without having any capacity for and knowledge of the awe and dread of Heaven, with the result that they took it all in a corporeal sense and so they went astray.

So you see, brother, how much care you must take in assessing yourself, in refining your physical matter. You must direct every one of your motions in the study of the Torah and in prayer to attach [yourself] in love to the Lord with all your heart, with self-sacrifice, and the end will be that the holy spirit will come to you of its own accord. As the rabbis say,* 'through him they enjoy counsel and sound knowledge'. Study for its own sake, and honour will come in the end. You should have nothing else in mind but to toil in the Torah, worship, and performing acts of benevolence in order to break the coarse physical matter and the evil inclination by means of the counsel provided by our rabbis, of blessed memory. Then you will be successful, and it will be well with you. And take care not to seek to draw the holy spirit to you until you know for certain that your physical matter has been refined, lest another spirit* should be substituted, Heaven forfend, for the holy spirit. You can see all of this in the *Sha'ar kedushah* especially in chapter 7 of Gate 3 and in Gate 4. Consult it and you will see the wondrous things of the Lord, blessed be He, and blessed be His name.

the Taz David Halevi, author of the *Tur hazahav* commentary on the *Shulchan arukh*, as mentioned earlier.

a separate sect the followers of the false messiah, Shabbetai Zevi (1626–76).

Elijah who appears to teach those worthy of the visitation.

'and the donkey kicked over the lamp' this saying occurs in a talmudic tale in Shab. 116*b* but E. evidently puns on *hamra*, 'donkey' and *homer*, 'matter' i.e. their grossly corporeal conceptions of the divine realm put out the light of knowledge.

lewd and adulterous forms the Shabbeteans were alleged to have engaged in illicit sex in order to resemble the 'copulations' on high.

As the rabbis say Av. 6: 1.

lest another spirit an unclean spirit, a demonic force.

THE FEAR OF THE LORD IS HIS TREASURE.* 'For all that, if there is the fear of the Lord, yes, otherwise, no.'* Now, brother, after all these true words, the rabbis can still be in doubt whether there is the fear of the Lord, 'such a treat for such a gift'*. But if you really merit the honour of studying the doctrines of the Ari, of blessed memory, on the mystery of the externals and internals and the numerous external externals and the numerous internal internals, endless and limitless *ad infinitum*, you will understand that this saying revolves around the Higher Ones of all the seven lower ones* of each *partzuf* up to the Higher Ones of the seven Perfections of the Head, all these clothing the seven perfections of Atik,* and Atik is the Malkhut of Adam Kadmon,* in the innermost root of the fear of the Lord. Then you will understand Knowledge and find the fear of the Lord. How far must a man ascend from stage to stage, from internal to more internal, until he reaches the stage of the fear of the Lord, the most internal of all in that all the worlds are garments of the fear of the Lord! Understand this, for I have taught you a great mystery. And you will see the hidden Wisdom, concealed from all who live. How great are Thy deeds, O Lord, how profound Thy thoughts, O God of Israel!

However, in a more simple account of our words, there is a further hint in 'the fear of the Lord is his treasure'. This is based on that which Ramban,* of blessed memory, writes on the verse: 'When thou doest that which is good and right' [Deut. 12: 28], quoted in the *Sefer ḥaredim*.* He writes as follows. 'According to our rabbis,* this is well explained as referring to compromise and to going beyond the letter of the law, and so forth. For first it is stated that we should keep His precepts, testimonies, and statutes which He has commanded. But you must also put your mind to that which He has not actually commanded you, namely, to do that which is

The fear of the Lord is His treasure continuing the exposition of Shab. 31*a*; even after all the things of wisdom have been achieved they are as naught without the fear of the Lord.

'For all that ... otherwise no' this is a quotation from the passage in Shab. 31*a*, meaning that even if you have such attributes as wisdom and so on, they are of no avail without fear of God.

'such a treat for such a gift' talmudic saying; Sanh. 94*b*.

seven lower ones the higher *sefirot* of each *partzuf* extend from world to world, reaching to the Perfections of the Head, i.e. to Keter and Arikh.

Atik the higher stage of Arikh.

Atik is the Malkhut of Adam Kadmon the highest stage of Arikh (= Atik) is the lowest stage (Malkhut) of Adam Kadmon.

Ramban Nahmanides on Deut. 6: 18 (E., quoting from memory, gives it as Deut. 12: 18); ed. Chavel, 376.

Sefer ḥaredim The 'Book of God-fearing Men', by the Safed kabbalist Eleazar Azikri (1533–1600).

According to our rabbis Chavel notes that this is Ramban's own remark and is not actually found in the Talmud.

good and right,* since He loves the good and the right. This is a great subject. For it was impossible for the Torah to mention all the various ways in which a man should conduct himself in relation to his friends and neighbours, his business affairs, and the improvement of society. So the Torah only refers to some of these, for example: "Thou shalt not go back and forth as a talebearer among thy people" [Lev. 19: 16]; "Thou shalt not take vengeance, nor bear any grudge" [Lev. 19: 18]; "Thou shalt rise before the hoary head" [Lev. 19: 32], and similar matters. But the Torah then states in a general sense that a man should do that which is good and right in whatever he does, to include compromise and going beyond the letter of the law ... even including that which the rabbis say* that a man should have a good reputation and speak gently* to others so that everything he does can be called good and right.' Here, too, my friends and brethren, after all that I have explained to the best of our ability on the different aspects of 'faith ... and knowledge' and their various stages, it still has to be said that you must have a treasure (of the fear of the Lord) to which Scripture does not refer directly. This is sufficient for my faithful brethren and friends.

He has not actually commanded you ... to do that which is good and right there is no detailed command, but there is a general command; i.e. one should go beyond the letter of the law to do that which is good and right.

the rabbis say Ta'an. 16*b*.

speak gently Yoma 86*a*.

WRITTEN UPRIGHTLY WORDS OF TRUTH

AFTER these rules, my brothers, I shall now relate to you the special function of this science and the purpose it serves. True though it is that it is only possible to comprehend these things I have set before you by means of engagement in this science, as I have explained, yet we shall add some further ideas, of which you should take note, in the following words, written uprightly, words of truth.

First, we must understand the ways leading to a true concept of the divine unity. The early ones* engaged in speculation but became so worn out that they were obliged to study Greek philosophy and learn from the uncircumcised sages, the unbelievers (the Greeks), from whom they learnt how to engage in speculation so as to desire to change their religion. (See the responsa of Rashba,* and the reply of Bedersi* to Rashba, and the *Minḥat kenaot*.)* Most of their speculations consisted of false problems, leading to the conclusion that the world is abandoned and there is neither Judge nor judgement,* Heaven forfend. My brethren, although Rambam, of blessed memory, in his work *Moreh nevukhim** rose to set at naught all their arguments, yet, for all that, this study caused impure thoughts to enter the hearts of the Children of Israel, casting doubts into their minds. How great was the groan of the early teachers because of this; they raised their voices on high against those who studied Greek philosophy. (Come and see the

the early ones the mediaeval Jewish philosophers.

Rashba R. Solomon Ibn Adret (1235–1310). His responsa on the subject are in *Responsa of Rashba*, nos. 614–18.

Bedersi Jediah Bedersi (d. 1340), quoted in *Responsa of Rashba*.

Minḥat kena'ot The text has here the abbreviation 'MR' but the meaning is obscure. I suggest that it is a printer's error for MK, the *Minḥat kena'ot* by Abba Mari Astruc (early 14th cent.), quoted in *Responsa of Rashba*.

neither Judge nor judgement a rabbinic term for atheism.

Moreh nevukhim Maimonides' *Guide for the Perplexed*.

responsa of Rashba and the responsa of Rosh.)* Woe to us for that shame and embarrassment of learning from the Greeks, the majority of whom gave up all religious belief, that they should teach us the nature of deity, God, holy in Jacob, mighty and tremendous; that they should inform us of the nature of our God who brought us out of Egypt.

But what option did they have?* In their day the wells of wisdom had been stopped up as a result of the great troubles and severe persecutions and harsh decrees which took place at that time. They misunderstood the Aggadot and Scripture, which seem to entertain a corporeal concept of divinity seemingly in contradiction to their tradition, and to that written in Scripture, 'for ye saw no manner of form' [Deut. 4: 15], that the Eternal God, the Lord, can never be depicted in any corporeal manner. They wanted to discover acceptable ideas in the science of the divine about God's nature, His quality, and quantity—without having access to the science of tradition, for as a result of the terrible persecutions it had been forgotten—so that what the prophet promised* might be fulfilled. One need not say much on this topic since it is so well known that every schoolboy knows it. They engaged in the study of natural science, with the result that Greek learning came to be accepted by the people of the God of Jacob.

Come now, my brother, and I shall show you, if you have not as yet entered into wisdom, how to find your hands and feet among the root principles of speculation by the early teachers, holy men of the highest degree, saints and righteous men of lofty and holy souls, men of renown, as our fathers have related to us, and as we see from their books their great holiness and asceticism in the toil of Torah and knowledge.

The saintly author of *Ḥovot halevavot**, a work that leads men to follow in the way of holiness, can still write as follows in chapter 4 of 'The Gate of Unity':* 'Before we make an enquiry into the subject of divine unity, the following has to be noted. Of anything about which we want to enquire, we must first ask whether or not it exists; and then, once we have established that it really does exist, it is necessary to enquire what it is, how it is, and why it is. But with regard to the Creator, may He be exalted, a man is only

Rosh R. Asher b. Yehiel (d. 1327); see e.g. *Responsa of Rosh*, iv. 20.

what option did they have? i.e. the Jewish philosophers.

what the prophet promised the general prophetic promise that the Torah will never be forgotten (Deut. 31: 21).

Ḥovot halevavot *Duties of the Heart*, by Bahya Ibn Pakuda, mentioned earlier.

'The Gate of Unity' *Sha'ar hayiḥud*, the first section of the book; each gate is further subdivided into chapters.

allowed to ask if He is; and once it has been established that He exists . . . we can then go on to enquire if He is One.'* How difficult are these words, O Lord God. My brethren, just look at how this saint can utter words that contradict the Torah, Heaven forfend, without adducing any proofs for what he says. He postulates that a man is only allowed to ask whether He exists, meaning, whether there is a God of the world, that is to say, if there is a Creator in existence. But one is not allowed to ask what and how He is, and why He is. In my eyes this is the exact opposite of the way of the Torah, given openly to six hundred thousand souls of Israel, the men apart from the children, at whose giving the whole world trembled. How is such a sin different from the sin of 'Is the Lord among us, or not?' [Exod. 17: 7]? On this verse, Rashi quotes the Midrash: 'Resh Lakish said: What was Israel like at that hour? A man who had a son whom he took on his shoulder to the market place, where the son, seeing something he wanted, asked his father to buy it for him and the father bought it for him, and so it was on other occasions. The son saw another man and asked him: "Have you seen my father?".' Now I ask you, are we allowed, as this beloved saint says, to ask if He is? Aha! Aha! Was it for nothing that the Lord our God brought us out of Egypt and showed us His greatness and His strong hand with signs and wonders? Was it for nothing that He divided the sea for us, gave us the manna and the Sabbath, and that the Lord our God opened the treasure stores of desirable vessels, the delights of his hidden store, when Israel stood at Sinai? That He caused His sanctity to reside among us when He built the Temple? And sent us His prophets and our feet stood at Sinai? 'In every generation a man is obliged to see it as if he had himself gone out from Egypt.'* And all the acts we have seen with our own eyes, and to this very day His love has not departed from us. These are His greatness and His power, one small lamb, etc.* Can we then dare to ask if He is? It is even more astonishing when he speaks of 'how He is', meaning, what is His nature, whether or not He is good; and 'what He is', meaning is He a living being, is He a man, and such like questions; and 'why He is', what purpose does He serve. This, the saint states, we have no right to ask. Consider for yourself, brother, whether or not this saint has spoken in contradiction to the Torah. Now of what He is, namely His essence, the Torah says: 'For the Lord thy God is a devouring fire' [Deut. 4: 24]; it does not say, 'Like a

we can then go on to enquire if He is One i.e. we cannot discuss His true nature but can only ask what is meant by His unity.

'In every generation . . .' a quotation from the Passover Haggadah.

one small lamb, etc. one small lamb existing among seventy ravenous wolves, i.e. a small nation with all the others pitted against it (Yoma 69*b*).

devouring fire'. So you see He is fire—imagine, spiritual fire—fire that burns fire, fire that consumes fire; from which you can see that the Torah has revealed to us what He is; and why should we not enquire and ask what is the nature of fire? And Ezekiel and the other prophets used similitudes, as it is said: 'And by the ministry of the prophets have I used similitudes' [Hos. 12: 11]. And why should we also not enquire as to how He is? Moses has proclaimed what His nature is: 'merciful and gracious' [Exod. 34: 5]. And Moses said: 'to walk in His ways' [Deut. 8: 6] and 'Unto Him shall ye cleave' [Deut. 13: 5], cleave to His attributes:* just as He is merciful, just as He is gracious. Why, then, should we not enquire into His quality of goodness? Moses, chief of the prophets, asked: 'Show me now Thy ways' [Exod. 33: 13]; see the exposition of our teacher, of blessed memory, in the first chapter of tractate *Berakhot*.* Why is He known to us? It is for us to reveal His divinity in all the signs. 'And God hath so made it that men should fear before Him' [Eccles. 3: 14]. Heaven forfend, the saint has opened to us an opening to err by adopting the exactly opposite opinion. Far be it from you, O holy saint.

Verily, brother, to what extent should you kiss the hands of Israelite wisdom, received by tradition from our ancestors, that you should understand the words of our rabbis and see that the words of the early teachers are built on the foundations of wisdom, for they were recipients of divine inspiration. First I shall try to make a little clearer the words of our master, the Ari, of blessed memory, in reply to the question raised by the early teachers, why was the world not created before the time it was? Here are his words:* 'Those who understand what we have said will discover much good taste once they have grasped it. Now for the question they ask, why this world was created at that particular time, neither earlier nor later? For the solution you must know what I have written in my work. (He did not just record a solution. For you should know that for the solution it is necessary to know the whole of the work. See later on for my exposition of his solution.) For, as is well known, the Supernal Light is higher and higher *ad infinitum*. Its name demonstrates that It cannot be reached at all by any kind of reflection, so that one cannot even think of It ... It has no time sequence, no before and no after. For It is always in existence without any beginning or end whatsoever. Now from the Ein Sof there evolved by emanation an entity ... called Adam Kadmon,* the first of all first entities,

cleave to His attributes Sif. on Deut. 11: 22.
Berakhot Ber. 7*a*.
Here are his words in the *Etz ḥayim*, I. 1. i. 25*a*.
Adam Kadmon Primordial Man.

and from this there evolved afterwards the illuminations which depend on this Adam Kadmon ... numerous illuminations called the World of the Points.* And afterwards there came the Four Worlds* ... In truth this Adam Kadmon does have a beginning and an end.' See there for the solution. You have the book. Look into it and see it for yourself.

The later teachers misunderstood this solution, inventing many ways of dealing with it. Hear, brethren, what I say to you. You should know that the question stems from the Greeks, who believed in the eternity of matter and that the world enjoys necessary existence as does the shadow of a wall in relation to the wall itself, and that the world was not created by a Will,* Heaven forfend. After these propositions their minds were nourished by the verse: 'For I the Lord change not' [Mal. 3: 6]. There are many profound ways of presenting the problem. See the beginning of the *Sefer ḥaredim*,* in whose sweet words the whole problem is adequately set forth. The book *Sha'arei gan eden** suggests as a solution to the problem that the world continues in a cycle* of jubilee and sabbatical years, and it is pointless even to attempt a refutation of what he says. (See how he makes that which is stated into that which is not stated;* see *Likutei torah*, 'Kedoshim'.) For, with respect, he did not understand the question, and his solution is no solution.

I have seen someone write in the name of our master, R. Dov Baer,* his soul is in Eden, a solution to this problem, according to which time is itself created, and at first time did not exist. I cannot believe that such an idea came from the mouth of this holy man. For on this too the question can be asked, why was time itself not created earlier? And what will the rabbi do with the statement in *Midrash rabbah** that there was a time sequence before the world was created? And the rabbis say in the Gemara* that the

the World of the Points the stage before the *sefirot* had received their separate identities.

Four Worlds Atzilut ('Emanation';), Beriah ('Creation'), Yetzirah ('Formation') and Asiyah ('Action').

not created by a Will in the Aristotelean view, the relation of the world to God is like that of the shadow of a wall in relation to the wall itself. The universe has always existed together with God so that there is no *creatio ex nihilo* and no creative Will to bring the universe into being.

Sefer ḥaredim 'Hamitzvah ha'ikarit', ch. 5, pp. 36–8.

Sha'arei gan eden by Jacob Koppel of Mezhirech (d. *c.*1740). The passage is in ch. 1, pp. 1*b*–2*a*.

a cycle i.e. that the world moves in cycles of seven thousand years each.

makes that which is stated into that which is not stated by the notion of the cycles he simply introduces a new problem.

Dov Baer the Maggid of Mezhirech.

Midrash rabbah Gen. R. 2: 7.

in the Gemara this is not, in fact, in the Gemara (the Talmud) but in Midrash Gen. R. 8: 2.

Torah preceded the world by two thousand years. What is meant by a year? So we see that time did exist beforehand. However, I recall seeing in a book that Rambam in his *Moreh nevukhim** does advance this theory in a different context, but I do not have the book in my possession at the moment.

However, brother, incline your ear and listen, make your ears as a sieve and understand, open your eyes and see—after I have laid down certain propositions. There, in the first branch,* the rabbi states, in the name of the early kabbalists, that the reason why the worlds were created is because God, blessed be His name, is, of necessity, perfect in all His acts and potentials and in all His attributes of greatness, excellence, and glory, and without Him actualizing his potential powers He would be imperfect, so to speak, in His acts and their potentiality, in His names and in His attributes. For the great four-lettered name is intended to denote His eternal Being, that He was, is, and will be,* before the creation ...* Had the worlds and all that is in them not been created, the true meaning of His Being, blessed Be His name, as past, present, and future would not have been realized, and He would not have been called by the name HVYH, and the same applies to the name Adonai* ... And so it is with regard to His attributes of being merciful and gracious ... He would not have been called by these names without creatures coming into being so that His potential might be actualized and that He might be perfect in all perfection without any imperfection whatsoever.

The idea behind this subject is explained in the Zohar, 'Pineḥas', p. 227*b*,* where the following is stated: 'The thirteenth principle is to know that He is called wise in all knowledge ... But before He created the world, all the stages were called by the names of the creatures to be created in the future. For had there have been no creatures in the world, how could He have been called merciful and gracious?' (Consult the passage and you will observe wondrous things.) And the Zohar, 'Bo', p. 42,* states: 'If He had not spread His light on all creatures, how would He have been acknowledged and how could it have been said that the whole earth is full of His glory?' Thus far the words of the master, of blessed memory.

Moreh nevukhim Maimonides, *Guide*, ii. 13 and 30.

in the first branch i.e. in the first section or branch (*anaf*) of ch. 1 of Gate I of the *Etz hayim*, quoted by E. at the beginning of this section.

four-lettered name ... was, is, and will be the Tetragrammaton is understood to be derived from *hayah*, 'to be', hence the meaning: 'He was, He is, and He will be'.

before the creation ... and after the creation.

Adonai meaning 'Lord', i.e. of Creation.

Zohar, 'Pineḥas', p. 227*b*. Zohar iii. 227*b*.

Zohar, 'Bo', p. 42 Zohar ii. 42*b*.

Now it is essential to understand what the rabbi says, that the Creator had to create the world of necessity, as it were, in order for Him to be perfect in His names without any imperfections. You must not mistakenly take this to mean that the Creator, blessed be His name, was then bound to make up that which He lacked. Brother, you must note how carefully chosen his words are. He uses the expression 'when it came up in His will'. He does not say, 'when He willed to create the world'. And in the Zohar, too, the expression used is always, 'when it came up in His will to create the world'. And see chapters 1 and 2 of 'The Gate of *Tikun*', and see the exposition of the Female and Male Waters. (That the words 'came up' refer to the Female Waters, he remarks there in the exposition of the Female and Male Waters, as follows.) This is what he says in Exposition 2: 'The first copulation, which took place when the world was created, was by a miracle of His own free choice, and by His simple will, as it is stated in the Zohar in many places: "When it came up into His will ..." It is necessary to understand why, whenever the reference is to the creation of the world or to the beginning of emanation, the expression used is, "when it came up in His will". But there are two aspects ...' See there where he continues: 'However, the first time and in connection with the first copulation, the Male impulse came of its own accord without any impulse from the Female, and there came up in Him a will to desire'* ... See it there. From this we learn that the words 'came up' refer to some act produced by an impulse from below. Now we have heard in the name of the *tzadikim*, and the idea is found at the end of the work *No'am elimelekh*, on the verse: 'He will fulfil the desire of them that fear Him' [Ps. 145: 19], that those who fear Him do not want anything since they lack nothing, as it is said, 'For there is no want to them that fear Him' [Ps. 34: 10], and the Holy One, blessed be He, makes them have a want. See there in 'Likutei shoshanah'.*

And so, too, in the Mishnah of *Pirkei avot** 'Make thy will as His will'. There can be a will that stems from free choice. (And the rabbis say:* 'He is to be coerced until he says, "I want it" '.) So it says here: 'When it came up in His simple will', meaning, that, as it were, the Ein Sof made a will for Himself. By His own free choice He made a will for Himself and, as it were, He made a lack and imperfection in Himself (the purpose of this was

a will to desire i.e. the first impulse was not caused by anything external but simply a will to will, not a will in order to satisfy some desire or to make good something that was missing.

'Likutei shoshanah' section at the end of *No'am elimelekh*, 103*b–c* (ed. Nigal, p. 554).

Pirkei avot Av. 2: 4.

the rabbis say Kid. 50*a*, i.e. although in certain circumstances where a person's assent is required the court can compel him to give it, it is ultimately of his own free will that he does so.

for the Torah to be established. For according to the way of the Torah, He is obliged to change one will for another, from that of exile to that of freedom, for example, or, Heaven forfend, vice versa: 'And He doeth according to His will in the host of heaven' [Dan. 4: 32]; 'He removeth kings and setteth up kings' [Dan. 2: 21]. According to the way of the Torah, there must be reward and punishment. Through the impulse from below, the impulse from above is awakened to give unto everyone according to his ways. Now the Torah is the impression of His divinity, so that, for the sake of the love of the Torah, He was obliged to create a want in the Light of His Essence so that He should will the creation of the world. Understand this), and a desire. Heaven forfend that it should be understood to mean that He was lacking in anything and not perfect in all perfections. Heaven forfend that such a notion be entertained, since He is certainly perfect to the utmost degree of sheer perfection. But He made a lack and a desire in Himself that they should acknowledge Him since He desires mercy and wishes to do good, and if He cannot do good He is not, as it were, in a state of utter perfection and is, Heaven forfend, lacking. It follows that, as it were, He makes this will for Himself, and it came up in His will without any compulsion whatsoever. But once He had made this will in Himself, He was then obliged to be perfect in order that they should acknowledge Him. Before He had made this will for Himself there was no necessity, and the change brought about by this will was a miracle, as above from the expositions of the Female and Male Waters.

Rashi says something similar in his comment on the verse, 'and He rested on the seventh day' [Gen. 2: 2]: 'He wrote of Himself that He rested in order that a lesson be taught *a fortiori* to human beings.' See it there. We see that although He requires no rest, for he neither becomes weary nor tired, but it is Torah and is required so that we may learn from it. (The reason why he calls the will 'a simple will' is because although He made a will for Himself, that will is simple since it was not caused by anything apart from Him, and not by any compelling cause, and had He so desired He had the power not to will. Understand this.)

How He comes to be recognized is known from the Zohar. The Holy One, blessed be He, created the Torah. He looked into the Torah and caused all the worlds to be emanated, created, and formed, as explained in the *Etz ḥayim*. Go forth and learn. I shall provide you with a premiss taken from the *Zohar ḥadash** on the verse, 'And God said, Let the waters be gathered' [Gen. 1: 9]: 'R. Isaac asked R. Eleazar a certain question as they

* *Zohar ḥadash* pp. 12*d*–13*a*.

travelled through the wilderness. He said: "I wish to ask a certain question if it is not sinful so to do" (meaning, if it is not sinful to raise questions concerning the creation of the world). He replied: "You may ask." He said: "The verse states: 'and God saw the light, that it was good' [Gen. 1: 4]. For Him to have said it before the act would have been suitable. But to say it after the act seems to imply that He did not know this beforehand ... but when the act had been done it seems as if He examined it ... since it is written that first He saw it and then He pronounced it good ..." He said: "You are not sinful and the question needs to be asked, and this serves as a warning to human beings. For R. Judah said: When a man studies the work of creation, the creative acts performed on each day, he should not ask concerning that to which an answer is not found, asking, why was this act performed in this way and that in a different way, since you must reply that God saw it was good to do it in that way and you cannot therefore question it." ' (According to this reply the meaning of: 'And He saw that it was good' is that this shows that you should not ask why was it done so, since in the eyes of the One who performed it, it was good in the form it assumed when it came up in His will. He saw that it was good; the Creator in His mighty wisdom, He Himself saw that this act was good, and we do not know what is good.) Furthermore, it was for the purpose of teaching men the proper way. For the act was revealed and known to Him before it had been performed, and yet He did not wish to pronounce it good until the work was finished. In the same way, it is not fitting that a man should praise a thing until it has been completed, otherwise it may be found to have some defect and he will then be caught out in a lie. R. Berakhiah said ... —see the whole passage. In this reply a satisfactory solution is found to all the problems. For you should know, brother, we have a tradition from our rabbis, as the *gaon* R. Menahem Azariah of Fano* writes at the beginning of his work *Yonat elim*,* that the world bears the impress of the Torah, and the Torah bears the impress of His divinity, blessed be His name. That is what he says there.

It follows that when the Holy One, blessed be He, caused His Holy Torah to be emanated from Himself, 'like that snail* whose garment is

R. Menahem Azariah of Fano Italian kabbalist (1548–1620).

Yonat elim where the doctrines of the kabbalah are described at length.

like that snail this saying is in the Midrash, Gen. R. 21: 5, in connection with the garments of the Children of Israel during their forty-year journey through the wilderness. As they grew, their garments grew with them, 'like that snail ...' But in Bacharach's *Emek hamelekh* (ch. 1, beg.) it is applied to Ein Sof and the *tzimtzum*. E. applies it here to the Torah in relation to God.

formed from its very self', the Torah being called the light of the garment of the Holy One, blessed be He, this light is illumined through the evolution of the worlds *ad infinitum*. This is the mystery of the evolution of the worlds, through which the light of Ein Sof, blessed be He, and blessed be His name, is clothed and perfected, as the rabbis say: 'Whence was the Torah created? It was created from the garment of the Holy One, blessed be He. And whence were the Heavens created? This teaches us that the Holy One, blessed be He, wrapped Himself in the light of His garment and caused to shine from it ... and He created the Heavens. And whence was the earth created? The Holy One, blessed be He, took snow from under His Throne of Glory ...'; see the beginning of *Pirkei derabbi eliezer.** Although Rambam* expresses his astonishment at this statement, from which it looks as if this holy man postulates, Heaven forfend, the existence of a primordial matter (see the work *Ginat egoz*, by R. Joseph Gikatila, for a solution to the difficulty), but to those who fear him it all hints at the deep mysteries known to those who have entered into the secret of the Lord. It is all derived from the completion of the evolution of the worlds in which world derives from world; this one a garment to the other; this one the brain, the other a casing; see the Zohar, 'Bereshit', p. 19;* and it is explained in the *Etz ḥayim* in these gates.

Now you may well ask, why did it have to be in an evolutionary process? Was it not within the power of the Infinite, blessed be He, and blessed be His name, to create them all at once, as Scripture says: 'When I call unto them, they stand up together' [Isa. 48: 13]? This is similar to the question put by the *tanna* in the Mishnah:* 'They could have been created by a single word ...'* But this is the correct solution: the Torah teaches us the way of the Lord in which we should go, the whole of the Torah revolves around this evolutionary way. We quote the words of the *Zohar ḥadash* 'Bereshit',* on the topic of the evolutionary process, on the verse: 'Let there be lights' [Gen. 1: 14]: 'R. Abahu, R. Hiyya, and R. Nathan were travelling on the way ... And I recall that they have said, the sun's light is derived from the lustre of the Supernal Brightness. That light, it appears, is not its own, as is written "Let there be lights". It should have said: "Let there be *orot*". Why does it say *me'orot*?* R. Zera said it means "from the

Pirkei derabbi eliezer ch. 3.
Rambam Maimonides, *Guide*, ii. 26.
Zohar, 'Bereshit', p. 19 Zohar i. 19*a*–*b*.
in the Mishnah Av. 5: 1.
'They could have been created by a single word ...' i.e. why was the world and all that is in it created by ten sayings, when they could have been created by a single saying?
***Zohar ḥadash*, 'Bereshit'** p. 15*a*.
me'orot *me'orot* is taken as meaning *from* the lights', that is, everything has come into being from the illuminations of the Torah.

Torah", the *mem* being an auxiliary letter and the word itself being *orot*. R. Hiyya said: "Do not be surprised at this since the Torah has been emanated from the Supernal Wisdom ... In the same way when it gazes at Wisdom whatever is above and below becomes emanated one from the other ..." And from the precious throne they begin to be emanated one from the other. (It would seem that the throne referred to is Malkhut in relation to Ein Sof from which He caused Adam Kadmon to be emanated.* And Malkhut of Adam Kadmon becomes Atik of Atzilut.* And so it follows in each world. Malkhut of Atzilut becomes Atik of Beriah and so on. And see *Sefer ha'atzilut* by R. Hayim Vital, and Gate Abya,* ch. 1.) R. Abahu said: "Let this present no difficulty for with regard to our procedure, with differentiation" (by this he means, in the manner in which we speak when we say 'with differentiation' between the sacred and the profane or between the great and the small) "they begin at first to study the Torah, and from the student it is conveyed to the interpreter, and from the interpreter to the one next to him, and from him to one next to him, so that at the completion of the study all of them depend on the one who begins it. This is the way it is on high and in all worlds." And R. Abahu said: "Moses received the emanation from the Supernal Brightness, Joshua from Moses, and the Elders received the emanation from Joshua ..." '

Now if you observe how things are ordered in the world you see that everything proceeds in an evolutionary process. In order for me not to go to great lengths in stating my own views on the topic of the true Unity, I shall quote to you the words of the *Tikunim* [*Tikun* 69, p. 116*b*]: 'R. Eleazer said: "Father, since the time is opportune ... What is the Man* that the Cause of causes* created in His image, since it is written that He has no image?" He replied: "My son, it does say here: 'In our image',* implying that He has an image. When it says: 'in His image', the meaning is 'like Him'. Just as He sees and is not seen, so He sees and is not seen. Just as He has no image, so He has no image. Just as He has none to precede Him, so He has none who precede Him. Just as He is the Cause of causes, One with no partner, and is not numbered,* He is like Him. And there is a Man of Beriah, Yetzirah, and Asiyah after a different fashion, with garments and a

Malkhut ... from which he caused Adam Kadmon to be emanated the lowest stage of Ein Sof, the Malkhut of Ein Sof, becomes the highest stage of Adam Kadmon.

Atik of Atzilut the highest stage of the World of Emanation.

Gate Abya in the *Etz ḥayim*.

What is the Man ... i.e. Primordial Man, Adam Kadmon.

Cause of causes Ein Sof.

'In our image' as earlier, in Gen. 1: 26.

and is not numbered i.e. He is not counted among the *sefirot* but is above them.

body outside ... There is a creation which He created below, but He has not been created ....' And there, page *a*, he says: 'Why does it say of the letter *yod* that He knows My name? Just as the letter *yod* is not associated with any other letter, so here, too, He has no associate, He is One and has no second. He is One and is not numbered. He created everything and there is no Creator above Him. Is there anyone who can create even a small gnat except Him? But water has the power to create trees and herbs and it has been created. But the Creator of worlds created, but none has created Him.' See there, up to the conclusion of the passage where it says, 'No mind can bear this except for those who know the mysteries.' And at the end of *Tikun* 19: '*Yod* of which there is none higher than He except for that One who created everything but none has created Him. For there is a creator that has itself been created. Water, for example, creates herbs and causes them to grow but is itself created, whereas that One creates but has not been created, for there is no god above Him.' See it there. 'He said to him: "From this it can be adduced that there is a Primordial Man, First of all firsts." ' See it there and in many other places, especially in the Zohar, 'Bereshit',* p. 24*b*. See it there.

Observe and see, brother, the ways of our Torah, which follows the evolutionary process, so that we see that the whole world follows a process of cause and effect. We see a father and the son to whom he gave birth, and the grandson and great-grandson, and cause producing cause. Water causes plants and herbs to grow. At first the plants are void and empty, but the soil, when it is watered, has the capacity to make them sprout in their appointed times. And observe from the words of the *Tikunim* mentioned above how far the power of emanation extends: that there is a Primordial Man emanated from that which is above Him, just as He is the Cause of causes and is not numbered and has no associate, reaching up to the First Cause, the Cause above all causes, the One whom none has created. Great profundities are here, the waters so rapid* that if a carpenter's axe was to be dropped in them, it would still not have reached the bottom after seven years. 'For one higher than the high watcheth, and there are higher than they' [Eccles. 5: 7].

It emerges from what has been said that this was the intention of the Creator of all worlds, that everything should proceed according to the way of the Torah; and that all the worlds—those that have been emanated, those created, those formed, and those made—which depend on His

Zohar 'Bereshit' Zohar i. 24*b*.
the waters so rapid based on *BB* 73*b*.

name, blessed be He, should all evolve in the way of the Torah, from cause to effect. This is the purpose of the Torah, that He be acknowledged. They said in the Zohar, 'Vayigash', p. 208*a*:* 'Come and see. The Holy One, blessed be He, created the wise and the foolish, the rich and the poor, the righteous and the wicked, in order that each may benefit the other', that there should be a giver and a recipient. He created everything according to the Torah. He neither caused to be emanated nor did He create without first looking into the Torah, and only then did He cause to be emanated and then did He create ... As it is said in the Zohar, 'Terumah', p. 161*a*:* 'The Torah preceded the creation of the world by two thousand years. (For the Torah represents the category of Ze'ir Anpin,* according to the mystery of "The Torah, the Holy One, blessed be He, and Israel are One."* The two thousand years represent Abba and Imma;* learn wisdom, learn understanding.* Later on I discovered this in the commentary on the *Sifra detzeniuta* by the Ari, of blessed memory. This is obvious. And there is another mystery here as well.) And when the Holy One, blessed be He, wished to create the world, He looked into each word of the Torah and made something in the creation of the world corresponding to that word, since all the things and events of the world are in the Torah ... If you will say, what could be called work for Him? But by the Holy One, blessed be He, looking into the Torah in this manner, all came into being without toil or effort. It was written in the Torah: 'In the beginning God created the heavens ...' [Gen. 1: 1]. He looked at this word and by so doing He created the heavens. It was written in the Torah: "And God said: Let there be light" [Gen. 1: 3]. He looked at this word and thereby He created light. And so, too, with regard to every word written in the Torah.' Consult the passage and you will observe in our Holy Torah the wondrous works of He who is perfect in knowledge [Job 37: 16].

Now since the creation of all worlds was in accordance with the Torah emanated from Ein Sof, blessed be He, and blessed be His name, which is the impress of God, and the world is the Torah's impress, how can you ask, my son, why it was not created before or after that particular time? For the

Zohar, 'Vayigash', p. 208a Zohar i. 208*a*.

Zohar, 'Terumah' p. 161a Zohar ii. 161*a*.

Ze'ir Anpin corresponding to Tiferet.

'The Torah ... and Israel are One' Torah represents Tiferet. The 'Holy One, blessed be He' is also the name for Tiferet, and among the three patriarchs it is Jacob also known as Israel, who represents Tiferet. Hence all three—Torah, Tiferet, Israel—are one; all three are names for the same entity.

Abba and Imma Ḥokhmah and Binah.

learn wisdom, learn understanding in Aramaic, learn is *alef*, which resembles the word *elef*, 'thousand'; hence the two injunctions to learn represent two thousand years.

Torah comes to teach us the time for every purpose and will. The Midrash *Bereshit rabbah** comments as follows: ' "He hath made everything beautiful in its time" [Eccles. 3: 11]. R. Tanhuma said: "He created the world in its time and it was inappropriate for it to have been created before that time, as it is said: 'And God saw everything that he had made, and, behold, it was very good' [Gen. 1: 31]. R. Abahu said: "From this we learn that the Holy One, blessed be He, was constructing worlds and destroying them. He said: This is suitable ..." '* And come and see what the Ari, of blessed memory, has revealed to us, that this Midrash refers to the breaking of the vessels.* He built worlds and destroyed them so that there could be reward and punishment, which God made for practical reasons, for it is all, all the Torah, for the purpose of divine worship. And so the evolutionary process is for the sake of divine worship and the Torah. Had the world have been created all at once, you would have asked why do we have fathers and children, plants, and the planetary influences that cause the plants to grow, and why does one give birth to another, evolving one from the other, generation after generation, from one metamorphosis to another, from one cause to another—He should have created them all at once. But this is the way of the Torah, stage by stage, and whatever the Holy One, blessed be He, created, He created only for His glory,* that is, the light of His garment, as in the expression used by R. Johanan,* who called his garments the things that caused him to be respected, in accordance with the way of the Torah. And the Torah shows us the way we should go, to give, through the Torah, satisfaction to our Holy One, the Holy One of Israel. Israel ascended first in thought, after which there evolved the innermost light, worlds and souls from the light of His essence from which the Torah was emanated.

According to the Torah, everything has its own particular time: a time for the study of the Torah and a time for prayer; a time for eating and drinking; a time for sleep and a time for rising from sleep; a time for Sabbaths and festivals; a time for the sabbatical year and the jubilee, laid down as a fixed rule not to be transgressed. (And this, too, is the reason of those who hold that the world proceeds in cycles of sabbatical years and jubilees, and they have some support from the *Idra rabba*,* p. 136*a*. Note

Bereshit rabbah Midrash Gen. R. 9: 2.

This is suitable ... and this unsuitable.

breaking of the vessels i.e. the worlds that were created and destroyed are the *sefirot* at the time of the breaking of the vessels before they were reconstituted as *partzufim*.

whatever ... His glory Av. 6: 11.

used by R. Johanan in BK 91*b*.

***Idra rabba*, p. 136a** Zohar iii. 136*a*.

this well.) And it all goes back to the First Cause, Adam Kadmon, First of all firsts. Will you then ask of Adam Kadmon why He* was not caused to be emanated beforehand? If you do, it is not out of wisdom that you ask it. For it was the will of the Creator, blessed be He, who gave the Torah to the Children of Israel of his own free will, that everything should be constantly renewed, as in the expression: 'renewed every morning' [Lam. 3: 23]. For His greatness is beyond searching, and His understanding has no end, and He shows His Infinite power in all the supernal worlds. For this reason He made it that a permanent delight is no delight, for He chooses new forms of divinity in order to show His Infinite power and greatness, blessed be He, and blessed be His name. And every day He renews the work of creation. Since you say that He must be a new creation with all the renewals evolving from Him one after the other, then just let your ears listen to what your mouth says. For if He had been created beforehand in time, He would certainly not be a new creation; and perforce He is required to be in time, with a beginning and an end when He will no longer be, and there has to be a state of non-being before He came into being. For if He had been created before the time when He was created, and if there had been no state of non-being before He came into being, He would not have been called Man of Creation (implying a creation after a state of non-being). Why is He called Man of Creation? Because he was created after a state of non-being. He is called The First, as stated in the *Tikunim*, since there were none before Him except the Ein Sof, blessed be He, and blessed be His name, because there was no state of non-being before He came into being. All the worlds were in Him *in potentia* until He actualized them by His own free will, blessed be His name, by means of the evolutionary process, stage by stage; descending from crown to crown, from diadem to diadem, crownlet to crownlet, all by the will that He, blessed be His name, made for the essence of His glory, in order that His glory be revealed to creatures, to benefit them, that there should be reward and punishment in accordance with the Torah that emanates from His light, blessed be He, and blessed be His name. And see the 'Sha'ar hakedushah', that the root meaning of Adam Kadmon denotes the holy *sefirot* which are arraigned as a human figure, as it were, and they are the essence of the Torah, 248 limbs,* 365 sinews,* for this is the whole of man revolving on ten sayings,*

He throughout this section (to 'perfectly clear', on p. 102), 'He' refers, with few exceptions, to Adam Kadmon rather than to Ein Sof.

248 limbs corresponding to the 248 positive precepts of the Torah.

365 sinews corresponding to the 365 negative precepts of the Torah.

revolving on ten sayings see Avot 5: 1, 'The world was created by ten sayings', interpreted by the kabbalists as referring to the *sefirot*.

words and praises. Now one cannot ask of the first being why He was not brought into being and not created beforehand. This is precisely why He is called First, and, as stated above in the *Tikunim*, He resembles the sanctity of the Ein Sof, blessed be He, and blessed be His name, just as He is the Cause of causes ... It follows from our words that the solution provided by R. Hayim Vital is based on the wisdom of the Torah. For as a result of the evolutionary process the whole creation advances from world to world from Adam Kadmon, and Adam Kadmon has been emanated from beginning and end (in the poetic language of the rabbi).* Consequently, He had a time (when He did not exist). For everything that has limits has a time (when it did not exist and it has a state of non-being before coming into being). See *Ḥovot halevavot*. However, see the above-mentioned *Tikunim*, p. 116*b*, where there is the hair-raising statement that Adam Kadmon is also called the Cause of causes, One and having no number, from whom all the worlds evolve and each one (non-existing until it came into being) in its time. Each one came into existence from a state of non-existence, according to the way of the Torah, for it is the way of the Torah to teach us this: that there is a time for everything, until this world—certainly created in its time and season—evolved (in accordance with His blessed will, without any external compulsion, after all the other worlds from which it has evolved).* There is no need for the forced solutions invented by the later scholars, and the subject is perfectly clear.

According to the above, the words of the author of *Ḥovot halevavot* become as clear as the dawn. For from the remarks of the author of *Ḥovot halevavot* it looks as though his words in 'The Gate of Unification' are derived from the words of R. Sa'adiah Gaon* in his book *Emunot vede'ot** and in his commentary on the *Sefer yetzirah*;* see there in chapter 10 of the gate mentioned. The Geonim,* without doubt, were initiates in the mysteries, and all their words are by kabbalah.* Now all the words of the aforementioned saint are based on the inquiry into the meaning of the true Unity [so as] to keep the precept stated in the [first] paragraph of *Shema*

the rabbi Hayyim Vital Luria, quoted earlier.

from which it has evolved E. means that all worlds follow the evolutionary process in time, so that when the 'time' came for this world to come into being it was the 'right time'.

Sa'adiah Gaon 882–942.

Emunot vede'ot 'Beliefs and Opinions'.

Sefer yetzirah 'Book of Creation' (ed. with Sa'adiah's commentary, Warsaw, 1884).

The Geonim the successors of the talmudic teachers in Babylon from the sixth to the tenth centuries were known as the Geonim, of whom Sa'adiah was one. The kabbalists believed that the Geonim were mystical adepts who knew kabbalah.

all their words are by kabbalah this is an early saying to the effect that the Geonim can be relied on as having an authentic 'tradition' (*kabbalah*). E. assumes this to mean that they were kabbalists.

yisrael, of unifying God with all the heart, the precept delivered to us, the people of the holy seed, from our old, holy father* who unified God, together with his sons, his perfect bed, when his soul ascended to the Unity of the world. The inquiry of *Ḥovot halevavot* was in order that it (his unification) should be a real unification and not the imaginary type familiar in the mouths of ordinary folk.

Now, brother, the methods of unifying the name—it is a tremendous thing—have been delivered to us in the Zohar and according to the methods of the Ari, of blessed memory, in the *Peri etz ḥayim*, to unify from below to above by way of the channels of all the worlds; to offer oneself to be slain for the sake of the sanctification of His name, blessed be He, and blessed be His name; the one who unifies the true Unity sacrifices himself* to be united with the generality of Israel, like Jacob with his sons before his soul departed. And every intelligent person must unite himself with the souls of the saints which ascend to become the Female Waters,* ascending and unifying from world to world: Female Waters to Male and Female, Male and Female to Abba and Imma, Abba and Imma to Arikh, reaching to the stage of Ein Sof. They draw down from Atika* in all the categories of *Shema*,* each in his own way. And they unify with all His names, blessed be He, to the degree that these souls expire in longing, to unify with true unification up to Ein Sof, blessed be He, the First Cause, the Cause of all causes, with none higher and none beneath and none in all directions. He fills all worlds and surrounds all worlds. Then, just as the worlds evolved from above to below, from cause to effect, according to His blessed will at the time of the Creation, so, too, do we unify His great name from below to above, from effect to cause, reaching up to the Cause of all causes, blessed be He, and blessed be His name, up to the One. This is the purpose of our worship in reciting the *Shema* and in prayer, and especially in the offering of the sacrifices;* see the Zohar ('Noaḥ', p. 65)* in the passage: 'R. Simeon said: "I lift up my hands in prayer"' (and in the Zohar, 'Pineḥas', p. 297*b** mentioned above). There you will see the wonders of our Creator,

holy father the patriarch Jacob.

sacrifices himself surrenders his individuality.

Female Waters produced both by human deeds on earth and by the souls of the righteous when they ascend to Heaven.

Atika 'The Ancient One', the highest stage of Arikh.

They draw down ... in all the categories of *Shema* while reciting the Shema they reflect on all the stages E. has mentioned.

offering of the sacrifices even though there are no sacrifices after the Destruction of the Temple, the rabbis ordained that references to these be included in the liturgy, the recitation being considered as if the actual sacrifices were offered in the Temple.

Zohar, 'Noaḥ', p. 65 Zohar i. 65*a*.

Zohar, 'Pineḥas', p. 297*b* Zohar iii. 297*b*.

praised and exalted, in the ascent from cause to cause reaching to Ein Sof. It is around this that the enquiry of the above-mentioned saint revolves when he says: 'This we must know before we begin to enquire about the Unity. We must ask if it exists ... But of the Creator we are only allowed to ask if He is.' According to what has been said, his enquiry concerns the First Cause alone (the Creator whose existence was not preceded by any state of non-existence, namely the Ein Sof). For, as stated above in the name of the *Tikunim*, 'there is a Creator and there is One* who created Him'. At the time when we perform the unification, however, we must unify Him with the Creator, the Cause of all causes whom none has created. This One is not mentioned in the Torah. He is higher than all emanations, and no thought can grasp Him at all. Certainly no one is allowed to ask how He is and what He is and what He is for; Heaven forbid that there is any thought of Him that He does not know; He is beyond knowledge and unknowable (as R. Hayim Vital says himself); and the whole book of the Zohar is full of this idea, especially in the *Idrot*. In the *Idra rabba* (p. 130)* it is stated as follows: 'It has been taught: Nevertheless the name of the Ancient One is concealed from above all and is not referred to in the Torah.' Now the Ancient One mentioned there is not the First Cause, Ein Sof, blessed be He, but has evolved from the Malkhut of Adam Kadmon.

Now the truth is that divinity resides in all the *sefirot*, and by them His names, blessed be He, are called, as I have explained. YAH is the name of Wisdom. EHYEH is the name of Keter or of Binah. Binah is HVYH pointed as Elohim, stated in the Zohar, 'Vayikra', p. 20,* and in the Zohar, 'Aḥarei' (p. 65).* For us these names have been explained in accordance with the words of the Ari, of blessed memory, thank God; I have explained why each aspect of the name is expressed by means of these particular letters (by which He is called, all founded on wondrous wisdom, and the Jerusalem Targum translates *bereshit bara Elohim* as 'with wisdom',* the quality of Ḥokhmah). And see the Zohar, 'Bereshit',* that *Elohim* here refers to Binah, from which has evolved Heaven and Earth, representing Tiferet and Malkhut. However, we unite all the *sefirot* reaching to the First Cause, Ein Sof, blessed be He, who by His work brings about the flow of grace

there is One the Ein Sof.

***Idra rabba*, p. 130** Zohar iii. 130*a*.

Zohar, 'Vayikra', p. 20 the page reference is a printer's error; it is in fact Zohar iii. 10*b*.

Zohar, 'Aḥarei', p. 65 Zohar iii. 65*a*.

'with wisdom' from Ps. 111: 10, 'beginning of wisdom', which E. identifies with Hokhmah.

Zohar, 'Bereshit' Zohar i. 1*b*–2*b*. Thus the verse is rendered: 'With Hokhmah the Ein Sof created Heaven (= Tiferet and the other lower *sefirot*) and Earth (= Malkhut).

and renews each day constantly the work of creation from the light of the flow of His hidden glory until all worlds are filled. If He were to be withdrawn from them they would all remain, even the holy divine names, like a body without a soul.

Come and see what Elijah says* at the beginning of the *Tikunim*: 'Thou art Wise but not known by means of Wisdom.' He means that even when His power extends to some *sefirah*, His nature, His essence, His being, and His purpose are not known to us. This is the true meaning of the command to recite the *Shema*, to unite all the worlds and all the souls in the generality of the souls of Israel reaching to Ein Sof, with self-sacrifice for the Lord's sake, and we then draw down from the light of His essence, blessed be He, for we elevate the worlds to their First Root, to Nothing,* by means of the Torah and the precepts, and from thence His will is drawn down for an additional renewal of the energy of the worlds. If you ask: What means this mode of worship for us* and for our children, the answer is that this is how it ascended in His will, blessed be He, and blessed be His name, that everything should proceed from the impulse from below, by means of the Torah and the precepts which He gave to the holy seed, the people of the Lord, the people of the God of Jacob. Now we are certainly entitled to ask whether there really is a First Cause, an uncreated Creator of all worlds, a Prime Being with none prior to Him. For this there is no proof, even from the creation of the world; for the Creator of the world may Himself have been created, and who is to say that there really is a First and Prime Cause?

And according to the secret path,* perhaps Keter is the First Cause.* Understand this well, for it is exceedingly profound. And we are obliged to unify *ad infinitum*, to reach that of which we are not allowed even to think. Now all the miracles which the Lord our God has wrought for us were performed by the power of His names in the *sefirot*. For example, the Exodus from Egypt was brought about by the Wisdom that opens gates,*

Elijah says in the Prayer of Elijah, *Tikunei zohar*, 2nd. Introd.

Nothing Ayin = Ein Sof.

what means this mode of worship for us in the Passover Haggadah, the wicked son asks 'What means this worship for you?' E. is obviously paraphrasing this, but by using 'for us' he implies that the offence of the wicked son lies not in asking the question but in excluding himself.

the secret path kabbalah.

Keter is the First Cause i.e. and there is no Ein Sof.

the Wisdom that opens gates see Prov. 1: 20–1; Wisdom (= Ḥokhmah) is present at the opening of gates. The daily evening prayer includes the phrase 'with wisdom He opens gates'. Hence here E.'s theme is that the Exodus, the opening of gates of the Egyptian prison, was through the agency of Ḥokhmah.

and the Lord our God* brought us out from there. (This is a proof of *creatio ex nihilo*); but in reality, Wisdom is emanated from that which is above it. The parting of the Sea of Reeds* was brought about by the revelation of the Holy Ancient One,* the Simple Will (and this is a proof of the Will, that by His own free will, without any external compulsion, it was decided to create the world; and the wise will understand); but this, too, was emanated from that which is even higher. And so, too, when it is said in the Torah: 'For the Lord thy God is a devouring fire' [Deut. 4: 24], this refers to the creative power as imagined by our weak intellect. It is a name given to the *sefirah* of Power,* which is the subtle, spiritual fire on high. When Malkhut receives strength from the Power on high it is called Esh.* (As is well known, there is here a unification of the divine name: Elohim filled out by *yods** has the numerical value of 300, and the *alef* of Esh hints simply at Elohim.* For us, when we wish to perform the unification that sweetens the judgement, we have in mind seven times* HVYH and seven times EHYEH, the Good Name. So the numerical value is the same as that of Esh, and it becomes white fire shining at night; and so, too, MTZPTZ, the name HVYH in code,* sweetens the name Elohim.) In the same way you can understand the other names. However, the First Cause is known to us by tradition, from the time of the unification at Sinai, and the wise will understand. Around this revolve the sweet enquiries of the saintly author of *Ḥovot halevavot* in order to bring it nearer to the grasp of the intellect, only on whether He exists. But the nature and being of the Ein Sof, blessed be He, cannot be known, and we are obliged to affirm the unity of the One whose unity is unique. But it is certainly forbidden to enquire of the being and nature of the Ein Sof, blessed be He, the First Cause. And it is certainly forbidden to enquire why He is. And it is forbidden even to enquire into His name in the unification of His names, for no thought can

the Lord our God 'the Lord' = Tiferet; 'our God' = Malkhut.

Sea of Reeds generally referred to in English as the Red Sea, although the literal translation of the Hebrew term *yam suf* would be Reed Sea.

Holy Ancient One Keter.

the *sefirah* of Power Gevurah.

Esh Hebrew for 'fire'.

Elohim filled out by *yods* i.e. with the *hé* spelled *hé*, *yod.* With this spelling, the total numerical value of Elohim is 300, as follows: *alef* = *alef* (1) + *lamed* (30) + *pé* (80) = 111; *lamed* = *lamed* (30) + *mem* (40) + *dalet* (4) = 74; *hé* = *hé* (5) + *yod* (10) = 15; *yod* = *yod* (10) + *vav* (6) + *dalet* (4) = 20; *mem* = *mem* (40) + *mem* (40) = 80, giving a total of 111 + 74 + 15 + 20 + 80 = 300. *Esh is alef* (1) + *shin* (300), giving a total of 301.

hints simply at Elohim i.e. *alef* = 1, hence the single name, i.e. without filling.

seven times seven is a sacred number, corresponding to the seven lower *sefirot.*

MTZPTZ ... in code in this code, the letter *mem* (M) stands for *yod*, *pé* (P) for *vav*, *tzadik* (TZ) for *hé.* Thus MTZPTZ (*mem*, *tzadik*, *pé*, *tzadik*) is the name YHVH in code.

grasp Him at all. Take careful note of this, brother, and then you will also understand his words in chapter 5 of the aforementioned gate (over which all his commentators have worn themselves out in trying to get it right, for they did not know the mystery behind the topic).

I have gone to great lengths on this topic, in obedience to the saying of the rabbis,* of blessed memory: 'Rabbi said:* "Be *shakud* [diligent] in the study of the Torah and know what answers to give to the unbeliever".' For the word *shakud* is connected with the word for almonds, as in the verse, 'a rod of *shaked*' [Jer. 1: 11]. For almonds blossom sooner than all other fruits. In the same way, a man should not wait until he reaches old age before studying this science. (Hence it says 'in the study of the Torah' and not: 'Be diligent for the Torah' or 'at the Torah', as in: 'to be diligent at my doors'.* The meaning is that you must understand the innermost part of the Torah, to study to the extent of the mystery of the *lamed*,* the tower flying in the air,* so that you know what answer to give to the unbeliever. There is no worse unbeliever than the evil inclination in the days of one's youth, which causes doubts to arise regarding the secret wisdom as a result of the enquiries found among the early teachers on the above-mentioned problems.) I come to urge you to study this science, in order that you may be saved from the doubts of the unbelievers, especially in this generation. If the early teachers cried like a crane, what should the hyssops of the wall do? We are like ants in the vineyard and lust prevails, as R. Zemah writes in his Introduction.* Consult it there. Contemporary unbelievers are not like those of earlier days, for in this generation they separate themselves for the slaking of their lust.* Believe me, brother, one who does not study this science is as one who lives outside the Holy Land and, since lust prevails, he is as one who has no God.* The enticement of the evil inclination causes

the rabbis Av. 2: 14.

Rabbi said printer's error; should be Rabbi Eleazar said.

'to be diligent at my doors' Prov. 8: 34. 'To be diligent' is *lishkod*.

mystery of the *lamed* 'to study' is *lilmod* with a *lamed*. The letter *lamed*, which stands higher than the other letters, represents the 'tower flying in the air'—Binah.

the tower flying in the air the Talmud (Hag. 15*b*) refers to a 'flying tower' around which three hundred halakhic discussions revolved. The commentators are uncertain as to its meaning, but it became a metaphor for the esoteric. The letter *lamed*, repeated twice in the word *lilmod*, to study, is shaped like a 'flying tower'; hence E.'s caveat that one should study all the mysteries.

Introduction to the *Peri etz ḥayim*, p. 3*c*.

they separate themselves for the slaking of their lust they separate themselves from the believers not out of philosophical conviction but in the pursuit of their lusts. Z.E. is probably right here when he sees E. as referring here to the Maskilim, the so-called 'enlightened ones' who were paving the way at this time in the departure from traditional Jewish practices.

has no God based on the talmudic saying (Ket. 110*b*) 'Whoever resides outside Eretz Yisrael, it is as if he has no God'.

doubts in matters of belief, and there are many proofs of this. But one who takes the risk* of studying the doctrine of the Ari, of blessed memory, and the Zohar, and understands these—good tidings are given in the heart of the wise-hearted that he will attain the comprehension of this science and the elevated fear of Heaven, clear, bright, and true, and no doubts will remain about the ways of the Lord in performing His wonders. He will know with certainty the unification of His name and he will grasp the main principles of the divine subjects of the God of Israel, and there will remain for him no doubt and no problem whatsoever. May the All Merciful give us the merit of worshipping Him in truth. (Come and see the problem of divine foreknowledge and human free-will which agitated to such a degree the early teachers, Rambam* and Ra'abad,* of blessed memory. And yet it is dealt with in the *Zohar ḥadash*, p. 120 in the Slavita edition.* Even though what is said there seems unintelligible, here is not the place to explain it. If you really want to know, ask us and, with God's help, we shall explain it to you in a manner that is sweet to the palate.)

Now the mystery of the special quality of this science consists of the unification of the deed, demonstrating the function of each motion and each limb and of everything done under the sun from beginning to end, whether it be the unification performed when reciting the *Shema* or when reciting the Prayer. It shows us how to unify Him through all the sources of the channels of the limbs, which point to the *shiur komah* of the Creator. It shows us how to serve Him with the service of the heart—that is, prayer—and how to depict the unification of His name, blessed be He, and blessed be His name, without entertaining a corporeal picture, Heaven forfend. For believe me, my friend, those who have not experienced the fragrant fear of the Lord* in the study of this science entertain corporeal notions regarding divine matters. Even though a man knows that it is forbidden to have a corporeal concept, what can he do since he is ignorant of the roots of the channels of unification to elevate everything to the One. When he comes across the words of some Aggadah or some scriptural verse where it is written 'the hand of the Lord', 'the eyes of the Lord', 'the ears of the Lord', though he tries to force his mind not to entertain a corporeal concept he is unable to do so, for why is it called a hand of the Creator,

takes the risk as E. has said at the beginning of this treatise, the study of kabbalah is risky but it is a risk that is worth taking.

Rambam *Mishneh torah*, *Teshuvah*, 5: 5.

Ra'abad stricture of R. Abraham Ibn David, ad loc.

Slavita edition and in current editions too, on pp. 120*c–d*.

the fragrant fear of the Lord based on Isa. 11: 3, 'and his delight (*vehariḥo*, lit. his fragrance) shall be in the fear of the Lord'.

blessed be He? Even though it may be explained to him that it is only a metaphor, he has not been told what it means. And if he is told that it merely means the operation of the divine quality of lovingkindness, it still remains difficult why a hand should be postulated for that which has neither hand nor the likeness of a hand, since it is a total abstraction. And come and see how R. Akiba entered safely and emerged safely, unlike Aher.* Aher, knowing that there is neither sitting nor tiredness nor any other corporeal concept on high (see the chapter 'They Do Not Inquire')* was puzzled to find Metatron sitting down, as a result of which doubts entered his mind. But as for R. Akiba, what did he expound? He said *tzevaot** means that He is a letter* among His hosts. For all the likenesses and corporeal pictures mentioned by the prophets and the rabbis, of blessed memory, all hint at various letters of the divine name. Of these it is permitted to have a picture in the mind, as it is stated in the *Raya mehemna*, 'Bo'.* However, it should be in the manner I have mentioned previously, black fire on white fire, and sometimes, as above, white fire. For even letters can be grasped in a corporeal manner, Heaven forfend, and it is written: 'for ye saw no manner of form' [Deut. 4: 15], and yet it is written: 'and the similitude of the Lord doth he behold' [Num. 12: 8]; see the above-mentioned *Raya mehemna*. And I, too, thank God, have my own way of explaining, as above, the statement that God is a devouring fire, in that Esh represents the letters of the divine name. Similarly, with regard to the hand of the Lord: *yad** is a simple HVYH and filled with four letters and ten letters; 'and under His feet . . .' [Exod. 24: 10], the mystery of the foot is explained in the section 'The Intentions of Ḥanukah',* that *regel* has the numerical value of the total of 72 and 161;* for the feet of a higher world are the instruments by which the intelligences of a lower world are pro-

R. Akiba entered safely and emerged safely, unlike Aher a reference to the story of the four who entered Paradise (Hag. 14*b*), in which Aher became an apostate and only R. Akiba emerged unscathed.

chapter 'They Do Not Inquire' in the story of Elisha ben Abuyah in Ḥag. 15*a*.

tzevaot See Ḥag. 16*a*.

a letter reading *ot*, 'a sign', as 'a letter'. The *tzeva'ot*, 'hosts' of the *sefirot* and their combinations, can only be depicted as letters.

***Raya mehemna*, 'Bo'** Zohar ii. 42*a–b*.

yad *yad* means 'hand', but the letters are *yod* (10) and *dalet* (4). The Tetragrammaton has four letters but when 'filled' it has ten letters, so *yad* represents this combination of divine names (10 letters + 4 letters).

'The Intentions of Ḥanukah' *Kavanot ḥanukah*, in *Peri etz ḥayim*, p. 94*a*.

***regel* has the numerical value of the total of 72 and 161** The numerical value of *regel* ('foot') is 233, as follows: *resh* (200) + *gimel* (3) + *lamed* (30) = 233. This corresponds to the total value of the Tetragrammaton filled out with *yods* (72, as shown elsewhere) plus EHYEH filled out with *yods* as shown below: *alef* = *alef* (1) + *lamed* (30) + *pé* (80) = 111; *hé* = *hé* (5) + *yod* (10) = 15; *yod* = *yod* (10) + *vav* (6) + *dalet* (4) = 20; *hé* = *hé* (5) + *yod* (10) = 15, giving a total of 111 + 15 + 20 +

duced. Happy are we, how good is our portion, that we have been given the merit of having revealed to us the profound mysteries of our God, the fount of His Torah.

You can fulfil the obligation of unification also through deed, with deeds that are for the satisfaction of bodily needs such as business affairs, eating and drinking, and sex, to an even greater degree than that stated by the author of *Ḥovot halevavot* in 'The Gate of Unification of Worship' and in 'The Gate of Divine Worship', which revolve around the verse 'save unto the Lord only' [Exod. 22: 19], so that a man eats and drinks and sleeps so that his body may be strong for the worship of his Creator. Similarly, his business affairs are conducted so that he may have enough to eat and to support his children. Now while it is true that such a person is good-hearted, doing everything for the sake of God, all his deeds directed Heavenwards; but, my brother, according to our tradition, even this does not constitute perfect worship. And so have I heard it said in the name of the rabbi, the Maggid,* in a comment on the saying of the rabbis,* of blessed memory: 'What constitutes complete worship? That after which there is no other act of worship.' Now when a man's intention when he eats is that his body be strong so that he can study the Torah and engage in worship, how can this be considered a completed form of worship? At the time of his eating he neither prays nor studies; so this is not worship in itself but a means to the worship that will come afterwards. But, on the other hand, when the eating is in accordance with the intentions of the Ari, of blessed memory, to engage in the selection process whereby the holy sparks in the food are elevated, to elevate to the good from that which has been selected from the Primordial Kings, and especially one to whom God has honoured by setting before his eyes and his intelligence the roots of His names, blessed be He (as explained in the section on the 'Intentions for the Scholar's Meal')—such a man can perform unifications in his eating as in his prayer. Happy is he and happy his portion.*

And so, too, all one's business affairs constitute a means of worship on their own if conducted in faith. And so, too, with regard to all this-worldly matters, from beginning to end: ploughing, sowing, reaping, and all labour in the field; see *Likutei torah*, 'Behar', and *Likutei torah* 'Psalms', section

15 = 161. The sum of the value of Elohim and EHYEH filled out in this way is 233 (72 + 161), which is equivalent to the numerical value of *regel*.

the Maggid Dov Baer, the Maggid of Mezhirech.

the rabbis Yoma 24*a*, with regard to sacrifices.

happy his portion i.e., happy is he in his portion.

'Ovrei be'emek habakha'; and see chapter 7 of the 'Gate of Prayer'. Especially, if you have the merit of being familiar with the unifications of His names, blessed be He, the remembrance of the name will constantly be before your eyes, to discover desirable things.* You will then be able to converse with your companion, to give and take in faith.

In every word that comes from your mouth, you can find, if you so wish and if you recall the days of your life, some unification of His Name, blessed be He, whether in the initial letters or the end letters or through the numerical value, or through an alphabet in code. The intelligent will find good sense and good taste even in any language spoken. Unifications of His names, blessed be He, will flow in every word spoken once one becomes familiar with the methodology of the unification of divine names, their numbers, their combinations in their fillings, so as to unite and bind up all his deeds to His name, blessed be He. This is the meaning of: 'Let all thy deeds be done for the name of Heaven',* and it does not say simply 'for Heaven'. In *Tikun* 21 it is stated: 'Happy is the man who, when he prays, lets his thoughts soar upwards; for names are produced by the mouth, and fingers write down the mysteries.'

For so it is when a man's thoughts are bound to the Creator, blessed be He, then he has the capacity to discover the unification of His name, blessed be He, in all matters, and he will know the origins of every thing in the root of the qualities and the channels of the supernal flow of grace. For instance, he will know that bread belongs to the mystery of *leḥem*, which has the same numerical value as *mazala*,* as is well known, and represents the love that flows from *mazala*, the root of the three HVYHs* of 'the Lord reigns, the Lord reigned, the Lord will reign', and from there is the mystery of sustenance, as we explained, thanks be to God: *ḥasdo** in the verse 'who giveth bread to all flesh for *ḥasdo* [His mercy] endureth for ever' [Ps. 136: 25] has the numerical value of *leḥem*. And in the same way, water represents the nine *yods** of the four names AV, SAG, MAH, and BEN. The wise man will find a way of performing a unification even when he says

to discover desirable things enabling you to discover desirable things.

'Let all thy deeds be done for the name of Heaven' based on 'for the sake' Av. 2: 12, 'Let all thy deeds be for the sake of Heaven'; Heb. *leshem*, lit., 'for the *name* of Heaven', is taken by E to mean for the name, i.e. of God.

leḥem* ... *mazala *leḥem* = *lamed* (30) + *ḥet* (80) + *mem* (40) = 78; *mazala* = *mem* (40) + *zayin* (7) + *lamed* (30) + *alef* (1) = 78.

the three HYVHs the root of the Tetragrammaton is *hayah*, conveying the idea of 'to be', and the term is often explained as 'He was, He is, He will be'; hence also 'He reigned' etc. All this forms the opening of the well-known hymn *Adon olam*.

ḥasdo *ḥet* (8) + *samekh* (60) + *dalet* (4) + *vav* (6) = 78 = *leḥem*, as shown earlier.

nine *yods* 9 × 10 (*yod* = 10) = 90. *Mayim*, 'water', is *mem* (40) + *yod* (10) + *mem* (40) = 90.

*Brot,** in German, since this has the numerical value of seven times El, for this is the lovingkindness of the *mazala* and the name representing lovingkindness is El, the primordial lovingkindness which goes together with His Bride. And so, too, *Wasser** has the numerical value of 277, the mystery of *ezer,** after the mystery of the drops of the *yods*;* see the exposition of Light, Water, Firmament in the expositions of the Female Waters and the Male Waters. The same applies, my brother, to every subject of every deed and spoken word in the world: if you have merited the good fortune that your mind is set to recall the Creator (for happy is the man who does not forget Him), you will discover the name of the Holy One, blessed be He, in every word. 'And David got him a name' [2 Sam. 8: 13], that is to say, he discovered a means of performing a unification in whatever he did; see the 'Unification when Giving Alms' in 'The Intentions of "And Thou Rulest Over All" ' and the Zohar, 'Beḥukotai', p. 113.* The whole work *Raya mehemna* is based on the attempt to discover in every *mitzvah* and in every act the unification of the name HVYH, blessed be He, as has been explained in the work *Reshit ḥokhmah*.

And this is the meaning of the saying of the rabbis, of blessed memory, in *Menaḥot*:* 'R. Simeon ben Yohai says: Even if a man has only recited the *Shema* morning and evening he has fulfilled the verse: "thou shalt meditate therein day and night" [Josh. 1: 8].' A strange statement. For what are the circumstances? If the statement refers to one who is engaged in the performance of a *mitzvah*, then he is obviously exempt from studying the Torah. If, on the other hand, he is engaged in optional pursuits, why should the command to recite the *Shema* be considered more important than the command to wear *tefillin* or to perform other *mitzvot*, and why should he be exempt from studying the Torah during the whole of the day? However, you should know that the whole purpose of this science is to elevate all things to their Source, to the Creator of all worlds, and that the intention behind all deeds is to engage in the selection process in order to rescue the souls sunk in the depths of the *kelipot*. All the *mitzvot* revolve around this idea, all as has been revealed to us by the Ari, of blessed memory, in the works *Etz ḥayim* and *Peri etz ḥayim*, from the first point of the first *tzimtzum** down to the final point, the navel of the earth and all that is in it. The picture of all the worlds and all things that come into being and

Brot *bet* (2) + *resh* (200) + *vav* (6) + *tet* (9) = 217; *El* = *alef* (1) + *lamed* (30) = 31 × 7 = 217.

Wasser *vav* (6) + *alef* (1) + *samekh* (60) + *yod* (10) + *resh* (200) = 277.

ezer *ayin* (70) + *zayin* (7) + *resh* (200) = 277.

drops of the *yods* the *yod* representing the drops of 'water'.

Zohar, 'Beḥukotai', p. 113 Zohar iii. 113*a–b*.

Menaḥot Men. 99*b*.

the first *tzimtzum* when the Ein Sof with-

lose their being, from beginning to end, of all of these the Ari, of blessed memory, has related to us their roots, ideas, sources, vitality, reasons, and profundities: how these are emanated from the quality of the Creator, blessed be He, and blessed be His name, who has caused them to be emanated, who has created, formed, and made them for His glory, blessed be He, in order to give satisfaction to His name and to fulfil His will according to His wisdom.

Now I have mentioned above, in the name of R. Menahem Azariah of Fano, that the world is an impress (of God) of the Torah, and the Torah is the impress of His divinity, blessed be He, and blessed be His name. Every intelligent person who wishes to serve the Lord in truth must have in mind that his deeds be dedicated to the fulfilment of the verse: 'In all thy ways acknowledge Him' [Prov. 3: 6]. As we say in *Berakhot*,* chapter 'Haroeh': 'On which small passage do all the main principles of the Torah depend? On the verse: "In all thy ways acknowledge Him".'

Now the mystery of knowledge is in both the general and the particular, as it is stated in the Zohar, 'Va'era', in the *Raya mehemna*, p. 25.* Very briefly, this is what is said there: 'The first command taught to us by Moses is: "And ye shall know that I am the Lord your God" [Exod. 6: 7] ... And then he taught it to us in particular, as it is said: "Know this day, and lay it to thy heart, that the Lord, He is God" [Deut. 4: 39], stressing "this day ... that the Lord He is God"—this is the particular way. How many secrets and mysteries in this word ... the first command is to know the Holy One, blessed be He, in general and in particular, beginning and end. And this is the secret of: "I am the first" referring to the general, "and I am the last" referring to the particular.' Consult the passage as a whole (and study it carefully, for a great and profound principle and a pillar of the source of Torah and worship is contained therein. Delve deeply into this passage and you will find delightful things for your soul's perfection.)

Now, to understand the meaning of the statement that 'the Lord, He is God' refers to the general and the particular: 'general' and 'particular' are Yesod and Malkhut,* and they have to become united through Knowledge,* as is generally known. Now, the name Elohim is so called after the particular name, that is, Malkhut, the performance of the Torah and

drew in order to make room for the sefirotic process to develop.

Berakhot Ber. 63*a*.

***Raya mehemna*, p. 25** Zohar ii. 25*a*.

'general' and 'particular' are Yesod and Malkhut Yesod brings the *generality* of the *sefirot* to Malkhut which embodies every detail, i.e. the particularity, of divine providence.

Knowledge Da'at, which flows into Yesod to effect the unification.

worship with the 248 positive precepts and the 365 negative precepts, for this is the whole of man,* constituting the form of a complete *partzuf.* I have explained, on the premisses laid down by the Ari, of blessed memory, that the name Elohim hints at the external aspect of the *partzuf,* the image of God. For the *alef* of Elohim hints at the skull;* the *lamed** hints at the three brains, Hokhmah, Binah, Da'at; the *hé** hints at the five limbs from Ḥesed to Yesod: Hesed, Gevurah, Tiferet, Netzaḥ, Hod; and the *yod** hints at Yesod, and the *mem** at Malkhut. I have expounded all this at length in a tract on the passage in 'Bereshit'* which begins with: 'At the beginning of the will of the King'. There, thank God, I have explained many marvellous things, that the name Elohim extends in the name of Power* and functions from one world to another, so that a judge* here below and a king and ruler is called by the name Elohim, which is not so with regard to any other of the divine names. And in my exposition on section 'Aḥarei' I have explained the roots of the subject.

The name HVYH is the mystery of the general, for it hints at the inner *partzuf.* Now the particular is the Kingdom of Heaven.* All events that take place in the world are expressed in detail in the Sovereignty holding sway over all worlds. And consult the intentions of the *baraita* of Rabbi Ishmael in the *Peri etz ḥayim.** This is the act when it receives its completion in this world; heaven and earth and all their hosts; herbiage, beasts, fowl, animals, and human beings—all are impressed in detail in Malkhut. The man who worships is a king in the general sense and he is Malkhut in the particular. In the book *Hakanah** it is also stated that the quality of Malkhut refers to all man's possessions and his deeds and all his instruments, the completion and end of every act that was there in the divine thought from the beginning. And so, too, in the above-mentioned passage, it is said: 'General and particular, beginning and end, this one male, the other female . . .'; see it there. All is brought about by means of the Torah and the *mitzvot,* of which the world is an impression. For the measure of the Torah is greater

the whole of man Eccles. 12: 13, interpreted by E. to mean which forms a complete *partzuf* of a 'man'.

the skull the highest aspect of each *partzuf.*

lamed = 30 = three tens, hence the three *moḥin.*

hé = five, hence the five 'limbs' of the 'body', the five *sefirot* from Ḥesed to Hod.

yod the first letter of Yesod.

mem the first letter of Malkhut.

'Bereshit' Zohar i. 15*a*.

name of Power Gevurah.

a judge the name Elohim is given to a judge or a ruler (Exod. 21: 6; Exod. 22: 27, as interpreted by the rabbis).

Kingdom of Heaven Heb. *malkhut shamayim* = Malkhut.

Peri etz ḥayim pp. 12*d*–13*c*.

Hakanah an early kabbalistic work attributed to R. Nehuniah ben Hakanah. The reference is to pp. 1*a*–2*a*.

than that of the world. Zechariah ben Ido* stated that the boundaries of the Torah are 3,000.

It has been explained that the thirteen principles* by means of which the Torah is expounded sprout from the thirteen qualities of mercy and they total 3,210,* teaching that the way of the Torah is 3,200.* For it is the heart* that the All Merciful wants, and the Torah begins with the letter *bet** and ends with the letter *lamed*,* pointing to the quality of the heart. And in every series of a hundred, blessing is found. The total number of the quality of mercy is ten more, teaching that the mystery of *yod*, the first point, is the fulcrum of the Torah and the *mitzvot*; and the door revolves on its hinges. The whole of the Torah and the *mitzvot* revolves around this, to attain the quality of the point of the *yod** (the elevated fear, the root principle). In a general sense it is the fear of Heaven; the fear of the Lord is His treasure. There is no need to dwell on this at length. Verily, all the events of the worlds have their impression in it. Happy is the man who contemplates this science. Approaching the creation in an intelligent manner, he will discover that it is ordered by the way of the Torah, the work of the Lord; [it is] tremendous. Everywhere he sets his eyes according to the Torah permits him to observe the inner workings of the order: how everything makes its impression before his eyes, to serve his Creator, whom he acknowledges, praises, lauds, and exalts; like our king, David, on whom be peace, who did not leave aside anything, small or great, without offering thanksgiving and song. Go forth and see the Psalm 'Let my soul bless'* and the Psalm 'Praise the Lord* from the heavens . . . and the waters above the heavens.' One who looks carefully into everything will find that all things are based on the roots of the qualities of the supernal, [the] divine *sefirot*. However, all the details which depend on the deed belong in the mystery of the name Elohim, the mystery of the human agent, the judge and king, represented by the name Elohim. For all the external aspects of

Zechariah ben Ido see Eruv. 21*a* for Zechariah and the measurements of the Torah.

thirteen principles there are thirteen hermeneutic principles by means of which the Torah is expounded by the rabbis, and these are said to correspond to the thirteen qualities of mercy in Exod. 34: 6–7. Thus these thirteen can be said to represent the Torah.

they total 3,210 the total numerical value of the letters in the Exodus verses is 3,210.

the way of Torah is 3,200 and with an added 10 for the *sefirot* = 3,210.

it is the heart 'the heart' = Heb. *lev* = *lamed* (30) and *bet* (2) = 32.

begins with the letter *bet* the first letter of *bereshit*, i.e. the first word of the Torah, Gen. 1: 1, is a *bet*.

ends with the letter *lamed* the last word of the Torah is *yisrael* (Deut. 34: 12), the last letter of which is *lamed*. *Lamed–bet* forms the word *lev*, 'heart'.

point of the *yod* representing Keter.

'Let my soul bless' Ps. 104.

'Praise the Lord' Ps. 148.

the *partzuf* point to this, to the deed done by the hands of the one who acts, and it is the particular (of the deeds of the one who acts). However, what unites them in a general sense is Yesod.* This is the name HVYH, blessed be He (the name HVYH is the mystery of the general for, as above, it hints at the inner *partzuf*). And see chapter 3 of 'The Gate of the Ḥashmal'.* It is the Torah, the names of the Holy One, blessed be He, and the Torah is the impression of His divinity, blessed be His name. It follows that every motion and act in the world, from beginning to end, hints at and performs the unification which unites the general and the particular. The Torah is called the general. Its measurement revolves around a single *yod* for the purpose of the service of the heart, the root of the name HVYH. And the world is its particular, detailed in the name Elohim,* (in order to select and refine the 286 sparks,* take out eight* and bring in nine in order that the right should prevail over the left).

Note. Not as it has been printed in a certain book compiled by a great and renowned contemporary sage. He expounded this, calling his work *Sha'ar hayiḥud.** Believe me, brother, that his ways are not all those upon which light dwells. He relies on speculations and parables which are neither beneficial nor useful; I have already warned you, brother, of this. For all his ways in the discussion of this topic are hazardous. He who guards his soul will distance himself from them. The Lord God knows and will testify that I am not saying this for my own glory but only in order to urge the companions to distance themselves from these types of speculation which are tainted by the speculations of philosophy. Enough said.

With this, brother, in great brevity, I shall make you to understand the mystery contained in the Zohar, 'Va'etḥanan', p. 264*a*,* that the higher unification is *Shema yisrael*, the unification of HVYH, and the lower unifica-

what unites them in a general sense is Yesod E. means that Yesod, the connecting link between all the *sefirot* and Malkhut, is the mystery of how the *sefirot* in general are organized.

'The Gate of the Ḥashmal' *Sha'ar haḥashmal* in the *Etz ḥayim*.

The Torah is called the general . . . and the world is its particular, detailed in the name Elohim the Torah denotes the general mode of worship, concentrating all the divine names on a single *yod*, but the name Elohim represents the details of the Torah.

286 sparks at the breaking of the vessels, 286 holy sparks were scattered among the *kelipot*, and these have to be redeemed for the sacred.

take out eight . . . unclear; perhaps take out the letter *ḥet*, which stands for *ḥet*, 'sin', and bring in the letter *tet*, which stands for *tov*, 'good'; see Zohar i. 3*a*.

Sha'ar hayiḥud by R. Dov Baer of Lubavitch, the second master of the Ḥabad school.

Zohar, 'Va'etḥanan', p. 264a Zohar iii. 264*a*.

tion is 'Blessed be the name of His glorious kingdom for ever and ever',* the unification of the name Elohim, the general and the particular. See it there. 'And until each one has been unified, each on its own, they cannot be joined one to the other that they both become one.' I shall explain this to you in a simple manner. In the unification of *Shema yisrael* we elevate the Female Waters by means of self-sacrifice to the Lord (the name HVYH). We include ourselves in the generality of all souls and all worlds to elevate them to the One, the Cause of all causes, who is One and is not numbered. The result is that the name Elohim, called the particular of all the deeds of the worlds, as above, is united with the name HVYH, up to the highest of all stages. They become united one to the other and they are included one into the other up to the One, the First Cause. This is called the higher unification, the elevation of all worlds to Ein Sof, blessed be He, higher and ever higher. After we have elevated them and have ourselves ascended there to be united with the truly One, we then, through the unification of 'Blessed be the name of His glorious kingdom for ever and ever', draw down the flow of blessing from His will, blessed be He, and blessed be His name, through the channels which flow from the One referred to above, the Male Waters, for additional blessing, and the drawing down of His grace to increase the intelligences of all worlds, from the name HVYH. This is called the general. It is the Yesod of Adam Kadmon, as I have explained elsewhere. This is drawn down to *olam va'ed*,* the particular, the mystery of Elohim, as above. This is called the lower unification. For we draw down the Most Ancient* of all ancients, that His name be united with us in the *olam va'ed*, namely, Malkhut, the root of our souls in which all are rooted, the gathering place of all. For by it all, details are actualized and experienced by us. This is called the lower unification. For here that which is higher becomes united with that which is lower, like the Father in the palace of the Son and Daughter,* see Chapter 1 of the 'Expositions of Female Waters and Male Waters'. It is to draw down blessing, the blessing of the Father, the blessing of the Son; the blessing of the Father is the blessing of the Son, *Shema yisrael* is the higher unification, that of the particular with the general, the unification of the Son with the Father in the Father's palace. That is why we recite 'Blessed be the name of His glorious kingdom for ever and ever' silently, so that the Outside Ones should not be

'Blessed be the name ... forever and ever' a phrase recited after the first verse of the *Shema* and which, according to the rabbis, has to be recited in a hush.

olam va'ed in full, the sentence reads: 'Blessed be the Name of His glorious Kingdom for ever and ever.' 'For ever and ever' is in Heb. *olam va'ed.*

Most Ancient Ein Sof.

Son and Daughter Tiferet and Malkhut.

nourished by the blessing that is drawn down. It is the parable of 'the king's daughter who smelled a spicy pudding.* Would it be considered disgraceful?' For when we have ascended and have sacrificed ourselves to the truly One, Ein Sof, blessed be He, we are like Moses who when he ascended to God did not say, 'Blessed be the name of His glorious kingdom for ever and ever', for he was like a son united with his father in the father's palace. At this stage, why should we wish to ask for worldly things? In his great humility, Moses was too ashamed* to bring the father to his house and his palace. Our father Jacob, on the other hand, performed the unification of the father with his sons, drawing down to them the unification in their palace and so he did say, 'Blessed be the name of His glorious kingdom for ever and ever.' Understand this. I have many more expositions on this topic but I have only referred to it here in passing. May the Lord give us the merit of serving Him with a sincere, undivided heart. My prayer is that you should study this topic and find rest for your soul. Go forth and study. I have revealed a great thing to you here, albeit in wondrous brevity, the concealed teaching embracing the whole doctrine. And Solomon said: 'I know that whatever God doeth it shall be for ever (it was, it is, and it will be for ever and ever; in the Torah it is stated that one must not add to it, "Thou shalt not add to it nor diminish from it . . ."); nothing can be added to it . . .' [Eccles. 3: 14]. And see the Zohar, 'Pineḥas', p. 239, where it is said: 'He is He, He was, He is, and He will be for ever. Hence it is said in the Torah: "Thou shalt not add to it nor diminish from it . . ." [Deut. 13: 1].' For the word *hu* points to HVYH, and He was before His world was created . . . The Zohar concludes that the word *hu* hints at Knowledge; and Elohim usually refers to the Power from Ein Sof, who is beyond all searching. And when you come to understand the mystery of the Lord, how many mysteries of the Torah will become clear to you through this passage in the Zohar! Here is not the place to go to any greater lengths on the sweet words we have on this topic.

However, what does emerge from this is that the doctrines of the Ari, of blessed memory, comprehend that the whole Torah is made up of the names of the Holy One, blessed be He. From it you will see how and in

'the king's daughter who smelled a spicy pudding' a talmudic explanation, Pes. 56*a*, of why 'Blessed be the name . . .' is recited silently. The 'spicy pudding' is the recital of 'Blessed be . . .' which was said not by Moses but by the Patriarch Jacob; see the passage in Pes., ibid.

Moses was too ashamed When Moses pronounced the Shema (Deut. 6: 4–9) he did not say 'Blessed be the Name', etc.; according to the Talmud, Jacob said it on his deathbed.

which way and to what extent His names, blessed be He, have their roots and branches, myriads and myriads, thousands of thousands of worlds reaching to Ein Sof, blessed be He. All this must the wise soul cause to be elevated when the *Shema* is recited, to unite, with self-sacrifice, to the Lord, the truly One. When he recites the *Shema* in the morning, he elevates all that took place during the night from the sleep in which he offered his soul as a deposit. For sleep is one sixtieth of death, and the righteous are greater in their death, for more holy sparks are elevated at that time. And he also elevates whatever he studied during the previous night. All these holy sparks he elevates on high. And he takes upon himself the yoke of the Kingdom of Heaven, completely with self-sacrifice. By this means he unifies all the deeds he will carry out during the day. All the sparks bound to his soul-root will be unified and ascend through his deeds. And he takes upon himself the four types of death.* Let everything happen to him, Heaven forfend, and he will allow himself to be slain rather than transgress. And so, too, with regard to the night-time *Shema*. This is the refinement of the deeds done during the day, causing all the selections to be elevated* with self-sacrifice to the Lord. And the Shekhinah says, 'See with what food I come to you'.*

This you must know, however. They say, in the name of the Baal Shem Tov, that a man must elevate everything to its root. For example, if some lust comes to him, he should know that it comes from the World of the Breaking*, and he should elevate it to its root, which is the quality of Lovingkindness.* The same applies to some untoward thought or to cantankerousness, and so forth. He should elevate it to its particular quality; see the well-known works of his disciples.* But you must know that he should elevate these in a spirit of self-sacrifice, taking upon himself the four deaths at the hands of the court* to the best of his ability and the

the four types of death the four kinds of death meted out by the Sanhedrin in Temple times were stoning, burning, killing by the sword, and strangulation (Mid. Sanh. 7: 1). E. means that the faithful worshipper should take upon himself that even if he be threatened by death by one of these modes he must suffer the martyrdom. In some Hasidic circles it was a common religious exercise to enter into a fantasy of martyrdom.

causing all the selections to be elevated the 'selections' are the holy sparks released from the domain of the *kelipot* as a result of meritorious deeds.

'See with what food I come to you' Shekhinah offers the holy sparks selected for release to her spouse, Tiferet, as spiritual sustenance.

World of the Breaking when the light of the *sefirot* descended from world to world.

Lovingkindness Ḥesed.

the well-known works of his disciples among the Hasidic works in which this idea is found are *Keter shem tov* and *Toledot ya'akov yosef.*

the court the Sanhedrin.

capacity of his thought. Remember what I say to you, for it is a great thing, and you will not make a fool of yourself. I shall go to no greater lengths on this topic. (But in our Introduction to the *Peri etz ḥayim* we explain it, with God's help, at greater length.) If you study you will learn the truth: there can be no ascent without self-sacrifice in thought and deed, to the utmost of one's strength and even more so, with all one's 248 limbs and 365 sinews, to carry our every *mitzvah* and every act with all the heart, soul, and might, even if He takes ...* From this you will understand that nothing should be optional.* That which is sometimes referred to as optional is only in relation to a *mitzvah*. In that sense only is it said to be optional. As we find in chapter 5 of *Beitzah*:* 'These are in the category of the optional: They do not sit in judgement and they do not carry out betrothals ...'; and also when it says that the evening prayer is optional, see Rosh* on the chapter 'Tefilat hashaḥar'. But everything, even secular pursuits, should be an act of worship by means of which you perform a unification. For this science will remind you to perform unifications in everything you do. You will find the name of the Holy One, blessed be He, the Torah, so that you will discover in all worldly pursuits, whether in eating ... that they be conducted in accordance with the Torah, with the greatest care being taken in performing the niceties of the precepts and with a leaning towards the stricter view. For you will become accustomed to think in this way of the unifications of His name, blessed be He, until it becomes habitual. Then, indeed, you will fulfil the verse: 'And thou shalt meditate therein day and night.' This is the meaning of 'And these words, which I command thee ... and thou shalt talk of them' [Deut. 6: 6–7], which our rabbis, of blessed memory, expound* to mean: 'and not of vain matters'. Brother, was this said only so that a man should not transgress a negative precept implied by a positive?* For, in any event, who would imagine that it be permitted to talk of vain matters? However, according to what we have said, this is in the nature of a promise: if you take upon yourself completely the yoke of the Kingdom of Heaven, to unify all to the One, then you will have

even if He takes ... Based on Mishnah *Berakhot* (9: 5): one should love God with all one's might 'even if He takes your life'.

nothing should be optional meaning nothing should be seen as optional, there is no room for voluntary action. For the mystic, everything is a matter of divine commandment.

Beitzah Mishnah Beitz. 5: 2.

Rosh Asher b. Yehiel, Ber. 4: 7, which says that although the Evening Prayer is called 'optional', this means only that there is no obligation to recite it, but doing so is a *mitzvah* none the less.

our rabbis ... expound in Yoma 19*b*.

negative precept implied a positive the Torah sometimes commands 'Do this' with the implication 'Do not do the opposite.'

the merit that these words will be on your heart so that you will talk of them and not of vain matters, for in your speech you will find pleasantries for your soul. Enough said. You will see it and you will enjoy serenity of mind. (You will find a support for this interpretation in the Zohar, 'Terumah', p. 162*b*,* where thirteen commandments found in the *Shema* are enumerated and 'These words shall be' is not counted among them. So it is certainly as I have suggested.)

You must also know that all the sciences in the world, such as mathematics, astronomy, and natural science, are as nothing and are empty unless you know the ways of the hidden wisdom. Take astronomy, for instance. The early astronomers postulated that there is a reflexive motion and there is its opposite, a voluntary motion. Why did the Lord arrange it so to be? But I shall not dwell on this at length, for just now I am not engaged in the study of the sciences, for why waste time on these? Thank God, even if a man were to live for a thousand years, and if our days were endless, we would still be incapable of comprehending even a single one of the thousand of thousands, myriads of myriads, of worlds which the intelligent soul longs to elevate on the ladder with its feet on the ground ... by means of our holy Torah, sweeter than honey and the honeycomb; though King David, on whom be peace, did say: 'Neither do I exercise myself in things too great, or in things too wonderful for me' [Ps. 131: 1]. In truth you must proceed gradually, not jumping suddenly from a deep pit to a high roof in an unbalanced way and without wondrous concentration. And see what the Saba of Mishpatim* said about himself and about R. Simeon ben Yohai. A good deal of this depends on the degree of awakening that comes into the intelligent soul at a given hour. We find that the Yanuka,* 'Terumah', p. 166,* sprang from a roof in order to hear the *Kedushah** recited together with the congregation ... One scriptural verse says: 'Do not walk the even path' [Prov. 5: 6], while another verse says: 'Make even the path of thy feet' [Prov. 4: 26], quite apart from what the rabbis, of blessed memory, say in *Ḥagigah*, chapter 1.* Brother, for this let

Zohar, 'Terumah', p. 162*b* Zohar ii. 162*b*.

Saba of Mishpatim the 'Old Man' who imparts mystical knowledge to the companions (Zohar ii. 94*a*–99*b*, esp. 99*a*).

Yanuka 'infant', a wise child who imparts mystical teaching in the Zohar.

'Terumah', p. 166 Zohar ii, 166*a*.

the *Kedushah* the prayer in the liturgy representing the ultimate sanctification of God.

***Ḥagigah*, chapter** 1 either this is a printer's error or E. is quoting wrongly from memory. The reference is to *Mo'ed katan*, ch. 1, where a solution is given to the apparent contradiction between the two verses. E.'s own solution is that at times there has to be a balance, while at other times an unbalanced attitude is demanded.

every saintly man pray that he may discover the appropriate time to jump over the wall, to spring over the mountains, to leap, with a courageous heart, from roof to roof, with love in the soul. No written document can give expression to that which is in the heart of the true lover, and no mouth can utter it.

To revert now to the subject of reflexive and voluntary motion of the spheres and the stars, for thus are their ways of divine worship, the two motions, reflexive and voluntary of the spheres and the stars. Each day it goes to the south* and turns about to the north, hastening to the place whence it has arisen. We cannot go to any greater lengths, for its measure is greater than the earth. However, on the simple level, there is a reflexive motion each day in that 'by necessity you live':* man works and acts after the manner of the world. This takes place daily. And the motion from east to west by way of the south* represents His lovingkindness, blessed be His name, in that He desires to bestow from the quality of His goodness, and He desires in His wisdom that the world should endure. 'From the east' belongs to the mystery of Abba, the mystery of Wisdom, sending forth the flow of His grace to the west.* Father* established Daughter.* The Lord establishes the earth with Wisdom. And returning to the north at night, representing the return in repentance, 'North' represents the mystery of Imma, Binah, Repentance, all this by means of the twelve combinations of HVYH, the twelve combinations of EHYEH.* It hastens to the place whence it has risen. This is the voluntary motion, from west to east, in order to restore the soul of the worshipper as it proceeds higher and ever higher to the Highest of all, by means of all the unifications and selections performed in a spirit of self-sacrifice in this world in order to hasten it to its place.

We have already proved that the world is the impression of the Torah. These are the seven planets, the seven that move well.* Each star has its own voluntary motion in accordance with its place in the Soul of

it goes to the south Eccles. 1: 5–6.
'by necessity you live' Av. 4: 22.
south south = Ḥesed, north = Gevurah, based on the talmudic saying (BB 25*a*) that the Shekhinah (i.e. Malkhut) is the west and Evil (i.e. the power of Judgement) comes from the north (Jer. 1: 14).
to the west = Malkhut.
Father Abba.
Daughter Malkhut.
twelve combinations of EHYEH i.e. the letters of the Tetragrammaton can be arranged in twelve different ways (e.g. YHVH, YHHV, YVHH, etc.) and the same applies to the name EHYH (EHYH, EYHH, YEHH, etc.).
the seven planets, the seven that move well the seven planets represent the seven lower *sefirot*. In the medieval picture, the heavenly bodies are sentient beings, moving of their own volition.

Yosher.* For the spheres belong to the mystery of Asiyah* in the firmament of the heavens; see chapter 2 of the 'Picture of the Worlds',* and there you will observe the marvellous things of our Holy Torah, and that the world is the impression of the Torah. And so we have the explanation of all the motions of the stars above the sun and in the midst of the sun, and the path of the sun and the moon; the revolution of the sphere, the head of the sphere and the tail of the sphere; how many great rules do we possess of the tremendous ways of the Lord! [All this] because I studied this science in my youth since Rambam, of blessed memory, in the 'Laws of the Sanctification of the Month',* states that this is the mystery of intercalation,* although this is not necessarily so. (For how can the term 'mystery' be applicable to the external sciences? Rambam, of blessed memory, testified of himself that he had learned this science from the works of the Greeks, not from the sons of Issachar* who know understanding. It has already been said: 'He hath not dealt so with any nation' [Ps. 147: 20]. 'The secret of the Lord is with them that fear Him' [Ps. 25: 15] it is written; see the Zohar, 'Aḥarei', p. 73.* And what will the rabbi* say of the statement, 'The doves are still tender and the lambs still young', and the statement, 'The offspring of Naḥshon wished to establish a *netziv* ...' in *Sanhedrin*,* pp. 11 and 12? And why is the month called a *netziv*? Thank God, we are in possession of many mysteries regarding the mystery of intercalation. May God give us the merit of sharing them with you, my brother, by the life of my soul, so that you do not enter the World to Come in shame.)

However, it is possible that the Sanhedrin and those who intercalated the year did know this science, since it is also required for the world to be

Soul of Yosher kaballah conceptualizes two ways of arranging the *sefirot*: in a vertical continuum, reaching from higher to lower; and in concentric circles, with the higher *sefirot* in the centre. 'Yosher' (rectitude', 'straightness') is an allusion to the vertical arrangement.

Asiyah The World of Action.

'Picture of the Worlds' in *Etz ḥayim*.

Rambam ... 'Sanctification of the Month' *Mishneh Torah, Kidush haḥodesh*, 6: 1.

mystery of intercalation *Sod ha'ibur*; Ket. 112*a*.

sons of Issachar 'And of the children of Issachar which were men that had understanding of *the times* to know what Israel ought to do' (1 Chron. 12: 32).

Zohar, 'Aḥarei', p. 73 Zohar iii. 73*a–b*.

the rabbi Maimonides.

the statement ... in *Sanhedrin* what follow are riddles about the calendar, implying that it was not derived from the Romans as Maimonides suggests. The passage in *Sanhedrin* describes a coded message. The Jewish authorities sent this message about a *netziv* ('ruler', i.e. the Roman governor) in connection with the 'mystery of intercalation', i.e. the addition of an extra lunar month so that the lunar year can be made to correspond to the solar year. It was done secretly lest the Roman authorities intervene. E. interprets this in kabbalistic terms.

established. But all this is at the natural level. From the spiritual point of view, on the other hand, we perceive it all according to the balanced rules of the principles of the hidden science. Once I had begun to enter into the doctrines of the Ari, of blessed memory, I observed mysteries regarding the paths of the stars and the planets and their basic ideas, and their roots from nothing and to nothing. The sun, for instance, encircles the earth in its middle course in 365 days. This has the same numerical value as Yosef the Tzadik,* 365. The sinews of the human body also have this number, for it is the source of the member, and seventeen streams issue from it,* in the Zohar, 'Bereshit', p. 52,* to draw the vital spirit from the brain to sustain the limbs; see the *Raya mehemna*, mentioned above, section 'Va'era', p. 25. We have an explanation for even the finest details. As for the higher course of the sun, which takes seventy years,* it hints at the growth of Ze'ir Anpin according to the mystery of the perfect knowledge, which draws down according to the mystery of human life, which has the numerical value of the letters of seven names–AV, SAG, MAH, BEN, 161, 151, 143;* and the secret of the Lord is with them that fear Him. And there is the course of the moon in twenty-seven days, which has the dependent sphere, according to the mystery of the dependent sphere and its heart, mentioned in the *Sefer yetzirah*, hinting at the fact that the moon has no light of its own—its life depending on the sun,* which illumines it by means of the twenty-two

Yosef the Tzadik Heb. *yosef hatzadik*, which also has a numerical value of 365, as follows. 'Yosef' is spelled *yod* (10) + *vav* (6) + *samekh* (60) + *pé* (80) = 156; 'hatzadik' is spelled *hé* (5) + *tzadik* (90) + *dalet* (4) + *yod* (10) + *kof* (100) = 209, giving a total of 156 + 209 = 365.

The sinews of the human body also have this number, for it is the source of the member, and seventeen streams issue from it 'The sinews' is an allusion to the male member, represented by Yesod, and Yosef is also an allusion to Yesod, which is sometimes called *hatzadik*; hence 'the sinews' share the same number, 365. Moreover, there are 365 sinews in the human body. A sinew in Hebrew is *gid*, which has a numerical equivalence of 17 [*gimel* (3) + *yod* (10) + *dalet* (4) = 17], hence the 'seventeen streams' issuing from the 'source of the member'.

Zohar, 'Bereshit', p. 52 Zohar i. 52*a*.

the higher course of the sun, which takes seventy years according to medieval astronomy, the sun also had a seventy-year cycle.

according to the mystery of the perfect knowledge ... which has the numerical value of ... seven names—AV, SAG, MAH, BEN, 161, 151, 143 'Perfect knowledge' is a reference to Da'at, which has a numerical equivalence of 474, as follows: *dalet* (4) + *ayin* (70) + *taf* (400) = 474. The values 161, 151, and 143 are the equivalences of three divine names: KSA [*kof* (100) + *samekh* (60) + *alef* (1) = 161], KNA [*kof* (100) + *nun* (50) + *alef* (1) = 151], and KMG (*kof* (100) + *mem* (40) + *gimel* (3) = 143], and have a combined value of 455 (161 + 151 + 143). By a complicated formula, the letters of the other four names can be manipulated to give a total of 19, and 19 plus 455 gives 474, which is equivalent, as shown above, to Da'at, Perfect Knowledge. But this equivalence is hardly immediately clear.

the moon ... the sun the moon represents Malkhut, the sun represents Tiferet.

letters of the Torah, when it copulates at the time when there is opposition.* Brother, I am not occupied with this just now since I cannot spare the time, occupied as I am with the love of the companions and of Israel in general. I come here only to point out to you that you should observe how all the sciences are tasteless without salt, their taste evaporating and their fragrance departing from them, and how the hearts of many of those who know these sciences are stopped up and their eyes closed. (And their basic principles are weak, having nothing on which to stand since they have no portion in the Torah, neither in general nor in particular.) Believe me, that in natural science they are certainly blind,* whereas we have seen numerous wondrous things in the works of God. For things of nature have their root in the name Elohim, which has the numerical value of *hateva*,* and it is the Throne of HVYH and Israel, the portion of the Lord is His people.* If a person is to be healed it is through the combination of these two names, in general and in particular.

There is no healing, Heaven forfend, if it is in a natural way, that is, with the name Elohim alone, when this is not combined with the name HVYH in order to sweeten it. If that happens then, Heaven forfend, through the act of healing itself, the judgements attached to the name Elohim prevail.* We find that Isaiah said to Hezekiah: 'Let them take a cake of figs, and lay it for a plaster on the boil' [Isa. 38: 21]; see Rashi there. And this is the opposite of the methods of healing; this is after the manner of that which the rabbis, of blessed memory say, in the Aggadah of *Ta'anit*:* 'He who said that oil should burn ...' For it is well known that the act of burning is through the power of the name Elohim, while saying is by the power of the name HVYH, according to the mystery of 'Ḥokhmah says, Binah says' referred to

when it copulates at the time when there is opposition the moon is opposed to the sun as its rival. But when the sun gives its light to the moon, the two are said to 'copulate'. All this refers to the 'copulation' of the sun (= Tiferet) with the Moon (= Malkhut).

in natural science they are certainly blind those who have immersed themselves in natural science are blinded to the truth.

hateva the word means 'nature' and thus corresponds to the 'natural science' mentioned earlier; its numerical value is 86 [*hé* (5) + *tet* (9) + *bet* (2) + *ayin* (70)], which is equal to that of Elohim, as given above.

the portion of the Lord is His people Deut. 32: 9. 'the Lord' (HVVH) = Tiferet; 'His people' = Malkhut.

There is no healing ... the judgements attached to the name Elohim prevail the name Elohim represents the divine judgements. The Tetragrammaton represents the divine mercy that 'sweetens' the judgement. The term 'sweetening the judgement' is Zoharic but seems to derive from the Spanish. When Elohim prevails there is only harsh judgement and no mercy.

Aggadah of *Ta'anit* Ta'an. 25*a*. the Talmud here tells of a saint whose daughter inadvertently put vinegar instead of oil into the sabbath lamp, whereupon her father said, 'He who said that oil should burn can also say that vinegar will burn.'

in the Zohar, 'Tazria'.* And so it is with regard to each of the sayings in the narrative of the creation, the combination of the two names HVYH and Elohim. Yet it is the name HVYH that rules, coercing the name Elohim to do as it wills, and the patient is then healed. On the other hand, one who is unattached to the name HVYH—one who has no portion in it, but only in nature—for him, to be sure, healing does come to him through natural means, since he himself belongs to the natural order. Now, after Hezekiah had been healed by means of the cake of figs, he hid the Book of Remedies (so I have seen it written). For he saw that it was not the cake of figs that produced the cure, but He who provides the energy and the will to all vitality in the world. My son, pay no heed to the opinion of Rambam, of blessed memory, in his explanation of why Hezekiah hid the Book of Remedies—see his *Commentary on the Mishnah*, at the end of chapter 'Makom shenahagu'*—for, Heaven forfend, Solomon would not have done such a thing. As for his objection to Rashi's explanation from sickness due to hunger, this presents no difficulty whatsoever; for there the Torah points to herbs for food, and in the days of Noah even animals became permitted, and for the worshippers of God this in itself is an act of worship. Cures effected by means of bitter medicines, on the other hand, certainly apply only to one who conducts himself in accordance with nature. It is certain that there is implanted in all things that which derives from the qualities of the Creator, blessed be He. Each herb has the potential to realize the foundation by which the angel urges it to grow,* deriving from that particular quality and *sefirah* of which the angel has provided the root. And it all proceeds by natural means. But when there comes into operation the power of the great and tremendous name, rooted in His people Israel, and especially in the days of Hezekiah, whose generation was almost like the generation of the Messiah, as is stated in *Ḥelek*,* there was surely no need for them to resort to cures by natural means, that is, by means of the bitter medicines which have their root in the name Elohim. Consequently, he hid the Book of Remedies. He did not destroy it altogether; he hid it in

Zohar, 'Tazria' is Zohar iii; E. does not supply the page.

Hezekiah ... hid the Book of Remedies Pes. 56*a*. The Book of Remedies was apparently a book containing prescriptions for healing.

'Makom shenahagu' Pes., ibid. In his commentary here, Maimonides quotes a view that Solomon composed the book of healing, and people relied on it instead of relying on God. Maimonides cannot see how relying on medicines involves lack of trust in God; does it betoken a similar lack of trust in God when a hungry man looks for food?

the angel urges it to grow Midrash Gen. R. 10: 7. No herb grows unless the angel watching over it strikes it and says, 'Grow!'

Ḥelek Sanh. 94*a*. The Holy One, blessed be He, wished to appoint Hezekiah to be the Messiah.

the sense of: 'He hid it for the righteous* in the World to Come,'—the righteous having the power to overturn the act rooted in the name Elohim. And see the meditation of RIV* for the prayer of Rosh Hashanah, that it is not the intention to nullify the judgements, only to sweeten them. Take note of this. For it was Hezekiah's intention for every man in Israel to be like him, elevated above the need to have recourse to natural remedies. His intention was that the impulse from below would result in an impulse from above, so that the people of the Lord would no longer have any need to resort to medicines to be healed, but God would be their Healer. And see the 'Commentary on the *Tikunim*'* printed at the end of the *Tikunim*, explaining the saying about the ten knockings.* This is why you find that Asa the Righteous* was punished for resorting to physicians when he was sick instead of to the Lord. And in this a solution is found to the difficulty raised by the Tosafists chapter 'Haḥovel,* on the saying of the rabbis, of blessed memory: 'From here we learn that permission was granted to the physician to practise his healing.' The Tosafists ask: why would we have thought that it was forbidden? But according to the ways of the Torah, we might have supposed that for Israel, attached to the portion higher than nature, it was forbidden until the Torah gave express permission for the healer to heal. And even here permission was only given to the healer (like Rambam, of blessed memory, who was an expert Israelite healer, walking in the ways of the princes of the Holy One of Jacob, to him permission was granted, hence he raised his objection), one who binds himself to the root of remedies.

We have a tradition from our teachers that the healing name is pointed with a *ḥolem*,* the same expression as in the verse: '*vetaḥalimeni*, and make me live' [Isa. 38: 16]. The vowel *ḥolem* is the vowel of Tiferet, and the power of the name HVYH is rooted in Tiferet, and this is the true healer. (As it is said: 'For I am the Lord that healeth thee' [Exod. 15: 26], the letters of 'thy glory',* as I have explained in my commentary on the Zohar, 'Beshalaḥ'.) Then it all depends on the intention of the healer, not on that which is intended by the remedies. That is why it says that permission is granted for the healer to practise his healing, not simply that permission is

hid it for the righteous Ḥag. 12*a*.

meditation of RIV *resh*, *yod*, *vav*; a divine name to be kept in mind during the prayer of Rosh Hashanah; see *Sha'ar* 25 in the *Peri etz ḥayim*, p. 116*c*.

'Commentary on the *Tikunim*' by R. Hayim Vital, *Tikunei zohar* (Constantinople, 1 19), p. 153*b*.

ten knockings the ten knockings at the door by the beloved in S. of S.

Asa the Righteous 2 Chron. 16: 12.

Tosafists, chapter 'Haḥovel BK 85*a*, s.v. *shenitenah reshut*.

ḥolem the long 'o' vowel.

the letters of 'thy glory' *pe'erkha*, having the same root letters (*pé*, *alef*, *resh*) as Tiferet.

granted to heal, since the healer has to have the intention to heal. He must intend to draw down the energy from the will of the Creator to the potential of the herb used in the preparation of the healing balm with which he heals. This is why the healer has a greater degree of responsibility, since he uses natural means rooted in the name Elohim. (The root of the *moḥin* of *katnut*,* to use which is fraught with great danger; and it requires great care, as is explained in the 'Intentions of the Seventh Day of Passover'.)* I shall not go to any greater lengths since I come here only to demonstrate, to bestir the hearts of the disciples. From this you can draw an analogy with regard to the other sciences. Thank God, we possess subtle ideas concerning the vowels and the musical notes from the sages of riddles,* on the riddles of the *sefirot* and the qualities, on the square that is a cubit ... and on whatever is a handbreadth* wide ... things sweeter than honey.

Not only this but the same applies to all the external sciences, inessential to the ways of the Torah, apart from the true science, as stated above. But, brother, many strange things are also found in the Talmud. There are many statements there which cry out: 'Seek me* and live.' For example, there is the passage in the chapter 'Shiluaḥ haken',* p. 139*b*: 'The Papunians asked R. Mattenah: "What if one found a nest upon a man's head?" He replied: "It is written: 'And earth upon his head" [2 Sam. 15: 2]'. Rashi, of blessed memory, explains that even if the earth is on a person's head it does not lose its name; and this shows that a man himself is earth, hence it does not say 'on the earth on his head'. Observe how strange this seems. Is it such a great thing to set puzzles? And can such a thing ever happen? Possibly it can happen on the head of Ḥoni the Circle Drawer, who slept for seventy years.* Was it necessary to pose a problem concerning such a rare individual? Rambam, of blessed memory, in chapter 13 of the 'Laws of Sheḥitah', tries to make it more reasonable by changing it to the head of an

moḥin* of *katnut the stage when the 'mind' of Ze'ir is immature and undeveloped.

'Intentions of the Seventh Day of Passover' in the *Peri etz ḥayim*.

subtle ideas concerning the ... musical notes from the sages of riddles the musical notes are the signs for the cantillation of the Torah reading. The 'sages of riddles' are the kabbalists, who decode these mysterious signs in accordance with the kabbalah.

square that is a cubit ... whatever is a handbreadth ... mathematical formulae in Suk. 8*a–b*.

Seek me Amos 5: 4. *dirshuni*, meaning here 'examine me carefully'.

the chapter 'Shiluaḥ haken' the reference is to the law requiring the mother bird to be sent away before disturbing a nest found on the ground (Deut. 22: 6–7). The Papunians asked what would happen if the nest were found on a man's head, to which the reply was that it would still be 'on the earth'.

Ḥoni the Circle Drawer who slept for seventy years Ta'an. 23*a*.

animal. But why, then, did the Papunians change it? But you will understand it when you enter into the secrets of the Lord, according to our way, the way of holiness. For the mystery of the law of sending away from the bird's nest is explained by the Ari, of blessed memory, in 'The Gate of Abba and Imma'.* The hovering of the mother-bird over the fledglings and the eggs hints at the time when Zun* has only six extremities,* and the Mother hovers over the nest in order to nourish the offspring Zun. This is the meaning of the question they set when they asked what is the case where the nest was found on a man's head. This refers to where Ze'ir Anpin is at the stage of growth and he has a head, showing that he has the *moḥin*, and yet he found only 150* and not 370* complete illuminations. What does the category of the Mother hovering over the nest hint at in this case? To this question R. Mattenah replied that Scripture speaks of earth on his head, meaning that even when it* is only in the external vessels, he still possesses a head; even though so far as the inner vessels are concerned he is at the stage of *katnut*, and the *moḥin* are imperfect. And so it is in reality, for even an infant has all the external instruments. And see 'The Gate of Ḥag hamatzot',* chapter 1, and take note of this. For the purposes of divine worship of the heart there is flaming fire in all this. And the wise will understand.

And so, too, we find in *Menaḥot*,* chapter 'Shetei haleḥem', p. 69*b*: 'R. Zera asked: "What is the law if the Two Loaves were made from wheat which fell from the clouds? When the Torah says: 'Out of your dwellings' [Lev. 23: 17], does this only exclude wheat from outside the Holy Land, but wheat from the clouds can be used, or does it exclude wheat from the clouds too?" ' Rashi, of blessed memory, explains that the case is one where clouds swallowed a ship full of grains of wheat and they came down with the rain. Rambam, of blessed memory, records this in chapter 8 of *Temidim umusafim*. The conclusion is that it was a miracle, since the Gemara asks: 'Can such a thing happen?'; see the Tosafists there. But, brother, let me tell you that the clouds hint at Michael and Gabriel, in the Saba, 'Mishpatim',* 98*b*, the angels of Lovingkindness and Power, and the Holy

'Gate of Abba and Imma' in the *Etz ḥayim*.

Zun Zun stands for Ze'ir Anpin and Nukba, the female, i.e. Tiferet and Malkhut.

six extremities i.e. only six *sefirot* and no *moḥin*.

150 This is a reference to the 'nest' mentioned earlier; 'nest' = *ken* = *kof* (100) + *nun* (50) = 150.

370 the total number of the illuminations of the *moḥin*.

even when it even when the Flow of Grace.

'The Gate of Ḥag hamatzot' *Sha'ar ḥag hamatzot* in *Peri etz ḥayim*.

Menaḥot Men. 69*b*.

'Mishpatim' Zohar ii. 98*b*.

One, blessed be He, makes peace between them constantly (peace is the foundation of Imma;* understand this), as when the rabbis say:* ' "Dominion" refers to Michael, "and fear" refers to Gabriel, "He maketh peace in His high places" [Job 25: 1].' 'And the Holy One, blessed be He, says like this one and that one', in the Aggadah of the *sefinah*,* in order to extend the flow of grace to His people and to humble their enemies. So the passage refers to the clouds swallowing a ship full of wheat from outside the Land of Israel, and the clouds brought it to the Land of Israel where it came down with the rain. Now a ship hints everywhere at Malkhut of Atzilut (as the rabbis say:* 'How do we know that a ship is pure?' and the wise will understand) which sails on the sea, namely, in the World of Creation. As I have explained elsewhere and as it is stated in the commentary by the Ari, of blessed memory, on the *Sefer yetzirah*, it is well known that wheat hints at the twenty-two letters of the Torah* (the same numerical value as *ḥitah*) which extend to Her from the Supernal Wisdom. Now when the Ship is outside the Holy Land, She bestirs Herself—that is, Malkhut descends to the place where the judgements are strong. The Outside Ones are nourished by Her, and She descends to that place in order to humble them. She elevates from there all the holy sparks and all the souls that have been swallowed, bringing them to the Land of Israel for Her copulation with Ze'ir Anpin. And She says to Him: 'See what food I have brought to Thee. See with what food I come before Thee.' As a result of this, the flow from Wisdom descends, according to the mystery of wheat.* At the time when She was outside the Holy Land She was the rose among the thorns, according to the mystery of: 'Let thistles grow instead of wheat' [Job 31: 40], see *Likutei torah*, 'Ekev'; whereas in the Land of Israel wheat grows instead of thistles, having been sweetened by the clouds. Hence he asks whether 'out of their dwellings' only excludes outside the Holy Land, but it is all right when it comes from the clouds, for then it is like rain sweetened by the clouds, as is stated in *Ta'anit*,* and it has been sweetened by the clouds. On the contrary, the Ship has brought it up from

peace is the foundation of Imma Imma means 'mother'; Binah 'mothers' all the other *sefirot* so that judgement and mercy are combined in Her word and peace prevails.

the rabbis say *Yalkut* on Job. 9: 12. Gabriel is the angel of judgement, Michael is the angel of mercy; respectively, they represent fear and love.

Aggadah of the *sefinah* BB 75*a*. Lit., the legend of the ship. The statement that a ship is pure (i.e. cannot be ritually unclean) is made to refer to the final stage.

as the rabbis say Mishnah Shab. 9: 2.

wheat hints at the twenty-two letters of the Torah wheat = *ḥitah*, which has a numerical equivalent of 22 [*het* (8) + *tet* (9) + *hé* (5) = 22].

the mystery of wheat the mystery of wheat is explained later in this passage.

in *Ta'anit* 9*b*.

the place of the *kelipot* and the judgements through the clouds, and the thistles have become wheat, and it is written: 'And if thou bring forth the precious out of the vile' [Jer. 15: 19]. Hence it is even better and it ought to be permitted to make the wheat into the Two Loaves. The mystery of the Two Loaves* has been explained to us in *Likutei torah*, 'Emor'. They belong to the mystery of the drop of the Kindnesses in which there are twenty-two letters, the numerical value of *ḥitah*, from which the child is formed.* Consult the passage. This is why they are two, for they are combined one with the other, fire with water, water with fire.

Incidentally, I want to tell you what I have said on this subject, that it has been explained that the mystery of bread belongs to the mystery of Malkhut, included in 'the bread that he eats',* the mystery of the Temple service. It is called *leḥem* to hint at that it is required to influence Israel to have two tables*—that there should be Torah and greatness in one place.* This is hinted at in the word *leḥem*. For sovereignty is acquired* by thirty qualities, and the Torah by forty-eight qualities, and this is the significance of *leḥem* (according to the mystery of *leḥem* with the same numerical value as *mazala*,* and there are two *mazlin*, one of *notzer* and one of *venakeh*),* that, as stated above, each is combined with the other. This takes place on the festival of Shavuot, when all the powers have been sweetened and the Ze'ir Anpin grows and ascends the Beard.* Reverting to what we have been saying, this is R. Zera's problem on whether wheat that comes down from the clouds [can be used for meal-offerings], hinting at the Kindnesses that have been sweetened from the Foundation of Imma. And so does it appear from the Zohar, section 'Bereshit', p. 31*b*:* 'R. Huna explained that *avim*

the mystery of the Two Loaves the mystery is that they represent Tiferet and Malkhut made out of wheat.

from which the child is formed an infant is nourished by bread = Ze'ir Anpin.

'the bread that he eats' according to the rabbis, said of Potiphar's wife (Gen. 39: 6), as above. Also, 'a wife' is a reference to Malkhut, the spouse of Tiferet.

two tables Ber. 5*b*, i.e. success in this world as well as bliss in the Hereafter.

in one place Git. 59*b*.

For sovereignty is acquired the Heb. term used in the saying in Av. 6: 5 is *malkhut* referring to human sovereignty but applied by E. to Malkhut. Human sovereignty requires thirty qualities whereas according to this Mishnah the student of the Torah requires forty qualities.

the mystery of *leḥem* with the same numerical value as *mazala* *leḥem* is spelled *lamed* (30) + *ḥet* (8) + *mem* (40) = 78; *mazala* is spelled *mem* (40) + *zayin* (7) + *lamed* (30) + *alef* (1) = 78.

two *mazlin*, one of *notzer* and one of *venakeh* *mazlin* is taken to mean flows. *Notzer* represents Ḥesed and *venakeh* represents Gevurah; this is based on the thirteen qualities of mercy enumerated in Exod. 34: 6–7, where *notzer ḥesed* and *venakeh* are mentioned.

the Beard the Beard represents the flow of divine grace from 'the Beard of the Holy Ancient One', a Zoharic expression.

Zohar, 'Bereshit', p. 31*b* Zohar i. 31*b*.

means *av* twelves',* and in *Likutei torah*, 'Job', it is said that they belong to the mystery of the powers (it seems to me that they are the powers of Abba and they become the Kindnesses of Imma, as is well known), and the rains are sweetened from the seal of Imma,* the filling of three times EHYEH (the numerical value of *shamayim*);* see the 'Intentions of Shemini Atzeret'. Note it well, brother, and you will discover how sweet are these words. And when the rains are sweetened they bring down the wheat on Passover, the time of the birth,* on the seventh day of Passover. And that wheat is outside the Holy Land, the place of the *kelipot*; and therefore the problem is posed: Since they are nourished from them, are they [the grains of wheat] fit for the Two Loaves?

Allegorically, they [the grains of wheat that come down from the clouds] may hint at the souls of the saints among the nations of the world, or the souls of converts. Are these fit for the Two Loaves, to be on the table of the inner Malkhut? Enough said, and the wise will understand. It is a hidden mystery. And he will proceed* from world to world, the mystery of the cutting and the rebuilding, Naomi and Ruth, the ship dances, the fire on the altar burns, and they are sweetened by the clouds which come after the rain, the mystery of Boaz and Naomi. He who covers the heavens with clouds makes ready *matar*, the *matrona*,* drawing out the fat gently, the fat of the wheat of Kardenuta, from the candelabrum of Kardenuta.

We have in our possession the explanation of many other passages in the Gemara and of the *halakhah* and they have been explained by us, such as the talmudic passage on the verse 'When a bullock, or a sheep, or a goat ...' [Lev. 23: 27], *Ḥullin*, 39*b*: ' "Under its dam", this excludes an orphan'; see the Gemara there, and the Tosafists, beginning with *ela zeh pirush* etc. And, indeed, all the passages regarding the animal going out at the side are

twelves *avim*, 'clouds', is spelled by an *ayin* followed by *yod* (10) and *bet* (2) = 12.

from the seal of Imma ... Imma impresses her seal on *shamayim* = Heaven = Tiferet.

shamayim *shin* (300) + *mem* (40) + *yod* (10) + *mem* (40) = 390.

the time of the birth the birth of Ze'ir, which takes place at the end of Passover.

And he will proceed ... The whole of this passage is obscure. The 'he' refers to the wise man mentioned earlier. The 'cutting' and 'rebuilding' refer to the division of the *sefirot* and their reconstruction into *partzufim*. Ruth, the convert, is embraced by her mother-in-law Naomi. The ship, discussed earlier, dances because here E. waxes poetical and uses rhymed prose: 'dances', Heb. *rokedet*, rhymes with *mokedet*—the burning fire on the altar.

makes ready *matar*, the *matrona* ... the meaning of this obscure statement seems to be that *matar*, the word for rain, represents the *matrona*, matron, corresponding to Malkhut, who causes the wheat to grow fat. The 'wheat of Kardenuta' means 'wheat from Kurdistan' in the Talmud, but the term is used in the Zohar for a 'dark candelabrum' (from *kadrut*, 'dark'), corresponding to Keter, giving rise to a mystical concept of 'dazzling darkness'. E. mixes his metaphors here.

extremely odd. But the sages of the Talmud arranged all their work on the mysteries of the Torah, as stated in the *Raya mehemna*, section 'Pineḥas', p. 245.* And there are countless *aggadot* that are frightfully odd, with neither a carpenter* nor a carpenter's apprentice able to provide a solution and show their relevance to the ways of worship. And there, too, in chapter 'Shiluaḥ haken', on the same page, on the subject of Herodian doves—we cannot understand the simple meaning, even though the later scholars do have some kind of a parable on the subject but are unable to provide any practical consequences for divine worship. This can only be attained through the hidden science, the fifty gates of understanding.

A further advantage of this science is repentance. I have already explained the Mishnah 'If there is no knowledge there is no understanding'. All that remains is to explain the reason for it in connection with practice. For, by means of this science, one can see and know in which *sefirah* one has caused a flaw, Heaven forfend, and how each *sefirah* divides into the categories of instruments of various kinds without number: whether Arikh Anpin, Abba and Imma, or Zun; the categories of the inner part of the vessel or the outer part; the inner light or the surrounding light.

Now when a man reflects on this science he will observe in great detail which limb* his flaw affects, and he will express his remorse in a spirit of self-sacrifice and carry out a *mitzvah* that relates to the generality of that limb. Here is not the place to go to any great lengths, for a huge work would be needed for this on the roots of the qualities. Nevertheless, I shall give you an illustration. For example, if he has sinned, Heaven forfend, by creating a flaw in the sign of the covenant, come and see in 'The Gate of Putting Sins Right' how many unifications are laid down for each category in particular. And so, too, once he has repented of his sin, he should pursue many *mitzvot* in order to rectify the flaw, pursuing peace and making peace between man and wife, between a man and his neighbour. For peace is the mystery of the covenant.* And he should keep the Sabbath, remembering and keeping to the greatest extent with the intention of rectifying that which he made crooked. He should serve the *tzadikim*, foundations of the world, in practical ways, being a faithful servant to them in actual practice, according to the mystery of the *tzadikim* are faithful [in following God], as stated at the beginning of *Etz ḥayim*. He should perform the *mitzvah* of *tzedakah** and thus join *tzadik* to *tzadik*. He

'Pineḥas', p. 245 Zohar iii. 254*a*.

neither a carpenter ... a talmudic expression (*Av. Zar.* 50*b*).

which limb which divine limb.

peace is the mystery of the covenant Num. 25: 12: 'My covenant of peace'.

tzedakah giving charity.

should study the Torah for its own sake; if he was accustomed to study one chapter [he should study two; if he was accustomed] to recite 'Amen, may His great name . . .' he should do so with all his strength and with all his might and with the fullest concentration. And this applies to all the numerous detailed categories [of the *sefirot*]. Any intelligent man who sincerely desires to repent must seek the sources of the detailed matters associated with each *sefirah* and quality he had flawed and put right [the flaw] by carrying out *mitzvot* and good deeds. When he engages in the study of this science, he will certainly discover [what he seeks], for I have quoted only an example. In every act he does he will perform unifications of the names since he will know that these names are applicable to that principle. He, blessed be He, and blessed be His name, will help you and open up for you the gates of light, as the Zohar says* on the verse: 'If his sin, wherein he hath sinned, be known to him' [Lev. 4: 23]. Certainly He, blessed be He, and blessed be His name, will not withhold the good from those who walk uprightly; and whoever wishes to be pure he is helped. With this, peace be upon Israel.

Now we have explained the First Three* in this science whose roots are found in the doctrines of the Ari, of blessed memory. To this you can compare the others, even to the seven measures of liquid that were in the Temple,* all are required in the study of this science which is the purpose of studying the Torah for its own sake. As it is said in the 'Chapter of Torah':* 'R. Meir says: He who studies the Torah for its own sake . . . it prepares him to become a righteous man, a saint, upright and faithful.' This means the study of the Torah for the sake of the Lord, as it is stated in the 'Intentions for the Study of the Torah for its own Sake', in the *Likutei torah*, 'Vaetḥanan', and in the *Siddur*. This means the study of the inner science for the sake of the Lord. These are the five parts of the soul rooted in the five *partzufim* of Atzilut, embracing, as is well known from 'The Gates of Abya', every portion of the worlds. And these are the measurements of the form of the Creator. Now the root of the *tzadik* is to be a living person, great in deeds.* *Tzadik* is called ḤY, the initial letters of Ḥokhmah and Yesod, because the *tzadik* draws down from the mystery of Ḥokhmah the energy for every act performed in the world, all the breaths and all the words and to all the senses, sight, hearing, smell, and speech. The main principle of vitality in the world is Wisdom [Ḥokhmah], as it is said: 'Wisdom preserveth the life of him that hath it' [Eccles. 7: 12]; and without

the Zohar says Zohar iii. 23*b*.

First Three Keter, Ḥokhmah, Binah.

seven measures of liquid that were in the Temple from *Men.* 87*b*, applied here to the seven lower *sefirot*.

'Chapter of Torah' Av. 6: 1.

Now the root of the *tzadik* is to be a living person, great in deeds the *tzadik*, the saintly person, truly lives—in Hebrew, *ḥai*, a

Wisdom, Heaven forfend, one has no life. Now the main part of all vitality in the world resides in the taste that is in all things, minerals, plants, animals, and humans, as we know from our teachers. And the taste that is in all existing things is the holy spark in the food. And all the taste in the Torah is the vital force of the Torah; those who taste it enjoy life. For the vital force which resides in the Torah gives vitality to one who engages in its study, as it is said: 'for that is thy life, and the length of thy days' [Deut. 30: 20]. And without Torah, a man with an Israelite soul has no life at all.

Now it is said in the Introduction to the holy book *Reshit ḥokhmah* that 'Torah for its own sake' means 'for the sake of the Torah', called thus because it shows the way of ascent of the mountain of the Lord, the Holy God of Jacob. Now, brother, will it be of any use to show the way* to someone who is lame, or to a blind man, or a man without intelligence who is like an animal? That is what the Zohar calls those who lack wisdom, those who do not taste the honey and the honeycomb of wisdom, those whose hearts are stopped up and whose eyes are blind. This is why the *tanna* speaks of the study of the Torah for its own sake. When the aim of the student is to understand and to grasp the vital force of the Torah, then it prepares him to be a righteous man, a saint ... That is to say, it makes him into a vessel ready to receive, so that he becomes a righteous man and a saint, and it shows him the way in which he should go. He will be neither lame nor blind but will have a complete human form with no limb missing. The rabbis, of blessed memory, say* that a limb too many is treated as a missing limb. If a man does not reflect on his whole form, his two eyes, two ears, ten fingers, and ten toes, and every part of his 248 limbs, so as to know what the function is of each of them and at what each of them hints, he has redundant limbs and it is as if he lacked limbs and is *terefah*, and is not fit to be righteous, saintly, and upright. And how can the Torah be for its own sake, how can it be a guide to such a person? Whom will the Torah teach, as it is said: 'Whom shall one teach knowledge?" [Isa. 28: 9], since he has no vessel with which to receive, neither a hand nor a foot, no eyes to see and no ears with which to hear? But if he is engaged in the Primordial Torah, called 'Torah for its own sake', and 'engaged' means that he toils over it and wears himself out over it, and breaks his body to engage in it with all his might, then it will be healing for your navel and it

word formed from the initial letters of the *sefirot* Ḥokhmah and Yesod, the *sefirah* also called *tzadik* which draws the flows of divine grace from Ḥokhmah to Malkhut, thereby generating, as E. explains, the energy for every act performed in the world.

to show the way the word Torah can mean 'to show' or 'the showing' i.e. of the way.

the rabbis ... say Ḥul. 58*b*.

will prepare for you garments of ministration to serve the holy—these are the senses: sight, hearing, smell, and speech. Then you will be sound in limb, and the Torah will show you the way to ascend so that your soul and your soul's root cleaves to your Maker. Now the *Raya mehemna*, p. 33, says of the term *ḥasid* that if a man is a scholar his being must combine the qualities of Ḥesed and Ḥokhmah, and with this *yod* the word becomes *ḥasid*.* For you should know that the love of mercy is a branch of wisdom, and if you lop off the branch from the tree its root becomes dried up wood. And of the term *tzadik* it is stated in the Zohar, 'Terumah', p. 155*b*:* 'Joseph the righteous is called *tzadik* after the moon ...' This means that the *yod*, the letter of Ḥokhmah, is drawn into the Holy King* and it becomes *tzadik*. And so when the mighty man subdues his inclination, it stems from the quality of power, a branch of Repentance. It is stated in *Likutei torah*, 'Shemini', that the sin of Nadav and Avihu* consisted of them taking the brains of Imma (which, as is well known, is Repentance) without the brains of Abba (which, as is well known is Ḥokhmah). In the *Etz ḥayim*, too, in the 'Exposition of Plagues', it is stated that this is the mystery of plagues and leprosy. One who takes the brains of Imma without the illumination from the brains of Abba has to be secluded.* From thence comes the enticement of the inclination: it causes the judgements of the stage of *katnut* to grow in man, Heaven forfend, and as a result the inclination prevails. If there is wisdom, there is the power to sweeten all the judgements, and different names are combined in order that the mystery of Ḥokhmah might rest upon him. Come and see what R. Zemah writes in his Introduction: 'Furthermore, it seems to me that the reason why this science has been revealed just now among the inferior generations is that we should now have a shield to walk towards our Father in Heaven with perfect heart. For in earlier generations the saints and the good deeds acted as a shield, protecting them from the accusers. But now we are far

and with this *yod* the word becomes *ḥasid* the quality of Ḥokhmah, wisdom, is represented in the Tetragrammaton by its initial *yod*. Adding this *yod*, representing wisdom, to the quality of Ḥesed, loving kindness, produces the *ḥasid*, the true saintly scholar.

Zohar, 'Terumah', p. 155*b* Zohar ii. 155*b*.

is drawn into the Holy King the Holy King is Malkhut, which embodies the quality of justice, *tzedek*. The addition of the *yod* of Ḥokhmah, representing wisdom, as explained above, to *tzedek* produces *tzadik*.

the sin of Nadav and Avihu Nadav and Avihu, the sons of Aaron the high priest, brought 'strange fire' to God's altar, a sin for which they were punished by death (Lev. 10: 1–7).

one who takes ... has to be secluded this refers back to the 'mystery of plagues and leprosy' mentioned earlier, which relates to the account in Lev. 12: a person afflicted by plague or leprosy has to be confined for a time to see whether the affected spot spread or diminished.

distant from the Supernal Root. We are like the sediment at the bottom of the barrel. Who can shield us except through the power of this wondrous science? ... And the hidden things have become revealed. For in this generation, fornication rules ... and the *kelipot* have spread ...' Thus far his words. So there you have exactly what I have said: that by your engagement in this science you will sweeten the judgements. Evil will have no power over you, Heaven forfend, and you will subdue your inclination. This is enough, and peace be to you.

May it be acceptable to the Ancient One ... that these words, uttered in sincere love of the companions, should make their impression in the hearts of the companions, to encourage them, to bestir them to awaken the love, that their heart may be inflamed with the burning fire of the Lord that the name of the Holy One of Israel be magnified and sanctified in their midst, and that there be an increase of true knowledge. Friends and brothers, be strong and of good courage, for the time of love is nigh when the Name of the King of kings will be sanctified in the midst of the Lord's people and the *tzadikim* and the *ḥasidim*. I beg you, my brethren, to reflect on these words. For I have spoken with all my heart to strengthen your hands so that you do not fear to draw near to the holy. You have found honey. Eat your fill ... to be sure each according to his stage and his intellectual capacity, to measure you yourself with the measure of the *mitzvah*. But there should be intelligence in the true heart so that you should not want anything at all except to know how to use your heart for the Torah, prayer, and *mitzvot*; to unify God with all your *nefesh*, *ruaḥ*, *neshamah*, *ḥayah*, and *yeḥidah*; to let your soul ascend to its Source, to its place, to its people and its birth-place, returning with all the good to its father's house; to fulfil the will of the Holy One of Jacob, blessed be He who spake and the world came into being; and to draw down energy from the Source of Blessing and the channels and the good tidings. May it be His will that blessing and life be drawn down for us and for all Israel. Amen.

COMPLETED AND FINISHED
PRAISE BE TO GOD
CREATOR OF THE WORLD

Bibliography

WORKS BY ZEVI HIRSCH EICHENSTEIN

Sur mera va'aseh tov [Lemberg, 1832; Pest, 1842] (Jerusalem, 1969).

Beit yisrael (Lemberg, 1834).

Peri kodesh hilulim [Lemberg, 1832] (Irsava, 1928).

Ateret tzevi, 2 vols. [Lemberg, 1871–2] (Photocopied edn. with additional material: New York, 1960).

For further details on the above see Meir Wunder, Me'orei galitziyah *(Jerusalem, 1978).*

WORKS QUOTED IN *SUR MERA*

The editions cited below are those most commonly used.

Early Rabbinic Works

Babylonian Talmud (Vilna, Romm edn.).

Jerusalem Targum (in Heb. edns. of the Pentateuch).

Midrash Proverbs (Constantinople, 1517).

Midrash Psalms, ed. S. Buber (Vilna, 1891).

Midrash Rabbah (Vilna, 1911).

Midrash Leviticus Rabbah, ed. M. Margaliot (Jerusalem, 1972).

Mishnah (Vilna, Romm edn.).

Sefer yetzirah (Warsaw, 1884).

'Shiur komah', in *Merkavah shelemah*, ed. S. Mussajoff (Jerusalem, 1922), 30*a*–40*a*.

Sifra (*Torat kohanim*), ed. I. H. Weiss (Vienna, 1862).

Sifre, ed. L. Finkelstein (New York, 1969).

Medieval Philosophy and Later Rabbinic Works

Asher b. Yehiel, *Responsa of Rosh* (Zolkiew, 1802).

Astruc, Abba Mari, *Minḥat kenoat* (Pressburg, 1838).

Delmedigo, Joseph, *Matzref leḥokhmah* (Warsaw, 1865).

Edels, Samuel, *Ḥidushei maharsha*, printed in the Romm edn. of the Mishnah.

Falk, Jacob Joshua, *Penei yehoshua* (New York, 1975).

Gerondi, Nissim, *Responsa of Ran* (Lemberg, 1851).

Halevi, David, *Turei zahav*, printed in the *Shulḥan arukh*, various edns.

Heller, Yom-Yov Lipmann, *Tosafot yom tov*, printed in the Romm edn. of the Talmud.

Ibn Adret, Solomon, *Responsa of Rashba* (Lemberg, 1811).

Ibn Pakuda, Bahya, *Ḥovot halevavot* (Duties of the heart) [12th cent.], ed. S. Yerushalmi (Jerusalem, 1972), published in Eng. as *The Book of Direction to the Duties of the Heart*, ed. and trans. Menahem Mansoor (London, 1973).

Karo, Joseph, *Beit yosef* (commentary on the *Tur*), various edns.

____ *Magid mesharim* (Amsterdam, 1706).

____ *Shulḥan arukh*, various edns.

Jacob b. Asher, *Tur*, various edns.

Landau, Jacob, *Agur* (Sudlikov, 1834).

Maimonides, Moses, *Mishneh torah* (various edns.).

____ *Moreh nevukhim* (Vilna, 1914).

Nachmanides, *Commentary on the Torah*, ed. H. D. Chavel (Jerusalem, 1959)

Rambam, *see* Maimonides, Moses.

Ramban, *see* Nachmanides.

Rashi, *Commentary on the Pentateuch*, various edns.

Sa'adiah Gaon, *Emunot vedeot* (Jerusalem, 1855).

Schor, Ephraim Zalman, *Tevuot shor* (Lublin, 1716).

Taz, *see* Halevi, David.

Kabbalah

Zohar, ed. R. Margaliot (Jerusalem, 1964).

Zohar ḥadash, ed. R. Margaliot (Jerusalem, 1964).

Tikunei hazohar, ed. R. Margaliot (Jerusalem, 1964).

[Abraham of Granada], *Berit menuḥah* (Warsaw, 1883).

Azikri, Eliezer, *Sefer ḥaredim* (Jerusalem, 1966).

Bacharach, Naftali, *Emek hamelekh* (Amsterdam, 1648).

Cordovero, Moses, *Or ne'erav* (Jerusalem, 1956).

____ *Pardes rimonim* (Jerusalem, 1962).

Dov Baer of Lubavitch, 'Sha'ar hayiḥud', in *Likutei biyurim*, ed. Hillel of Poritch (Warsaw, 1865).

Dov Baer of Mezhirech, *see* Meshullam Phoebus of Zbarazh.

Elimelekh of Lyzhansk, *No'am elimelekh*, ed. G. Nigal (Jerusalem, 1978).

Gikatilla, Joseph, *Sha'arei orah* (Jerusalem, 1970).
Hayyat, Judah, *Minḥat yehudah* (also called *Sefer haḥayat*), (Mantua, 1558).
Horowitz, Isaiah, *Shenei luḥot haberit* (Jerusalem, 1963).
Ibn Gabbai, Meir, *Avodat hakodesh* (Jerusalem, 1973).
Jacob Koppel of Mezhirech, *Sha'arei gan eden* (Jerusalem, 1971).
—— *Siddur ha'ari* (Slavita, 1894).
Menahem Azariah of Fano, *Yonat elim* (Lemberg, 1884).
Meshullam Phoebus of Zbarazh, 'Yosher divrei emet', in *Likutim yekarim* (attributed to Dov Baer of Mezhirech but probably the work of Meshullam Phoebus), (Jerusalem, 1974), 110–44.
Nathan of Chelma, *Sha'arei tzion* (Tel Aviv, 1961).
No'am elimelekh, *see* Elimelekh of Lyzhansk.
Poppers, Meir, *Hilkhot derekh eretz* (Ostrog, 1821).
Recanati, Menahem, *Perush al hatorah* (Sudlikov, 1832).
Ricchi, Immanuel Hai, *Mishnat ḥasidim* (Jerusalem, 1982).
Vidas, Elijah de, *Reshit ḥokhmah* [Amsterdam, 1708] (Jerusalem, 1984).
Vital, Hayim, *Etz ḥayim* (Warsaw, 1891).
—— *Likutei torah neviyim uketuvim* (Zolkiev, 1773).
—— *Peri etz ḥayim* (Koretz, 1785).
—— *Sha'ar hagilgulim* (Premisla, 1875).
—— *Sha'ar hakavanot* (Jerusalem, 1962).
—— *Sha'ar hayiḥudim* (Koretz, 1783).
—— *Sha'arei kedushah* (Vienna, 1854).
—— *Zohar harakiyah* (Koretz, 1785).
Zemah, Jacob, *Nagid umetzaveh* (Jerusalem, 1712).

GENERAL WORKS CITED IN THE INTRODUCTION AND NOTES

Anon., *Shivḥei habesht*, published in Eng. translation as *In Praise of the Baal Shem Tov*, trans. Dan Ben-Amos and Jerome R. Mintz (Bloomington, 1970).
Band, Arnold G., *Nahman of Bratslav: The Tales* (New York, 1978).
Ben-Jacob, I. A., *Otzar hasefarim* (Vilna, 1880).
Berger, Israel, *Eser kedushot* (Jerusalem, 1973).
Berl, H. J., *Rabbi Yitzhak Eisik of Komarno* (Jerusalem, 1965).
Bodek, Mendel, *Seder hadorot* (n.p., n.d.).
Braver, Michael, *Tzevi latzadik* (New York, 1976).
Buber, Martin, *Tales of the Hasidim* (New York, 1948).

Bunim, H. I., *Mishneh ḥabad* (Warsaw, 1936).

Dresner, Samuel H., *The Zaddik* (London, 1960; paperback edn. New York, 1974).

Dubnow, S., *Toledot haḥasidut* (Tel Aviv, 1967).

Elior, Rachel, 'Between *Yesh* and *Ayin*: The Doctrine of the Zaddik in the Works of Jacob Isaac, the Seer of Lublin', in Ada Rapoport-Albert and Steven J. Zipperstein (eds.), *Jewish History: Essays in Honour of Chimen Abramsky* (London, 1988), 393–456.

Epstein, Yitzhak Isaac of Homel, *Ḥanah ariel* (Berditchev, 1912).

Fine, Lawrence, 'The Contemplative Practice of Yihudim in Lurianic Kabbalah', in Arthur Green (ed.), *Jewish Spirituality* (2 vols.; New York, 1987), ii, 64–98.

Green, Arthur (ed.), *Jewish Spirituality* (2 vols.; New York, 1987).

Harfenes, Y. D., *Yisrael vehazemanin* (New York, 1987).

Hundert, Gershon David (ed.), *Essential Papers on Hasidism: Origins to Present* (New York, 1991).

Idel, Moshe, *Kabbalah: New Perspectives* (New Haven, 1988).

—— *The Mystical Experience in Abraham Abulafia* (Albany, 1988).

Jacobs, Louis, *Hasidic Prayer* (London and New York, 1972; paperback edn. London, 1993).

—— *Jewish Mystical Testimonies* (Jerusalem, 1976; New York, 1977).

—— *Seeker of Unity* (London, 1966).

—— 'The Uplifting of Sparks in Later Jewish Mysticism', in Arthur Green (ed.), *Jewish Spirituality* (2 vols.; New York, 1987), ii. 99–126.

Y. A. Kamelhaar, *Dor de'ah: Tzadikei hador* (Bilgorey, 1933).

—— (trans.), *Tract on Ecstasy*, by Dov Baer of Lubavitch (London, 1965).

Lamm, Norman, *Torah lishmah: Torah for Torah's Sake in the Works of Rabbi Hayyim of Volozhin and His Contemporaries* (New York, 1989).

Loewenthal, Naftali, *Communicating the Infinite: The Emergence of the Habad School* (Chicago, 1990).

Mahler, Raphael, *Hasidism and the Jewish Enlightenment* (Philadelphia, 1985).

Markus, Aaron, *Haḥasidut*, trans. M. Shenfeld (Tel Aviv, 1954).

Milsehagi [Samiler], Eliakim, *Sefer raviah* (Ofen, 1837).

Rosman, Murray J., 'Miedzyboz and Rabbi Israel Baal Shem Tov', in Hundert (ed.), *Essential Papers on Hasidism: Origins to Present* (New York, 1991), 209–25.

Otto, Rudolf, *The Idea of the Holy*, trans. J. W. Harvey (Oxford, 1957).

Scholem, Gershom G., *Kabbalah* (Jerusalem, 1974).

—— *Major Trends in Jewish Mysticism* (3rd edn., London, 1955).

—— *Sabbetai Ṣevi: The Mystical Messiah, 1626–1676* (London, 1973).

—— *The Messianic Idea in Judaism* (New York, 1971).

—— 'The Historical Baal Shem Tov' (Heb.), *Molad*, 144–5 (1960), 1–24.

Shar, M. M. *Hagaon malbim* (Jerusalem, 1976).

Steinsaltz, Adin, 'Zhidachov', in *Encyclopedia Judaica*, xvi. 1009.

Tishby, I., *Torat hara vehakelipah bekabalat ha'ari* (Jerusalem, 1965).

Walden, Aaron, *Shem hagedolim heḥadash* (Warsaw, 1879).

Wunder, Meir, *Me'orei galitziyah* (Jerusalem, 1978).

Index of Biblical References

Index of Rabbinic Works

Index of References to the Zohar

Subject Index

A

Aaron of Starosselye xxxiii n. 22
Abba ('Father') xix, xx, 64 n., 71, 132, 133
  and east 122
  as fear of the Lord 61–2
  and Ḥokhmah xvii, xviii, 23 n., 99, 99 n.
  as wisdom 59–60, 99
Abraham of Granada, *Berit menuḥah* 55 n.
Abraham ibn David of Posquières xxviii, xxx, 108
Abulafia, Abraham xxvii
Adam Kadmon ('Primordial Man') xvii, xix, 45, 117
  and creation 101–2, 104
  and emergence of *sefirot* xvii, 60 n., 90–1
  and Malkhut 85, 97, 106
Adonai 34, 35, 58, 70, 92
Agur (Jacob Landau) 82
Aher, *see* Elisha ben Abuyah
Akiba, R. 10, 20, 28, 32, 36 n., 57, 109
  Torat kohanim 44–5
allegory 132
amen, and *gematria* 70–1
Amidah 52
Amram, R. xxviii
analogy, use of xxxvii, 64–5
Ari, the, *see* Luria of Safed ('the Ari'), Isaac
Arikh Anpin ('Greater Countenance') xviii, xix, 60, 64 n., 77, 103, 133
asceticism, in Hasidism xiii
Asher b. Yehiel (Rosh) 88 n., 120 n.
Asiyah xix, 97–8, 123
astronomy 121–4
Astruc, Abba Mari, *Minḥat kena'ot* 87 n.
atheism 87–8
Atik 85, 97
Atika 103
Atzilut ('emanation') xviii–xix, xxxiv, 43 n., 53 n., 63 n., 91 n., 97–9, 101–2, 130, 134
AV xviii–xix, 111, 124
Ayin ('that which is not') xv, 77, 105 n.
Azariah of Fano, Menahem, *Yonat elim* 95, 113
Azikri, Eleazar, *Sefer ḥaredim* 31 n., 40 n., 85 n., 91

B

Baal Shem Tov, Israel (the Besht) xiii, xx–xxii, xxxii, 24, 39, 45, 49, 65, 84, 119
Bacharach, Naftali, *Emek hamelekh* 39, 95 n.
Bahya ibn Pakuda xxxv
  Ḥovot halevavot 11 n., 61–2, 88–9, 102–3, 106, 110
Bedersi, Jediah 87
Beit Yosef (Joseph Karo) 75, 82
BEN xix, 64–5, 111, 124
Ben Yohai, Simeon xiv
Berger, Israel xiv n.
Beriah xix, 97–8
Berl, H. J. xix n.
Besht, the, *see* Baal Shem Tov
Bet El xxxi
Binah ('Understanding') xvi–xvii, xix, 58 n., 60, 69 n., 70
  and creation xvi
  as EHYEH 104
  and *gematria* 13–14, 106
  as Imma xvii, xviii, 7 n., 25 n., 60 n., 80 n., 99 n.
  and knowledge 80–1, 107 n.
  and north 122
  and repentance 7 n., 18 n., 22 n., 23
bitul hayesh ('annihilation of selfhood') xxiv
Bodek, Mendel xiv n.
Book of Remedies 126
brains, three 58, 114

Z

Printed and bound by CPI Group (UK) Ltd, Croydon, CR0 4YY

13/04/2025

14656581-0005